Reshaping Ministry
Essays in Memory of Wesley Frensdorff

Josephine Borgeson
& Lynne Wilson, Editors

Copyright © 1990 by Jethro Publications.

All rights reserved. No part of this book may be reproduced or transmitted in any form or by any means, electronic or mechanical, including photocopying, recording or by any informational storage or retrieval system — except by a reviewer who may quote brief passages in a review to be printed in a magazine or newspaper — without permission in writing from the publisher. For information contact Jethro Publications, 6066 Parfet Street, Arvada, Colorado 80004.

First printing 1990

ISBN 1-879145-00-6

Chapter 8, "Because of People," is based on the introduction to a book presently being written by Bishop Richard Kraft. It is used here with the author's permission. Copyright 1990 by Richard A. Kraft.

Chapter 11, "Baptism, Ordination and Deacons," is reprinted with changes, from a book to be published by Cowley Press, 980 Memorial Drive, Cambridge, MA 02108, by permission of the publisher. Copyright 1990 by Ormonde Plater.

Printed in the United States of America

Reshaping Ministry
Essays in Memory of Wesley Frensdorff

Editorial Board

Phina Borgeson, Chair
Dee Frensdorff
George Harris
Dick Hayes
Steve Kelsey
Tom Ray
Lynne Wilson

Reshaping Ministry
Essays in Memory of Wesley Frensdorff

Produced by the Wesley Frensdorff Memorial Project,
The Diocese of Northern Michigan, Sponsor

Made possible by grants from:
  The Lilly Memorial Fund of St. Paul's, Indianapolis
        and
  The Roland Allen Symposium Steering Committee
  The Board for Theological Education
  The Robert Paddock Trust
  The William Cooper Procter Fund
  Sindicators
        the dioceses of
  Eastern Oregon
  Minnesota
  New York
  Olympia
  Rio Grande
  West Tennessee

        and contributions of the following bishops:

  George E. Bates, Bishop of Utah
  David B. Birney, IV, Assistant Bishop of Massachusetts
  Frederick H. Borsch, Bishop of Los Angeles
  Edmond L. Browning, Presiding Bishop
  E. Otis Charles, Dean, Episcopal Divinity School
  David R. Cochran, Retired Bishop of Alaska
  Robert H. Cochrane, Retired Bishop of Olympia
  William C. Frey, Dean, Trinity Episcopal School for Ministry
  George C. Harris, Bishop of Alaska
  Joseph T. Heistand, Bishop of Arizona
  Harold A. Hopkins, Jr., Director of the Office of Pastoral Develop-
        ment
  Robert L. Ladehoff, Bishop of Oregon
  Gerald N. McAllister, Retired Bishop of Oklahoma
  C. Shannon Mallory, Former Bishop of El Camino Real
  William B. Spofford, Retired Bishop of Eastern Oregon
  Leigh A. Wallace, Bishop of Spokane
  Vincent W. Warner, Jr., Bishop of Olympia
  William G. Weinhauer, Retired Bishop of Western North Carolina
  Stewart C. Zabriskie, Bishop of Nevada

In thanksgiving

for the life and witness of

Wesley Frensdorff

Book design: Lynne Wilson

Contents

Part III: Synthesis and Unfinished Business

FOREWORD

Anyone who came in contact with Wes Frensdorff was richer for the experience. With his humor and his deep compassion for the individual, Wes would touch you to the depths of your heart and soul. And in that touching you approached the wholeness of personhood, to which Wes' ministry was dedicated. His selfless dedication to people given to his care characterized a truly servanthood ministry to this church.

It was because of this dedication that Wes developed his vision for total ministry. In our many conversations about total ministry, Wes taught that all persons were called to share in the ministry of this church through their baptism. By the grace of God, each person was called to ministry within the community of faith. While Wes served as my mentor, I came to a much deeper appreciation of the connection between ministry and baptism. And it was probably from this early relationship that my understanding of an inclusive church began to take shape.

The full impact of the person and work of Wes Frensdorff is yet to be appreciated. This volume is a first attempt to describe Wes' vision and his contribution to total ministry. I pray that it will enable us to see how Wes Frensdorff set the direction for total ministry in the Episcopal Church, and our part in that ministry.

Edmond L. Browning,
Presiding Bishop

i

INTRODUCTION

This volume was conceived at the February, 1989 meeting of Sin-dicators, an informal group of total ministry advocates and Frensdorff associates. The project, as it emerged from that meeting, was a collection of Frensdorff-authored and Frensdorff-inspired essays, in his memory, that would be a serious educational resource for parochial, diocesan and national church leaders, schools of ministry and seminaries, and anyone interested in ministry. The purpose of the book would be to keep the issues of total ministry development before the church.

The Diocese of Northern Michigan agreed to be the formal project sponsor, responsible for fiscal accountability to project contributors. Names were suggested for an editorial board, with Phina Borgeson serving as chair. This group would be responsible for book content, recruitment of authors, and, with the help of other readers, critique of draft manuscripts. The board would also be responsible for oversight of the total project. CRW Management Services assumed responsibility for project management; Jethro Publications, Lynne Wilson, editor, for book design, style and final editing.

Implementing the plan has been a kind of continuing journey with Wes, with him very much a part of the dialogue. We open the volume with his dream for the church. In his own words that vision is then spelled out in detail in Chapter 3, "Ministry and Orders: A Tangled Skein," which is his most thorough single statement of his cause. We don't have a date for this manuscript, but it was circulated and refined over a period of several years and eventually printed by the Education for Mission and Ministry unit of the Episcopal Church in 1985. While the field in which Wes' initial conceptual work was carried out was mostly rural and small town, he soon saw that the principles were applicable in many settings. So in 1980, he argued before the Urban Caucus for a trial of those concepts in the inner city. Ten years later we asked two recognized urban specialists to join that dialogue: the substance of Chapter 4. Finally, Wes' direct engagement in the dialogue is picked up again in Chapter 14: "Authority and the Theological Enterprise," which was probably the most difficult chapter to assemble and perhaps the most open-ended or unfinished — characteristics we intended for the whole book.

In the four chapters of Part I, we have endeavored to set the stage for the balance of the book: the dream, a brief biography by Bill Spofford, and the case for total and indigenous ministry.

Part II then reports on the experience — the dream lived out — in six very different settings. These might be thought of as case studies or stories. The writers' styles vary a lot, but the idea is to report on the action in specific situations.

In Part III we seek to address, forcefully and substantively, continuing issues in thematic chapters that we hope will stimulate, drive and broaden the dialogue over the years ahead. We intended these chapters to pose more questions than answers, generate beginnings rather than offer conclusions.

I join with the editors in thanking all who contributed, in devotion to Wes and with conviction of the need, to making this memorial possible; the list is long. First is Dee Frensdorff, Wes' widow. We felt her full moral support at every step, but she counted on us to chart the course and create the product. Then there are the editorial board, sponsor, writers, critical readers, funders and others who knew of the project and kept our enthusiasm going. Thanks, all. We hope we have earned the confidence you placed in us.

Charles R. Wilson
CRW Management Services

Part I

THE MAN
AND
THE VISION

Chapter 1

THE DREAM

Wesley Frensdorff

And it shall come to pass afterward,
>   that I will pour out my spirit on all flesh;
Your sons and your daughters shall prophesy,
>   your old men shall dream dreams,
>   and your young men shall see visions.
Even upon the menservants and maidservants
>   in those days, I will pour out my spirit.

Joel

Wes Frensdorff is well known for his pioneering work in total ministry development and that is indeed the focus of this volume. However, the vision of total ministry is much broader than generally perceived. It has implications for justice, ethics, stewardship, evangelism — everything involved in being the church. It is the purpose of this first chapter to set the substance of the book into that more encompassing vision.

Wes put forth his dream for the church on numerous occasions. We have text and notes on four such addresses or sermons delivered at major church events during the period 1981-85. The sermons are, of course, tailored for the specific occasion and they are full of the little asides, anecdotes and stories characteristic of Wes — his playfulness and his humor. However, the dream, which is the core of each address, is, in substance, pretty consistent.

I have, accordingly, lifted the dream from the four sources, distilled it into one version and edited it for print rather than preaching. In this form it is more of a poem than a sermon. But the flow, the choice of words, the turn of a phrase remains. It is, I'm confident, an accurate rendering of the Frensdorff dream.

Charles R. Wilson

L et us dream of a church

> in which all members know surely and simply God's great love, and each is certain that in the divine heart we are all known by name.

> In which Jesus is very Word, our window into the Father's heart; the sign of God's hope and his design for all humankind.

> In which the Spirit is not a party symbol,
> > but wind and fire in everyone;
> gracing the church with a kaleidoscope of gifts and constant renewal for all.

A church in which

> worship is lively and fun as well as reverent and holy;
> and we might be moved to dance and laugh;
> > to be solemn, cry or beat the breast.

People know how to pray and enjoy it — frequently and regularly,
privately and corporately, in silence and in word and song.

The eucharist is the center of life
      and servanthood the center of mission:
the servant Lord truly known in the breaking of the bread.
With service flowing from worship, and everyone understanding
      why a worship is called a service.

Let us dream of a church

      in which the sacraments, free from captivity by a professional
            elite,
    are available in every congregation regardless of size, culture,
           location or budget.

      In which every congregation is free to call forth from its midst
    priests and deacons,
            sure in the knowledge that training and support services
            are available to back them up.

      In which the Word is sacrament too, as dynamically present as
    bread and wine;

      members, not dependent on professionals, know what's what and
            who's who in the Bible,

      and all sheep share in the shepherding.

      In which discipline is a means, not to self-justification,
            but to discipleship
    and law is known to be a good servant but a very poor master.

A church

      affirming life over death as much as life after death,

      unafraid of change, able to recognize God's hand in the revolu-
            tions,

affirming the beauty of diversity,
abhorring the imprisonment of uniformity,

as concerned about love in all relationships as it is about chastity,
and affirming the personal in all expressions of sexuality;

denying the separation between secular and sacred, world and
church, since it is the world Christ came to and died for.

A church

without the answers, but asking the right questions;

holding law and grace, freedom and authority, faith and works
together in tension, by the Holy Spirit, pointing to the glorious
mystery who is God.

So deeply rooted in gospel and tradition that, like a living tree, it
can swing in the wind and continually surprise us with new blos-
soms.

Let us dream of a church

with a radically renewed concept and practice of ministry
and a primitive understanding of the ordained offices.

Where there is no clerical status and no classes of Christians,
but all together know themselves to be part of the laos —
the holy people of God.

A ministering community
rather than a community gathered around a minister.

Where ordained people, professional or not, employed or not, are
present for the sake of ordering and signing the church's life and
mission,
not as signs of authority or dependency,
nor of spiritual or intellectual superiority,

but with Pauline patterns of "ministry supporting church" instead of the common pattern of "church supporting ministry."

Where bishops are signs and animators of the church's unity, catholicity and apostolic mission,

priests are signs and animators of her eucharistic life and the sacramental presence of her Great High Priest,

and deacons are signs and animators — living reminders — of the church's servanthood as the body of Christ who came as, and is, the servant slave of all God's beloved children.

Let us dream of a church

    so salty and so yeasty that it really would be missed
        if no longer around;
    where there is wild sowing of seeds
        and much rejoicing when they take root,
    but little concern for success, comparative statistics, growth
        or even survival.

    A church so evangelical that its worship, its quality of caring,
    its eagerness to reach out to those in need cannot be contained.

A church

    in which every congregation is in a process of becoming
        free — autonomous — self-reliant — interdependent,

        none has special status:
        the distinction between parish and mission gone.

    But each congregation is in mission
    and each Christian, gifted for ministry;
        a crew on a freighter, not passengers on a luxury liner.

    Peacemakers and healers
        abhorring violence in all forms (maybe even football),
        as concerned with societal healing as with individual
        healing;

with justice as with freedom,
prophetically confronting the root causes of social, political and
economic ills.

A community: an open, caring, sharing household of faith
where all find embrace, acceptance and affirmation.

A community: under judgment,
seeking to live with its own proclamation,
therefore,
truly loving what the Lord commands
and desiring His promise.

And finally, let us dream of a people called

to recognize all the absurdities in ourselves and in one another,
including the absurdity that is LOVE,
serious about the call and the mission
but not, very much, about ourselves,
who, in the company of our Clown Redeemer can dance and sing
and laugh and cry in worship, in ministry and even in
conflict.

Chapter 2

WESLEY FRENSDORFF:
The Man and the Mountains

William B. Spofford

There are, in my mind's eye, two geographic views associated with the life of Wesley Frensdorff. The first is one enjoyed from the patio of the home he and his wife, Dee, had in North Tucson. Sitting there, perhaps watching Wes swim his daily laps while listening to a learning tape of some sort, one's eyes move up Pusch Ridge of the Catalina Mountains which enclose the burgeoning southwest city on the north. From those expanding suburbs of that Sunbelt sprawl, one looks past ascending cacti, alive with birds, to the higher ridges. There, between the folding mountain waves, is a big "W." Each evening the descending desert sun makes it glisten. Each morning, as that sun comes up, there it is, outlined in black. Because of the "W," his wife and friends gave the ridge the name, "Wes' Mountain." Following his sudden death that "W" felt like an icon of his life. The second geographic view is also of a mountain. But more on that later.

Born in Hanover, Germany, Wes was baptized in the Evangelical Lutheran Church. His mother, Erna, was Christian while his father, Rudolf, was born into the Jewish community. In 1938, with the increasing viciousness of the Nazi regime, the family sought ways to leave Germany. The Quakers in England provided the needed help; thus the beginning of Wes' attraction to people of that faith community. The youngest child, Wes at age 12 was the first member of the family to leave Hanover for England. Over a period of time his brother Karl and sister Marlys, and then his parents all made their escape. Wes seldom talked (at least to me) about this period and perhaps it was not a time he remembered all that well. In England the siblings were lodged in different households, with Wes landing in the home of a wealthy citizen of that land apparently desiring to assist in a program of refugee resettlement.

During his stay in England Wes developed a taste for English wartime food (such as bread with drippings and salt) in which, later on, the Sisters of Charity of the Wellspring Retreat Center, Boulder City, Nevada, and the cooks at the diocesan camp would occasionally indulge him.

In 1940, the family sailed for New York and settled in Elmhurst on Long Island. He attended St. James' Episcopal Church, where the future clergyman and author, Robert Capon, was active with him in the parish youth group. Following graduation from Newtown High School, he entered the Army, serving with counter-intelligence for a year in Japan. After demobilization he attended Columbia University, doing well in his studies although English was, of course, his second language.

While at Columbia he had a moment of panic when he first heard the university hymn. Set to the tune "Austria," it revived all his old fears of the Nazis. Later in life, however, the hymn to that tune, "Glorious Things of Thee Are Spoken," became one of his personal favorites. At the time, the Rev. Dr. Shunji Nishi was university chaplain and later in the West these two maintained their relationship and many common interests, while Nishi was professor of theology and sometime acting dean of the Church Divinity School of the Pacific, Berkeley, California.

Throughout his life Wes' mind was quick and perceptive. He had the ability to cut through to the essence of issues and to their resolution. The quickness was displayed frequently in his ability to pun on words. He would often get in such contests in the middle of meetings of the diocese or the House of Bishops. As with all devotees of the art of punning, the preliminary groans of his auditors never deterred him from going ahead with the play on words, followed by an insightful smile.

Straightway on graduation from university Wes entered General Theological Seminary in New York City. His bishop, James DeWolf of the Diocese of Long Island, was at the time one of the leaders of the church's

Anglo-Catholic constituency, a formative influence on Wes at the time, and one that would continue with him.

The post-war seminary years were exciting. The student body and many of the tutors were returning military personnel who tended to be somewhat older than previous members of the academic community and, due to war service and work, were strongly moved by a vision of a world which needed redemption and re-creation. Among the tutors at General when Wes attended were Paul Moore and C. Kilmer Myers. Among his classmates were Otis Charles, Robert Cochrane, Robert Rusack and William Weinhauer. In subsequent decades the ministries of these men as bishops would touch the dioceses of California, Utah, Olympia, Los Angeles and Western North Carolina, as well as Nevada, Navajoland and Arizona.

During his seminary years Wes spent some time exploring non-urban areas of ministry. He spent one summer in the National Town-Country Church Institute program, in and out of Roanridge, Parkville, Missouri, under the supervision of the Rev. Henry Robbins in Shenandoah, Iowa. He also spent some time in Western North Carolina at Valle Crucis in the Blue Ridge Mountains under the supervision of the Rev. Dr. E. Dargan Butt who, in winter terms, taught town-country ministry at the Seabury-Western Seminary in Evanston, Illinois.

In his seminary years he was whole-heartedly Anglo-Catholic in his theological understanding and practice, particularly in terms of centering the life of the church in the eucharist. Over the decades his theology and practice of ministry broadened. However, that Anglo-Catholic background served him well when, in later years, he would begin exploring the use of local priests and deacons in Nevada and elsewhere.

Wes was graduated from General in 1951. By invitation of Bishop William Fisher Lewis, he became vicar of a three-point mission in the mining and cattle area of north-central Nevada. A hard, beautiful and wide land, the environment was far different from Long Island and New York City. Uncrowded, it was very cold in the winter and hot in the summer. It featured communities and people who were separated geographically, but very neighborly. Like most clergy in the Intermountain West, Wes learned to drive many miles, in his case between St. Mary's, Winnemucca; St. Andrew's, Battle Mountain; and St. Anne's, McDermitt. The last, up on the high desert border of Eastern Oregon, was, basically, a mission with and to the Paiute people — in light of the vicar's subsequent career in Navajoland, a seminal experience.

It was in Winnemucca that Wes met, wooed and ultimately married Dolores Stoker, better known as Dee. A marriage of love, humor, challenge, devotion and world travel ensued. They had a family of five —

Andrée, Kerry, Donald, Victoria and Mark. Over the years they opened their home to many others of varied ages who needed a home and family.

In 1953 my wife Polly and I, then serving on the staff of Roanridge, moved to rural Idaho to establish the Western Extension Center of the National Town-Country Church Institute. Through our mutual concern for small town church work, the Frensdorffs and the Spoffords enjoyed a growing personal as well as professional relationship. We shared many ministries and trained seminarians and clergy out of various centers: Roanridge, the College of Idaho in Caldwell, St. Luke's in Weiser, Idaho; at Glenbrook and the diocesan camp and conference center in Nevada. During those ventures persons such as Bishop William Lewis, William Wright, who later succeeded Lewis as bishop of Nevada, and Norman L. Foote, director of the program at Roanridge and later bishop of Idaho, assisted us in training and supervising students.

Fundamentally, these programs attempted through research, action and training to help ministers, most of whom were seminarians, and basically urban-oriented, to understand and function in the various rural areas of the American scene. For a period, while he was in Winnemucca, Wes served as director of the program for western America, since I had returned to Boston to be the chaplain at the Massachusetts General Hospital.

From 1954 to 1959, the Frensdorffs carried out their ministries in the two-point field of St. Paul's, Elko , and St. Barnabas' and St. Luke's, Wells, Nevada: sociologically and economically similar to the Winnemucca/Battle Mountain/McDermitt field. They guided the Elko congregation through a new church building program. Increasingly during this period Wes was being recognized as one of the church's leaders in the area of small town work.

In 1959, Wes was called to a tri-point mission in the Washington Cascades through the invitation of Bishop Lewis, who had been translated to be the bishop of Olympia in western Washington. Working through the Churches of the Transfiguration in Darrington, St. Martin's in Rockport and St. Francis in Newhalem, Wes was further refining his theology of ministry and mission in light of persons and their community needs and challenges.

In 1960, I was called by Bishop Foote to be dean of St. Michael's Cathedral in Boise, Idaho. I accepted the call contingent on the cathedral becoming a training center for seminarians. Since it did, we moved back to the Intermountain West. Very quickly Wes, together with the Rev. Charles Wilson and the Rev. Robert Anderson and others, was restructuring the modes of training for town-country clergy and seminarians, and we gathered in both Boise and Salt Lake City for supervisors' training.

In 1962, Bishop Richard Watson and the chapter of St. Mark's Cathedral, Salt Lake City, extended a call to Wesley to become dean of that significant diocesan and urban congregation. Wes very quickly became an important community leader and force. There, in an environment predominantly Mormon, he started to bring into focus his ideas on the basic priority of the baptized ministry of the laity and to develop models to stimulate it. Since the LDS community functioned with a total "lay ministry," perhaps Salt Lake was an ideal setting to do this.

Wes was instrumental in bringing the Rev. Otis Charles (then executive secretary of The Associated Parishes, concerned with liturgical renewal in the Episcopal Church) to Utah for some parish workshops. Subsequently, upon the retirement of Bishop Watson and perhaps under the influence of these workshops, Otis was elected Utah's bishop. The consecration centered in a fiesta spirit of songs, colorful vestments, balloons and Hispanic and Native American dances — enjoyed by all, but destined to raise some conservative eyebrows, Episcopal and Mormon. As a team of bishop and dean, Otis and Wes shared training programs, retreats at a Trappist monastery in the snows of the Wasatch Range and many community activities involving such issues as those pertaining to the Navajos in southern Utah and atomic blast fallout blowing out of Nevada. It was a short-term arrangement, however, as Wes was soon to return to Nevada.

As deans — Wes in Salt Lake City and I in Boise — we ran what we jokingly called the "western Minsky circuit." He would get a guest preacher or teacher in and then send the individual on to Boise for a repeat, while I would send my guests east to shake up Salt Lake City. Among these "troopers" were the retired bishop of Washington, Angus Dun, the bishop of Bengal, India, and seminary professors innumerable and diverse. Since we were both in what were called "fly-over" areas, such stimulating input was always appreciated.

In 1968-69, Wes took a sabbatical in the Diocese of Nicaragua and, together with Dee and the children, became familiar with the issues confronting the culture, people and churches of Central America. Being in a post-Vatican II Roman Catholic area, he further explored the relationship of any church's ministry in light of the needs of society and culture. Those were the early days of what later became known as liberation theology. It included the development of dynamic ecclesial "base communities" with their emphasis on lay study of the Bible, eucharistically-centered churches, and home and family ministries by lay persons, all of which Wes was to develop later on in Nevada, Navajoland and Arizona.

Shortly after his return, Wes was elected to succeed Bishop William Wright as bishop of Nevada, and although he and Dee had some doubts about returning to her home turf, they both knew that it was their kind of diocese and challenge. He was consecrated in the Sahara Club, Las Vegas, on a hot day in 1972. The Presiding Bishop, John E. Hines, was chief consecrator; Otis Charles and I (by then bishop of Eastern Oregon) were co-consecrators.

I'll never forget one side incident that day. While we were vested and lining up for the procession, I plugged a quarter into a slot machine (and believe me, I am no gambler!) and rackety-rackety, out came fifty dollars. I hastily shoved this metal through the pocket in my rochet. During the offertory I asked the Presiding Bishop what I should do with the extra cash. He ordered me to give half to Wes' discretionary fund and to spend the other half to buy myself a new tennis racket. This I did, buying the racket on my way out of town. I still have "Wes' tennis racket" in my exercise equipment.

Wes served as bishop of the geographically large Diocese of Nevada (which, basically, has two metropolitan centers — Reno and Las Vegas — and much "outback") until September, 1985. Living in Reno, where he and Dee soon built their first home, he focused on issues of ministry: its nature, its development, its deployment. Inspired by the work of Bishop William Gordon in Alaska and subsequently by the writing of former missionary in China, Roland Allen, Wesley developed and put in place modes and models for expanding the ministry of the laity, for using and deploying permanent and functional deacons, and for training and deploying what, today, would be called local priests, functioning always under competent supervision in a team model.

A pivotal point during this period was a diocesan clergy-lay vicars' conference in 1974. Otis Charles addressed the group on the theology of the proposed initiatory rites, and Bill Gordon on TEAM (Teach Each a Ministry). A conceptual model for total ministry was beginning to take shape across the diocese. As far as ordained ministry was concerned, the attention was on priesthood. For the sacraments to be available in the villages and small towns a priest was required (a Gordon emphasis), and the vocal liberals were celebrating the ordination of the Philadelphia Eleven. It wasn't a particularly friendly environment for an unemployed, newly ordained, outspoken deacon.

Nevertheless, a year later saw Deacon Phina Borgeson on the diocesan staff and in the fall of 1976, launching a diocesan-wide ministry education effort which she would lead for the balance of the Frensdorff Nevada episcopate. It was a mutually stimulating relationship — Wes and Phina. The diaconate became an important component in Nevada's total ministry development, and Nevada, a big influence in the renewal of the diaconate nationally.

Because of Wes' zeal in advocating a reshaped ministry for Nevada, he influenced ministry development across the country and around the world. In 1976, he called together representatives from dioceses and programs using the canon for local clergy to discuss strategies and educational programs. Sindicators (another Frensdorff punny name) grew out of that gathering and continues as a think tank, dream factory and peer support group for a network of slightly crazy people concerned with total ministry development. Wes also helped to keep the emerging issues in ministry as he saw them before traditional church bodies dealing with ministry, such as the Board of the General Theological Seminary and the Council for the Development of Ministry. As a member of the CDM, he was instrumental in beginning the major revision of Title III, so that the canons on ministry would reflect the best renewed theological thinking and practice.

The basic battery of the diocese, and for Wes and Dee the retreat par excellence, was Camp Galilee on Lake Tahoe. It was there that they shared their lives with their co-workers, their family and friends, and their many diocesan guests who came to teach and explore.

He took seriously his responsibilities in the House of Bishops and in the national and world church. In all such settings, Wes was known as that quick, humorous guy who, leaving his cross-stitch frame, would approach the microphone to sharpen an issue, share a joke, say where he stood or enter debate. And when he did, the audience, whether ecclesial or otherwise, listened because, agree or not, they knew they would hear something worth pondering.

In 1983, John M. Allin, Presiding Bishop, asked Wesley whether he had the time and energy to function as the interim bishop of the Navajoland Area Mission, a unique extra-diocesan jurisdiction established by the House of Bishops to assure that Navajo needs and hopes were significantly addressed. After numerous consultations and making appropriate arrangements with the leaders of the Diocese of Nevada and the jurisdictions of Coalition 14 (the budgetary negotiating group of non-self-supporting dioceses, which were generally rural and western), Bishop Frensdorff agreed. He served in this capacity until, flying back from a visitation to Navajoland, he died when his plane crashed at night on the north rim of the Grand Canyon.

Dee and Wes always planned to retire in the Reno vicinity since that is where four of their five children and their families live. Given his work in the Four Corners area of Navajo country and believing it would be easier to move back to Reno if he had been away, and since Dee was suffering from a physical disability which might be alleviated in a warmer climate, he accepted the invitation of Bishop Joseph Heistand to become the assistant bishop of Arizona in 1985.

From that moment until his death, he was extremely busy learning a new diocese and its personnel, developing ideas and models for ministry (both for Arizona and Navajoland), traveling much and, with Dee, enjoying a teaching-exploring trip to New Zealand and Australia (as guests of the Aboriginal and Maori people).

Frensdorff was always in demand as a teacher and conference leader while he was in the episcopate. During those years he took part in the consecration service of Bishop Desmond Tutu, future Nobel Peace Prize recipient, in South Africa. (Desmond and Leah Tutu had been houseguests of the Frensdorffs years earlier when the future bishop had been called in by Wes as a diocesan guest speaker.) He and I shared two weeks of mission, in churches and in the streets, on Exuma Island in the Bahamas while enjoying sun-bathing and diving with our wives — all of us guests of Bishop Michael Eldon of that jurisdiction. Also, together with then bishop of Hawaii, Edmond Browning, and the assistance of bishops from North and South America and the Philippines, he organized the Pacific Basin Conference in honor of Roland Allen. This particular gathering called together Anglicans from all dioceses of the Pacific Rim to explore the issues of mission, ministry and continuity that would be important to the church in that particular part of the world during the coming century.

I have said little about Wesley Frensdorff as a human being or as a man. What he was in his vocation and calling, I would say, was what he apparently lived out as a husband, parent, colleague, friend and prophet. He had one of the world's great collections of clown figures and paintings. Following a House of Bishops meeting in Mexico, and while Wes, Dee, Polly and I were doing Mexico by third class buses, I recall that we looked for clown artifacts in every town we visited. When, prior to the Lambeth Conference in Canterbury in 1978, we spent a week canal boating out of Stratford-Coventry, he looked for similar works. He showed up for that adventure with a lot of books but quickly learned that, when canal boating, one doesn't get much reading done. Every time you think you can, you are interrupted by the appearance of another lock to be either opened or raised, while your spouse is buying bread in the lock house nearby.

While Wes was a superb joke teller, he could also listen well and respond appropriately. He had dreamed dreams as a youth and he maintained and expanded his vision continuously.

It is obvious that the life and works of Wesley Frensdorff were full and broadly shared. It is true that his was a life cut short. The shock and trauma of his accidental death were devastating. His gifts to the church and society were manifold, and in this book his colleagues and friends share some of this. They are gifts that will endure. His life was centered in the Bible, well-worn the many times I saw him using it in hotel rooms, camp and retreat settings, in conference or recreational environments. His humanity was enriched at the altar and in and through the community of Christ.

Which, now, at the close, brings us to that other geographic icon, another mountain balancing the "W" mountain in the Catalinas north of Tucson. This one you have to view through the glass window serving as a reredos for St. John's Chapel at Camp Galilee on the eastern shore of Lake Tahoe. Across the deep blue of the lake are the Sierra Mountains. The one you see through the window has a permanent snow cross lodged in a crevice about three-quarters of the way up the mountain. It is slightly askew, suggesting that through the eons it has been continually battered, melted and re-frozen. But there it is . . . to be seen by all. Surely, for Wesley Frensdorff, it was a subject for meditation and reflection almost his entire life and ministry. And, one must believe, most significantly when he stood in front of that chapel altar, with the bread and wine in front of him for blessing, then to be shared — the power of Christ — with his family and friends in communion. Wes chose Camp Galilee for his final resting place.

Wesley Frensdorff:
Searcher, Caretaker, Bishop and Human
1926-1988
Bishop of Nevada: 1972 - 1985
Interim Bishop of Navajoland: 1983 - 1988
Assistant Bishop of Arizona: 1985 - 1988

Chapter 3

MINISTRY AND ORDERS:
A Tangled Skein

Wesley Frensdorff

M inistry, as the sharing of God's gifts in service, is the personal privilege and imperative of every member of the church by virtue of baptism. There is little debate about that.

> *Whatever gift each of you may have received, use it in*
> *service to one another like good stewards dispensing the*
> *grace of God in its varied forms.* I Peter 4:10.

The church is a ministering community, a community of ministers: interrelated, interdependent, proclaiming and sharing the love of God, in Christ Jesus. There is little debate about that either.

> *For Christ is like a single body with its many limbs and*
> *organs which, many as they are, together make up one*

> body. *For indeed we were all brought into one body by*
> *baptism, in the one Spirit whether we are Jews or Greeks,*
> *whether slaves or free men, and that one Holy Spirit was*
> *poured out for all of us to drink.* I Corinthians 12:12,13.

Yet somehow, the church has not always been able to make this a reality in its life and mission. Happily, in this past decade or two, there has been considerable concern with these matters in many traditions and denominations, and certainly in the Episcopal Church and the Anglican Communion. Ultimately, it is a matter of ecclesiology. Examining ministry and the ordained offices in the total ministry of the church forces us also to a reexamination of some aspects of the theology of the church.

These ministry explorations have necessarily also resulted in a reexamination of the place and role of the ordained offices because of their importance in both the tradition and practice of the church's life and mission. The episcopate has received a certain amount of attention. The diaconate, as a distinct order, is being studied extensively, resulting in a significant renewal. The presbyterate is experiencing significant changes.

Out of the reexamination and remodeling of the ordained offices, a number of questions and issues have emerged that beg for further exploration. Some of these are theological, some institutional and some more personal. All are intertwined and interrelated. Most relate particularly to the place of the presbyterate in our tradition. I would like to suggest some approaches to these questions and perhaps raise some additional issues.

In introducing the articles from the 1981 Trinity Institute Symposium on Priesthood, Dean Durston McDonald writes:

> *There are other signs that we must rethink our theology of*
> *priesthood. The large increases in the numbers of "nonsti-*
> *pendiary" clergy, the ordinations of a variety of "sacra-*
> *mentalists," of rectors also working in secular jobs, as*
> *well as changing relationships between clergy and laity*
> *and the increased stress upon clergy and upon parishes*
> *economically, are phenomena which have implications not*
> *only for policy but also for our understanding of the nature*
> *of priesthood.*[1]

Let me suggest the image of the tangled skein. Those who knit, do needlepoint or other handwork, as well as those who recall their mothers doing such things, remember a skein of wool that has been hopelessly entangled. The tendency in the process of disentangling is to pull on one or another strand. But that tends to tighten the knot and usually is not effective.

The wool in such a skein can be restored to usefulness by fluffing it so that gradually the knots are loosened. Pulling on one strand, or one issue, tends to harden the knot. Therefore, we want to examine the variety of questions and issues with the hope that out of the tangle the strands of ministry and orders can be loosened and freely examined.

However, before examining the strands themselves, let us set forth some definitions. I find it most helpful to think of the church in terms of its life and its mission. Rather than focusing on the now all too common phrase, "the mission and ministry of the church," for me it is clearer to focus on the life of the church and the mission for which that life exists. Ministry is the instrument of both. I am aware that the life and the mission of the church are essentially one, but in functional terms it is, for me, clearer to distinguish between them.

The life of the church begins and is centered on its worship — the offering of praise and thanksgiving focused in the eucharist. This life takes place in the context of a caring, loving community and includes the growth and nurture of the members. Ministry in the life of the church involves all of those activities in which the members offer their gifts for worship, community life, caring and nurture, as well as the organizing and administration that are necessary.

But the life of the church, as the body of Christ, exists primarily for the sake of its mission. The church is sent to make known the good news of God's total love as revealed in and through the life, death and resurrection of Jesus Christ and to the servant of God's children in his name, binding up their wounds and participating in establishing the kingdom of God on earth. Ministry, in the mission of the church, is the activities of its members in carrying out evangelization and servanthood.

> *All members are called to discover, with the help of the community, the gifts they have received and to use them for the building up of the church and for the service of the world to which the church is sent.*[2]

Some systemic problems

In my mind there are two basic systemic problems, which are interrelated. One of these deals with our ministry delivery system, and the other with our system of leadership and governance. These are, in practice, too intermixed and intertwined to distinguish easily. Disentangling them may be helpful for the purpose of this exploration.

Our ministry delivery system, the delivery of service in the name of Christ, is basically the English village model, but in overload. That model is centered and heavily dependent on the "cleric," who at one time was the most educated person in the village and thus also the primary teacher. The church buildings, as a result, are set up as classrooms. This model tends to create vicarious religion, centered on the priest as the holy person, in whom is focused the religious power and knowledge. It also tends to create dependence, rather than interdependence. If the priest is "father," church members are children, who never reach sufficient adulthood in Christ to exercise much of their ministries. If the priest is pastor, members are always sheep intended to follow, not lead. Furthermore, this ministry delivery system is highly professionalized; at the center stands a professional with professional training. The model is highly hierarchical and economically dependent in that it cannot function in its presently accepted traditional form without money. Furthermore, as a result of setting priesthood in a professionalized and economically dependent ministerial system, we have created a "sacramental captivity." Sacraments are primarily available where a professional, stipendiary priest is available. As a result there is a high degree of sacramental deprivation where the conditions of the model can't be met. (Parenthetically, we might note such deprivation is even more extreme in the Roman Catholic system because celibacy and other factors have further limited the number of priests in relation to membership.) As Roland Allen pointed out more than fifty years ago, we have a situation in which we claim that the eucharist must be central to the life of the church wherever it gathers, but we have locked up its presidency in a professional, highly educated order. This clerically-centered model of congregational life and mission increasingly limits both ministry delivery and the sacramental life of the church.

But this system is also tied up with our governance system. It has separated, or at least created a distance between, the church's primary leadership and the community of faith. As far as the local congregation is concerned, the primary leadership, by design, is *imported*. That, however, is not as true with bishops because they are called by the diocesan community through an extensive process, and often from that community itself. With regard to the congregation, the exercise of leadership takes second place to that of the imported leadership of the priest. Furthermore, because primary leadership has been focused in the ordained offices, the governance system has been largely clerically dominated. While the laity have exercised strong leadership at all levels of the Episcopal Church, in the minds of many — and in practice — such leadership is heavily clerical. The governance system has not been clearly defined and the hybrid ecclesiastical democracy that is ours does not function with clarity. For example, a vote by orders is used as much to impede change as to develop consensus.

Our congregational leadership system can be diagramed as follows:

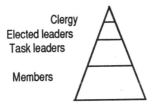

However, because we want to be a servant community, we often think of our congregational leadership this way:

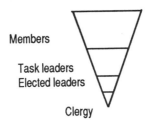

In this form the system is very unstable and top-heavy; no wonder it tends to keep falling over.

In New Testament terms a congregational leadership model might look like the figure below. (The diocesan model would look similar and include the interrelationship of congregations.)

An ellipse, rather than a circle, is a better way to diagram the church's life and mission because it has two interrelated focal points. Around the edge is the leadership team. Mutuality is at the heart of Christian community and therefore mutuality in leadership is more authentic than in a hierarchical model, even an upside-down one. We are reminded of this by Jesus' conversation with Peter at the washing of the feet at the Last Supper:

> *When it was Simon Peter's turn, Peter said to Him, "You, Lord, washing my feet?" Jesus replied, "you do not understand now what I am doing, but one day you will." Peter said, "I will never let you wash my feet." "If I do not wash you," Jesus replied, "you are not in fellowship with me." "Then, Lord," said Simon Peter, "not my feet only; wash my hands and head as well!"* John 13:6-9.

Both systemic problems — leadership and ministry delivery — create much discomfort because they are basically inconsistent with our faith convictions. There is a gap between the message and the medium. That creates pressures, both on the church and on the persons in the ordained offices. As Christians we are committed to a basic view of life that has interdependence at its heart. The world, in our understanding, is not hierarchical, but interrelated, and all parts are considered of equal value. However, our systems further either a high degree of dependence or a high degree of independence, but fall short in creating interdependence. Our present ways of doing things impede a personal and institutional life that reflects effectively the kind of body images that St. Paul uses so effectively.

We are uncomfortable with hierarchy because we are servant-oriented by our faith commitment. We are committed to the servant principle, but we have difficulty in living it out. Jesus obviously had the same problem with the disciples. We accept mutual servanthood in principle, but our lives do not reflect that too well. We have a yearning for communal sharing — to have all things in common — but we find it difficult to realize that ideal. We claim and affirm gifts for each disciple, yet both the negative spirituality, which is part of our inheritance, and the customary ministry delivery and leadership systems prevent our actualizing the offering of those gifts. Our members are largely convinced that they are giftless, especially for ministry. In our spirituality we are committed to a noncompetitiveness, yet our culture manages to press us in the opposite direction. Furthermore, we have tended to support a two-class spirituality — one for clergy, one for laity. We explore this topic later.

A bit of history

In order to understand these systemic problems a little more clearly, or perhaps as a way of clarifying the issues further, it might be helpful to look at a bit of history. Dr. Bernard Cooke is the author of one of the thorough studies of the development of leadership and ministry in the first four centuries of the church's life; his book is called *Ministry to Word and Sacraments*. In a lecture given at the Roland Allen conference in Hawaii in the summer of 1983, he pointed to three major shifts or movements that occurred in the first two centuries of the present era. These shifts have not been reversed; rather, in some cases, they have become even more entrenched. First, he pointed to the shift from itinerant ministry and leadership to resident ministry and leadership. Jesus was itinerant, and he demanded the same from his followers. In the early church leadership ministries were also itinerant, but many soon settled down. While there has always been some itinerant ministry, for example through missionaries, most primary leadership in the church has been "settled" since those early centuries.

The second shift to which Bernard Cooke points is one from charismatic to official leadership. The early leadership patterns were based on gifts given to individuals, because of which they were then called to carry out certain functions. Paul has a number of these lists. But soon the institutional leadership needs tended to shape these functions into offices. This shift, Cooke points out, was heightened by the second-century gnostic crisis. "In the face of these two challenges, both the ministry of prophecy and the ministry of teaching have their autonomy diminished, almost eliminated."[3] Other similar challenges tended to solidify this movement toward more "official" leadership.

The third shift:

> ... that from secular to sacred, is perhaps the most important because it deals not with who does ministry, but with the very nature of what it is that is done. At the same time it is inseparable from what we have just seen because it is the key element in the process towards attributing sacrality to official church leadership; the shift towards contributing to such leaders' sacred power by virtue of which their ministerial activity is salvifically effective.[4]

Here are sown the seeds of what later developed into a view of actual superiority of the clergy by virtue of ordination.

In contrast, Cooke points out, primitive Christianity:

> ... really saw its own existence with that of Jesus as "secular." They believed that a radically new form of sacrality had entered the picture with the advent of Jesus, and above

all with his death and resurrection. This new sacrality had nothing to do with some special realm of sacred religious activity. It dealt with the sanctifying presence of God's spirit in Jesus and thereafter in the church. It was this Holy Spirit that made Jesus the new and definite "holy of holies" and the Christian community the temple in which God dwelt; it was this creative spirit that came in fullness with Jesus' resurrection to transform the face of the earth; it was this spirit that was the life force animating the church as body of Christ, filling both vine and branches with new and unending life; and it was this spirit of sanctification that rooted all of the early manifestations of Christian ministry. The entire community was believed to be empowered by Christ's spirit, and empowered to share in the on-going mission of the risen one.[5]

By the end of the first century, all of this was beginning to change. There was a shift to the sanctuary with images of priesthood praising God on behalf of the people. In the second century "the sacred character of the Episcopos and the sacred nature of his role are explicitly and consistently mentioned."[6] This appears to reverse earliest Christianity's reluctance to apply sacred terms to any individual in the church. "From the third century onward we can speak of holy orders in the life of the church."[7]

Edward Schillebeeckx, in his book, *Ministry—A Study of Ministry in the Life of the Church*, supports Cooke's thesis and especially the third shift.[8] He points out that the trends Cooke identifies reached new heights in the Middle Ages and that we are still stuck with them. Schillebeeckx then goes on to point out that at that time the shift from leadership rooted in community to leadership with "private" power came to new fulfillment.

This shift could be diagramed this way:

	Jesus	→	the people of God	→	clergy and leaders
to	Jesus	→	clergy and leaders	→	the people of God

Our theology and tradition still claim the first picture while our practice and ecclesial culture point in many ways to the second. It is also interesting to note that while the Reformation sought to make basic changes in some of these areas, it was largely unsuccessful. Even though the various traditions differ with us in their historical and theological views regarding ordained leadership, their basic situation is the same. Even though their polity may differ with ours, the basic issues we are discussing in this article are shared in every tradition. Aidan Kavanagh puts the matter as follows:

*The upshot of all this is that the Western churches in the first
half of this present and perhaps most egalitarian of centuries found themselves with a highly undiversified ministerial structure focused on a "learned" and thus ineluctably
hieratic and elite group of people who were now regarded
by many as "first-class Christians," a church of the chosen
within a far larger church of the unchosen who constituted
a baptized proletariat of Christians of the second, third, or
even fourth kind. The effects of this are presently all around
us. The other Christian ministries, where they survived,
have been presbyteralized, and the rest of the church has
been deministerialized. Charisms have not been restricted
by this situation, for the Spirit persists in blowing, discon-
certingly, where it will. But there can be no doubt that this
constricted ministerial situation has made it all the more
difficult to discern diaconic (i.e., service) charisms when
they occur, and made it all but impossible to recognize them
publicly and employ them effectively to the churches'
good.[9]*

The most significant thing to recognize is that in this process the
ordained offices have been uprooted from community. They are privatized
and clericalized. Equally important, sacramental power leads to leadership,
rather than leadership leading to sacramental ministry. In the earliest church
tradition, a leader was identified, called and then given sacramental responsibility. Now, because of these shifts in our practice, someone offers him or
herself to the church and, if affirmed, is trained. Then, through ordination,
sacramental authority is given; only after this comes the call to specific
leadership. The primary criteria are leadership *potential* and intellectual ability, rather than *already established* leadership in the community of faith. *Simply put, in the early church, leaders became eucharistic presidents, while in
our system we make eucharistic presidents and then call them to leadership.*
The sacraments are the lifeblood of the church. The present system
gives their control to *potential* leaders rather than to established leaders.
Then, add the economic factor. While there are increasing variations, it is still
largely true that the availability of money controls the availability of
sacramental leadership for most local congregations.
If we are going to free the life and the mission of the church from
these clerical and sacramental captivities, we must understand our history,
disentangle the issues and "reform" the systems, in order that every community of laity, in Schillebeeckx's words, "may have a full ecclesial life." Only
then is the church truly empowered for mission. Now let us take a look at
some other strands in the tangled skein.

Some strands to be examined

Several of the strands are related to what I consider confusions. We can identify three of them. One is a role and expectation confusion. The second is an identity confusion. The third is a call and career confusion.

The *role and expectation confusion* can be illustrated from our ordination liturgy. An analysis of the liturgy for ordaining a priest reveals a multiplicity of references to roles, function, lifestyles and expectations.[10] The pastoral and preaching aspects of the office appear more important than the priestly and sacramental functions. Teaching and eldership are also referred to. The examination declares that it is the task of the priest to "proclaim by word and deed the Gospel of Jesus Christ and to fashion his or her life in accordance with its precepts." It next mentions the call to love and serve the people and to caring for all sorts and conditions. Then it goes on to say "you are to preach, to declare God's forgiveness to penitent sinners, to pronounce God's blessing, to share in the administration of Holy Baptism and in the celebration of the mysteries of Christ's Body and Blood, and to perform the other ministrations entrusted to you." Presidency in the community's celebration of "word and sacrament" is certainly not primary; it almost appears as an afterthought. The rest of the service puts more emphasis on the pastoral and teaching aspects of the office than on the sacramental aspects. It also focuses the spotlight on extensive lifestyle expectations. Even in the actual ordination prayer, we do not find a clear picture of the office itself. While it begins with the recognition that the priest is to "offer spiritual sacrifices," and "rightly administer the sacraments," there is really no direct reference to eucharistic presidency. The prayer does contain a plea to make the ordained a "faithful pastor, patient teacher and wise counselor," none of which are, while most desirable, theologically or even historically *essential* elements of the presbyteral office. These are, or can be, broadly shared by others in the church. In the attached appendix I have attempted a sample rewrite of part of the liturgy for the ordination of priests for a clearer focus and order. The liturgies for ordination and consecration of a bishop and of a deacon are a bit clearer, but they could also benefit from describing each office more clearly and distinguishing between function and other expectations.

The role and expectation confusion is also illustrated by a recent study done for the Board for Theological Education. *We Need People Who* (as the report is entitled) is described as "an exploration of criteria for ordained ministries in the Episcopal Church.[11] In this study Margaret Fletcher Clark, the director, sets forth ten different models for ordained ministry. They are listed as follows:

1. Counselor/Healer/Caretaker	6. Ring-leader
2. Minister of the Word	7. Community Personage
3. Administrator/Manager	8. Celebrant
4. Prophet/Social Activist	9. Spiritual Guide
5. Social Examplar	10. Witness

Referring to the study in an Alban Institute article, Clark points out that it is "important to know that we use 'model' here to describe neither an ideal nor theological tradition. It is more like a person's dream house; more an abstraction of reality than a description."[12] These models came from church members, commissions on ministry and clergy. Clark notes that the study committee was surprised by the variety of role expectations and by their seeming discrepancies, even apparent contradictions. For me it is of interest that the categories leave out a clear indication regarding "authority," even though the priest in most situations is considered the primary leader and by canon has many prerogatives. But even more important is the fact that eucharistic presidency is merely listed as one among ten functions, whereas in our theology and spirituality this is considered central to the priestly office. The multiplicity of roles tends to blur the primacy of eucharistic presidency in the office of priest.

More than a decade ago, David G. Jones developed a table of how clerical expectations were enlarged in this century. He lists as many as twenty-four different roles. As congregational life developed and as the mission of the church was expanded, the model that had professional leadership at its apex tended to assign primary responsibility for implementation to the clergy; since much of this accumulated without clarity, it is not surprising that overload stress among the clergy became common.

Now let's add to all of that the even more undefined and subtle expectations or images, such as prophet, guru or shaman, and we see another dimension of this confusion.

"Prophet" does not even appear in the ordination liturgy, yet it is a part of the collective consciousness of the church for the ordained. The supposed prophetic role of the clergy needs examination, because it is often misused as a way to excuse the rattling of the cages. It is generally agreed that prophets are called by God in peculiar ways and that the most disturbing, and thus the most effective, are not necessarily among the ordained. It may in fact be impossible to be priest and prophet at the same time. There is enough in the history of Israel and the life of the church to support that statement. The *church* is indeed called to be prophetic, but who within the church becomes its instrument is another matter.

The "guru" expectations of the clergy add another dimension. The guru is the answer person, the one who has the "knowledge" and on whom the people can depend for the "correct answer." Partly because of this, the Episcopal Church has the interesting phenomenon of having one of the most highly educated memberships, but also one of the most biblically and theologically illiterate. This, by the way, is not an indictment of our membership, but rather an indictment of the system that tends to promote vicarious religious knowledge, as well as vicarious spirituality. Happily, recent years have tended to bring this to our attention and we are making some progress in providing more incentive and opportunities for education for our people, but it is my conviction that until we make more radical reforms, such progress will not be significant.

Priesthood also takes on the role of "shaman," or healer. As in other religions, it is understandable that some such role expectation is attributed to those who exercise sacramental and other spiritual leadership. However, it becomes a great personal burden when the officeholder moves from being a sacramental channel to being sacralized as a person.

The titles we use for clergy also point to the role and expectation confusion. Take the term "father." In a normal family the children are expected to grow into adulthood, capable of parenthood. However, in the church a male priest is the father and the members of the congregation are the children and remain so forever. Once in a while somebody may be called to become another "father," but then probably not in that household. The use of the term "pastor" conjures up similar dependency images. The priest is the shepherd; the people are the sheep — always. In the early church and in the scriptures there is very little reference to church leaders as shepherds. Clergy and people are sheep of the Good Shepherd even as they share in his shepherding. It is my conviction that the bishop carries a shepherd's staff not so much as the symbol of the chief shepherd, but rather to call the church to its shepherding vocation.

Earlier in this essay, reference was made to the leadership aspects of the ordained offices. We need to rethink the nature and way of servant leadership. Servant leadership cannot be hierarchical; it is without rank or title. As the conversation between Jesus and Peter at the Last Supper makes clear, servanthood must be mutual. It is *not* a reverse kind of ranking. We must also learn how mutual, shared leadership is effectively exercised. Our present models are as hierarchical as the society in which we live; they have their roots in the Roman and feudal systems of the Middle Ages. The essentially communal character of the early church was set aside soon after Constantine. Furthermore, as indicated earlier, we need to consider further the way leadership is called and affirmed. Is the present practice and process effective? We will examine this later.

With regard to leadership as a function of the ordained offices, there are additional anomalies or at least differences between theory and practice. The presbyterate has a strong tradition of collegiality and collegial leadership. The very origins of the office lie in shared eldership. But here also we have problems in practice. For historical reasons the governance system of the Episcopal Church has strong democratic elements. Yet, as indicated earlier, it does not function with clarity and is clerically dominated. Furthermore, nowhere, as far as I know, is there a presbyteral college, simply functioning with the bishop as an accepted authority. Indeed, presbyters take their "share in the councils of the church,"[13] but in practice they do so by virtue of election rather than ordination.

Recently we have rightly made it possible for deacons to serve as clerical deputies in the General Convention. Many dioceses seeking to reestablish a renewed and effective diaconate and increasingly aware of the disenfranchisement of their deacons, are making similar appropriate changes in diocesan leadership structures. But what about the tradition that deacons are directly under the authority of the bishop? The ordination liturgy includes such reference. The implication is that they do not share in the same kind of collegiality as do presbyters. Though there is some historical basis for such tradition, do we need to maintain it in our time? The diaconate was nominal for centuries. Does its revival preclude its inclusion in a system of collegial and communal leadership that is more biblical than the tradition on which the single bishop and deacon authority line is based?

If we can disentangle the leadership strand from the other strands of the role and expectation confusion, we might be able to achieve not only an increased clarity and effectiveness, but also greater consistency with biblical principles.

Now to another strand in the tangled skein. I call it the *identity confusion.* As a result of the "sacralizing" of the ordained offices, as explained by Cook and Schillebeeckx, those who are ordained tend to place their primary Christian identity in their ordination rather than in their baptism. Two theological terms, "character" and "indelibility," play a part in the disentangling of this confusion.

In reference to the shift from a secular to a sacred understanding of the ordained offices, Bernard Cooke wrote: ". . . when we come to official church leadership we are dealing with more than a common social phenomenon. We are faced with an explicit claim to distinctively sacred status and role."[14] Schillebeeckx points out that this shift reached its zenith in scholastic doctrine, which led to an "even magical sacerdotolizing of the priesthood."[15] The notion of "character," he writes, "seems to be a particular medieval category which expressed the ancient church's view of the permanent relationship between the minister and the gift"[16] . . . given through ordination. But what started out to be a theological explanation of sacramental grace — gifts received for special ministry — became related to "personal power" and status.

In a 1972 article, Herve-Marie Legrand, a Belgian Roman Catholic, relates character to indelibility and to the tradition that the sacrament of ordination is not repeatable. He writes:

> *At the seventh session of (the council of) Trent, a definition was issued which received no dogmatic codicil since then: "If anyone says that in the three sacraments of baptism, confirmation and orders there is not imprinted in the soul a character, that is a certain spiritual and indelible sign from which it follows that they cannot be repeated, let him be anathema.*[17]

In the subsequent discussion Legrand expresses the opinion that the preoccupation with "sacramental character" was a way of dealing with the prevailing theology of the presbyteral office, which emphasized status rather than function.

Our new Prayer Book moves in the right direction as it attempts to be clear about the relationship of baptism and confirmation. The latter is at most a reaffirmation of the Baptismal Covenant, not the establishment of a new membership status, as was often implied in previous practice. Furthermore, when confirmation is talked about as the ordination of the laity, there is an implied denial of the primary ministerial identity accepted in baptism. Such a view of confirmation also plays into the hands of that which makes a categorical difference between laity and clergy.

Even at Trent, Legrand claims, the intention was not to establish a connection between the understanding of "character" and the nonrepeatability of the sacrament of orders. "Just as someone who has been confirmed can no longer be considered as never having been confirmed, so one who has been ordained."[18] Someone ordained may cease to function, or even be prohibited to do so, but when restored or recalled to function in the ordained office, such a person is not reordained. However, that is *not* because some indelible character has been bestowed in the ordination, but rather that a previously authorized office is being reauthorized. Legrand says:

> *When thought on this subject starts with the concept of character it is no longer based on the notion of ministry, that is of service to the people of God, but on a theology of cult: the priest becomes the one who is personally empowered to offer the eucharist.*[19]

Both the Anglican and Roman Catholic (ARC) and the Lutheran and Roman Catholic statements on the ministry of the church make reference to the permanence of ordination. Regrettably, both use "ministry" to refer to the clergy. The ARC statement says:

> *Just as Christ has united the church inseparably with Himself . . . so the gifts and calling of God to the ministers are irrevocable. For this reason ordination is unrepeatable in both of our churches.*[20]

We may note that the word "indelible" has been avoided. The Lutheran and Roman Catholic statement is more explicit:

> *By means of ordination Christ calls the ordained person once for all into the ministry of the church. Both in the Catholic and Lutheran understanding, therefore, ordination can be received only once and cannot be repeated.*[21]

> *There follows a discussion of the question of indelible character that rejects the notion of personal sanctification and seeks to understand it more "in terms of the promise and mission which permanently marks the ordained and claims them for the service of Christ."*[22]

Aidan Kavanagh, in a Trinity Institute article, deals with identity as follows:

> *Christians thus do not ordain to priesthood, they baptize to it. While the episcopacy and the presbyterate do come upon one for the first time at ordination, priesthood per se does not; it comes upon one in baptism, and thus laos is a priestly term for a priestly person. The vocabulary of priestliness, with which Christian tradition is ingrained, denotes a christic, i.e., a messianic-sacerdotal-royal quality which all the baptized share in the Anointed One himself and is expressed in a vast symphony of charisms, all of which originate from his own spirit given for the life of the world. To lay this on the Procrustean bed of a single order of ministry, or even on that of two orders of ministry, and then analytically chop away with modern scientific tools, is to engage in a reductionism of so severe a kind that it closely approaches an invalidation of the*

> *results of the process. Christians must not be led astray*
> *by it, especially Christian-presbyters and bishops.*[23]

Urban T. Holmes, in his book *Spirituality for Ministry*, attempted to get away from the view that clergy are in a special class, but he did not quite succeed. He wrote:

> *The priest or pastor objectifies in his or her person, and*
> *by what he or she does as the one preaching and presiding*
> *at the liturgy, a constellation of images that serves as a*
> *symbol of God's presence . . . . I am not implying that*
> *ordination effects some kind of characterological change*
> *in a person. It is not clear what such a change might*
> *mean. It does appear true, however, that within the*
> *consciousness of a community that recognized a person as*
> *ordained and within the awareness of its individual mem-*
> *bers he or she becomes a symbol. He or she represents*
> *and shapes a sense of the divine that wells up from deep*
> *within the corporate and individual memories of the people*
> *of God.*[24]

> *The power within the ordained person is what in fact the*
> *community gives to him or her as a sacrament of Christ,*
> *who is in turn the primal sacrament of God . . . . The*
> *pastor or priest is rooted in a world of symbols and takes*
> *on the character of his or her environment. There is an*
> *expectation that gathers about the person which, while*
> *not of his or her making, is real . . . .* The ordained person
> is expected to be a person of prayer that the person in the
> street cannot be.[25] (Emphasis mine.)

Many persons in the street are, in fact, more fully persons of prayer than some of the clergy.

We do indeed need to explore in greater depth the matter of sign and symbol. The ordained offices do serve as "living reminders" of the central elements of the church's life and mission: the bishops are signs of unity, catholicity, and apostolicity of the church; presbyters are signs of the whole body's priesthood and the deacons are signs of its servanthood. But they do not thereby become a separate class. Furthermore, symbol and function are related. A priest who does not exercise the office is not a sign or symbol to anyone. A sign that cannot be seen is not a sign. In that sense the indelibility question is moot.

The important World Council of Churches document *Baptism, Eucharist and Ministry* touches on a number of these questions:

> *The authority of the ordained minister is rooted in Jesus Christ, who has received it from the Father (Matt. 28:18), and who confers it by the Holy Spirit through the act of ordination. This act takes place within a community which accords public recognition to a particular person. Because Jesus came as one who serves (Mark 10:45; Luke 22:27), to be set apart means to be consecrated to service. Since ordination is essentially a setting apart with prayer for the gift of the Holy Spirit, the authority of the ordained ministry is not to be understood as the possession of the ordained person but as a gift for the continuing edification of the body in and for which the minister has been ordained. Authority has the character of responsibility before God and is exercised with the cooperation of the whole community.*[26]

Obviously all of the questions and discussion related to the ordination of women to the three orders will also continue to force the Episcopal Church into a new awareness of all of the significant symbolic and psychological questions. The male images and the patriarchal elements of both our theology and our practice are now being examined with a new scrutiny and with refreshing new insights. Similarly, when we accept the fact that clerical power is at stake in the reform of our practice of the ordained offices, we will be able to deal more creatively with such alternative models that welcome the leaders of minorities and of the poor to the ordained offices through "paths" that are appropriate to their context:

> *The absence in many modern churches of significant and deeply rooted orthodoxy in baptismal theology and practice turns seminaries into catechumenates, ordination into baptism, and clergy into "first-class" ecclesiastical citizens freed of obligations to the tradition and to proletarian communities of the merely baptized.*[27]

There is one church, one laos. Indeed, "Christians do not ordain to priesthood, they baptize to it." We may well wonder if it is not our holding on to the medieval vestiges of "character" and "indelibility" that continues to press in the direction of maintaining a distinctive status for the ordained. Maybe ordination ought not to be considered quite so permanent!

It would be a way to reestablish, periodically, the relationship of the ordained to the community of faith. At least this matter deserves some continuing reexamination.

For me, two of the most significant aspects of the foregoing discussion are these. First is the distinction between laity and clergy. Even our new catechism almost makes that implication when it asks the question, "Who are the ministers of the church?" and responds with the statement: ". . . ministers are lay persons, bishops, priests and deacons"[28] as if there were four orders. I have often heard statements to that effect. Even in common vocabulary, lay means uneducated, unknowledgeable, unprofessional. Perhaps the language battle is lost. Yet, the laity are *all* the people of God, including the clergy!

The second and more serious concern relates to the distancing of ordination from community. To me this is symbolized by the tradition that the call to presbyterate and diaconate generally originates with the person and is then given to the church for affirmation. The primary call is understood as coming from God, by the Spirit, to the individual. However, with the call to the episcopate both the theory and the practice are different. There the primary call comes from the community and is followed by assent and affirmation from the individual called. It seems to me that that is the way it might also be for the other offices. Both Canon III.8 and III.10 move in this direction, but community call is not generally practiced even in their use. *(The reference here is to the* Constitution and Canons of the Episcopal Church. *Title III (on Ministry), Canons 8 and 10 provided for ordination under "unusual" circumstances (peculiarities of the place or age of the individual) with somewhat relaxed academic standards. In subsequent years, under Wes' and others' influence, these canons were revised. Today what was once seen as unusual or exceptional appears in the canons as normative. A new Canon 1 calls each diocese to "make provision for the development and affirmation of the ministry of all baptized persons." Canon 3 establishes procedures and standards for a range of licensed lay ministries. The old Canon III, 8 as revised is now Canon 9, Of the* Ordination of Local Priests and Deacons, *which explicitly refers to persons "called by their congregations and the Bishop. . . ." - Eds.)*

In the Diocese of Nevada, in calling persons to the ordained offices, we have focused on such a community call process. There is strong evidence that the Spirit acting through the community in calling persons to presbyterate and diaconate is often more, or at least equally, effective than through the "traditional" approach.

The third confusion I call the *career and call confusion.* It relates to vocation, profession and employment. On the one hand we believe that God and the church call someone to these offices, but once employed, such a person is also concerned with job, career and professional service. The tension is immediately posed when it is realized that while a priest may well be a shepherd, even among other shepherds, he or she is also a hireling. It is quite difficult to keep that tension from becoming a stressful conflict. Some of this is reflected in the "lifestyle" expectations and requirements expressed even in the liturgy; some of it is expressed in the ill-defined professional criteria, some in concerns about compensation standards and tenure.

It is interesting to explore in what way the question is related to vocation and community call, and in what way it is related to professional protection. If we believe that a community calls a person to career responsibility in one of the ordained offices, why is it not equally possible for the community to withdraw that call? We certainly believe that the individual who has responded to such a call can feel called to another community for the exercise of that office. Why not the other way around?

These questions merely illustrate the need to disentangle the vocation and career confusion that is part of the entangled skein.

Some conclusions

Where, then, are we led by these discussions? First, we are called to develop a renewed theology of the church. Then, as we continue to explore and work at the renewal of the church in ministry, we need to continue to rediscover the biblical understanding of ministry as shared by every member of the body of Christ. Furthermore, we need a more focused understanding and modeling of the ordained offices based on the renewed and clearer New Testament understanding of the church.

Second, we need to continue the process of "fluffing the tangled skein" by describing the offices more clearly, distinguishing them from employment, understanding them in a variety of settings, and achieving some clarity regarding role and function. In the process we might discover that clergy can be volunteers and laity can be employees in the life of the church. We will discover that shared ministry avoids distinction in status. As we continue the process of desacralization and declericalization, the ordained offices will become more open to varieties of persons in varieties of situations. Preparation will be less academic and more situational. Spiritual formation will be less monastic and less concerned with creating a separate ministerial status.

Third, it is equally important for us to continue to explore the meaning of shared leadership in order to make our governance system more consistent with our gospel commitment. The medium must be brought closer to the message.

And last, the ordained offices must be more firmly rerooted in the community by which they are called and for the sake of which they exist:

> All members of the believing community, ordained and lay, are interrelated. On the one hand, the community needs ordained ministers. Their presence reminds the community of the divine initiative, and of the dependence of the Church on Jesus Christ, who is the source of its mission and the foundation of its unity. They serve to build up the community in Christ and to strengthen its witness. In them the Church seeks an example of holiness and loving concern. On the other hand, the ordained ministry has no existence apart from the community. Ordained ministers can fulfill their calling only in and for the community. They cannot dispense with the recognition, the support and the encouragement of the community.[29]

Furthermore, every community of faith, no matter what its size, no matter where it is situated or how little money it has available, must be enabled to have a complete life and thus be empowered for a comprehensive mission.

> As for the community and the Eucharist, the ancient church and the modern church cannot envision any Christian community without the celebration of the Eucharist. There is an essential link between the local ecclesia and Eucharist. Throughout the pre-Nicene church, it was held evidently on the basis of Jewish models, that a community of which at least 12 fathers of families were assembled had the right to a priest or community leader and thus to the Eucharist, at which he presided. In the small communities these originally episcopal leaders soon became presbyteral leaders, parish priests. In any case, according to the views of the ancient church, a shortage of priests was an ecclesiastical impossibility. The modern so-called shortage of priests stands to be criticized in the light of the ancient church's view of church and ministry, because the modern shortage, in fact, has causes which stem from outside the ministry.[30]

David Paton points to the main thesis in Roland Allen's writings:

> *The heart of Allen's understanding is that the church lives by faith in Christ, whose gifts are sufficient for its life. At every level the church is empowered by Christ to be itself, from the almost illiterate little congregation in a village to the Vatican Council itself; and the deepest considerations apply as much to the one as to the other, and to all other levels between.*

> *This conviction, that no part of the church is too small or too lowly to be the church and be responsible as the church for being Christ to the world around it, rests upon two convictions which Allen held with a depth of passion of which he may himself have been unconscious. They seemed to him obvious, and they continued to seem so even when he had become reluctantly aware that many sincere Christians did not hold them as he held them. These convictions are (1) that the gifts of God in the "signs of the Kingdom" — in the Gospel and the Gospel sacraments and the life of the Spirit-filled Body itself — are sufficient; (2) that ordinary human beings — yea, . . . Chinese peasants or . . . African tribesmen — are able to receive and use these gifts.*[31]

In conclusion, we must recall that the primary reason for the reform and remodeling of the ministries and ordained offices of the church is to continue the renewal of her life and the strengthening of her mission. *Baptism, Eucharist and Ministry* provides us with a helpful summation:

> *The ordained ministry should be exercised in a personal, collegial and communal way. It should be personal because the presence of Christ among his people can most effectively be pointed to by the person ordained to proclaim the Gospel and to call community to serve the Lord in unity of life and witness. It should also be collegial, for there is need for a college of ordained ministers sharing in the common task of representing the concerns of the community. Finally, the intimate relationship between the ordained ministry and the community should find expression in a communal dimension where the exercise of the ordained ministry is rooted in the life of the commu-*

nity and requires the community's effective participation in the discovery of God's will and the guidance of the Spirit.[32]

It is indeed one of the major challenges and opportunities of our time to develop both the systems and the theological understandings that will enable this to become a reality. When it does, the church's life will be more vital and her mission more effective.

Appendix

Following is a suggested revision of two parts of the Liturgy for the Ordination of a Priest. The beginning of the Examination is rearranged and slightly rephrased. The questions are rearranged. The Prayers are slightly edited to make them applicable to various ways in which priesthood is exercised, without changing the essence. Not all priests need to be pastor, teacher and counselor, all three. This way emphasis is on word and sacraments. "Proclaim" is broader than "preach."

The Examination

My *brother*, the church is the family of God, the body of Christ, the temple of the Holy Spirit. All baptized people are called to make Christ known as Savior and Lord and to share in the renewing of his world. You share this call with all the people of God, but you are now also called to the office of priest in the church.

As a priest it will be your primary privilege and responsibility to share with the bishop in the administration of Holy Baptism and to gather the church, where you serve, for the celebration of the mysteries of Christ's Body and Blood. You also will take your place with others in the councils of the church.

Together with those among whom you serve, it will be your task to proclaim by word and deed the Gospel of Jesus Christ, and to fashion your life according to its precepts. You are to love and serve the people among whom you serve, caring alike for young and old, strong and weak, rich and poor. As a priest, you are also to declare God's forgiveness to penitent sinners and to perform the other ministrations entrusted to you.

In all that you do, you are to nourish Christ's people from the riches of his grace and strengthen them to glorify God in this life and the life to come.

Bishop My *brother*, do you believe that you are truly called by God and his church to this priesthood?
Answer I believe I am so called.

Bishop Will you undertake to be faithful to all whom you are called to serve, laboring together with them and with your fellow ministers to build up the family of God?
Answer I will.

Bishop Will you respect and be guided by the pastoral direction and leadership of your bishop?
Answer I will.

Bishop Will you persevere in prayer, both in public and in private, asking God's grace, both for yourself and for others, offering all your labors to God, through the mediation of Jesus Christ, and in the sanctification of the Holy Spirit?
Answer I will.

Bishop Will you be diligent in the reading and study of the Holy Scriptures, and in seeking the knowledge of such things as may make you a stronger and more able minister of Christ?
Answer I will.

Bishop Will you do your best to pattern your life (and that of your family, or household) in accordance with the teachings of Christ, so that you may be a wholesome example to your people?
Answer I will.

Bishop May the Lord who has given you the will to do these things give you the grace and power to perform them.
Answer Amen.

The Consecration of the Priest
(last paragraph only)

The Bishop then continues:

May *he* be exalted by you, O Lord, in the midst of your people; offer spiritual sacrifices acceptable to you; boldly proclaim the gospel of salvation; and rightly administer the sacrament of the New Covenant. Grant that in all things

Frensdorff

he may serve without reproach, so that your people may be strengthened and your Name glorified in all the world. All this we ask through Jesus Christ our Lord, who with you and the Holy Spirit lives and reigns, one God, for ever and ever.

The People in a loud voice respond:

Amen.

Notes

1 *Anglican Theological Review*, 66 (Suppl. Series 9): 1, 1984 (subsequent notations, ATR).
2 World Council of Churches, "Ministry, 1, 5,"*Baptism, Eucharist and Ministry* (Geneva, 1982) p. 20 (subsequently BEM).
3 Bernard Cooke, "Early Christian Ministry," unpublished, a paper presented at the Roland Allen Conference, June 1984, p. 16 (subsequently Cooke).
4 Ibid., p. 20.
5 Ibid., p. 22.
6 Ibid., p. 23.
7 Ibid., p. 25.
8 Edward Schillebeeckx, *Ministry* (New York: Crossroad, 1981).
9 *ATR*, pp. 38-39.
10 *Book of Common Prayer*, pp. 525ff (BCP).
11 Margaret Fletcher Clark, *We Need People Who*, (New York: Board for Theological Education, September 1982).
12 Alban Institute, *Information*, Nov.-Dec. 1983, p. 2.
13 *BCP*, p. 531.
14 Cooke, p. 20.
15 Edward Schillebeeckx, "A Creative Retrospect as Inspiration for the Ministry in the Future," *Minister? Pastor? Prophet? - essays on grassroots leadership in the churches*. (New York: Crossroads, 1981), p. 67 (MPP).
16 Ibid., pp. 76-77.
17 Herve-Marie Legrand, " The 'Indelible' Character and the Theology of Ministry," *Concilium*, 74:54, 1972.
18 Ibid., p. 59.

19 Ibid., p. 61.
20 *ARCIC Final Report*, the Canterbury Statement, p. 15.
21 *International Lutheran/Roman Catholic Agreed Report*, p. 36.
22 Ibid.
23 *ATR*, p. 40.
24 Urban T. Holmes, *Spirituality for Ministry* (San Francisco: Harper and Row, 1982), p. 32.
25 Ibid., p. 34.
26 *BEM*, p. 22, Ministry I, 15.
27 *ATR*, p. 44.
28 *BCP*, p. 855.
29 *BEM*, pp. 21-22, Ministry II, 12.
30 *MPP*, p. 77.
31 David Paton (Ed.), *Reform of the Ministry*, (London: Lutterworth Press, 1968), p. 26.
32 *BEM*, pp. 25-26, Ministry III, 26.

Chapter 4

RENEWAL OF THE CHURCH
IN THE CITY

Wesley Frensdorff
with responses by Roger J. White &
Enrique R. Brown

In January 1980, Bishop Frensdorff addressed a meeting of the Urban Caucus, Episcopal Church. The following is the text of that address. We append to this — now ten years later — responses by the Rt. Rev. Roger J. White, Bishop of Milwaukee, and the Ven. Enrique R. Brown, Archdeacon of New York.

- Eds.

A mong the several items on the agenda of the February Episcopal Urban Caucus is renewal of the church in the city. Our experience in dioceses which are rural/small town, and whose urban areas are relatively new, may not offer much insight in addressing the serious social, economic and political issues of the inner city. There is, however, good reason to believe that our experience in ministry development might contribute significantly to the church renewal portion of our church's urban strategy. Only if the church, as a gathered, worshiping, ministering community, is a *significant* part of the life of the people of the city will she be able to have a *significant* share in the renewal and rebuilding of the city itself. Only a congregation present and alive — locally — can witness effectively, through its worship, its life, its ministries, to God's great love of the people of its community. Then, also, together with the church elsewhere, she can engage the various issues related to social change.

For the church to be vital, alive and truly present in the city, it must be owned by the people of the city. It is my conviction that our traditional models of church life (ministry, organization and decision-making) are too hierarchical, too money dependent and too centered on highly educated, professional, stipendiary clergy who normally come from the middle and upper classes. It is these models and these dependencies which unnecessarily prevent effective renewal in life, ministry and mission.

My limited comprehension of liberation theology leads me to understand both "presence" and "ownership" as related to "control." Ownership and control are interrelated: two sides of the same coin. They are essential to presence. Hugh White has said, "... people who own have control."[1] It appears to me that, together with the host of other problems, the church in the city must deal with the problems related to "indigenization" and, in this case, they are not that different from churches in a variety of cultural and ethnic situations.

Among the recommendations resulting from the urban hearings sponsored by the Urban Bishops' Coalition, we read:

> *We must be willing to choose a new kind of presence in the cities which calls less for money than for personal involvement in the struggles of the poor . . . . We must decide to be present in the cities wherever the poor are struggling to be free and not just in discreet "church" programs and operations.[2]*

Also:

> *In a dramatically surprising way, the most urgent plea to the church presented by those who spoke as or on behalf of the cities was not for money, but for the church's presence and involvement in their struggle.*

> *The effort to raise massive sums of new income leads to*

the assumption that nothing can be done until that income is raised. The evidence presented at the hearings is clearly that additional funds may well prove to be needed, but much more can be done now with existing resources if the church will change its sense of priorities, its style of operation, and its basic commitments.[3] (Emphasis mine)

In the 1920s, having served for eight years in China and subsequently studying Anglican missionary methods, Roland Allen, an English priest, wrote:

We constantly hear men use these three terms, self-support, self-extension, self-government as if they were distinct and separate things . . . they cannot be rightly so treated. . . thus self-support and self-government are closely knit. As for self-extension, it is surely plain that a church which could neither support itself nor govern itself could not multiply itself. Thus self-extension is bound up with self-support and self-government: these three are intimately united.[4]

Is there a relationship between these assertions and Roland Allen's conclusions? The common denominator is the incarnation — our Lord Jesus, fully present in and through the church, his body, indigenous in place, time and culture, among the people who are its life, who exercise its ministry, and who carry out its mission.

The rather ambitious proposals of the Urban Bishops' Coalition, contained in *The Challenge for Evangelism and Mission,* target some very important issues which seek to deal with the complex underlying causes of many of our social ills. Experience makes it a bit difficult to gather much optimism for the funding of these proposals. However, as *To Hear and To Heed* has pointed out, there's much to do that does *not* require money, though it will require basic changes in the way we do ministry, call and train persons to Holy Orders, and model our life for leadership and decision making. Our traditional, suburban, middle class models are no longer adequate for the church in the city to be truly indigenous. Herein lies a significant part of the challenge to evangelism and mission.

Is not much of our present paralysis in the inner city due to our lack of real identification with the people who are there? There are many aspects of the crisis of the cities. Most of these are beyond the church's ability to shape and change. But questions of indigenization, i.e., presence and identification, can be faced.

> *A pivotal issue which relates to the church's stake in the
> city is the question of identification. To what extent is the
> Episcopal Church willing to identify the people of the
> cities as its people? The Episcopal Church moved toward
> the suburbs in the '50s and '60s because that was where
> "its people" were present in ever increasing numbers.
> This exodus left the cities inhabited by people that the
> Episcopal Church has never identified as "its people."* [5]

If our church is to participate in both the pain, as well as the opportunities for renewal of the city, this withdrawal has to be reversed by engagement and identification with the cities' people. So far we have not been able, significantly, to deal with this problem.

Roland Allen concluded that the Anglican Communion — contrary to St. Paul's methods — had saddled its "missions" with methods of life, ministry or organization which were foreign to their situation and culture, resulted in a paralyzing dependency, and kept the church deprived of the very sacraments which are its lifeblood.

In our concern for the renewal and revitalization of the church in the city, we do well to consider some of these same matters. A truly indigenous church, Roland Allen pointed out, must be truly self-governing. It must own and control. The conclusions of the urban hearings point in the same direction.

> *We must decide to be involved as a servant church which
> recognizes the priority and authority of the people it seeks
> to serve. As a servant church, we must listen and must be
> directed by the voice of the Lord as expressed by the poor
> and concede to them a decisive role in the determination
> of the priorities, program and shape of the church's life
> and expenditures.* [6]

To be indigenous, to own and control, requires more than self-government. It also requires self-support. It involves autonomy, not in the sense of isolation, but in the sense of being responsible or response-able. Autonomy, in my mind, is not mere independence. It is to be capable of interdependence. "Autonomous" means having a strong sense of identity, purpose and ownership with the will and ability to act, and to act interdependently. A dependent person cannot be effectively interdependent; neither can a dependent congregation. However, our models for autonomous (in the above sense) congregational life — a parish, we call it — is based on having sufficient money to support buildings, diocese and stipendiary clergy.

As such, the model *guarantees* dependence on outside support for virtually every inner city congregation, as it does for small rural ones.

Real indigenization, with effective self-government and self-support, will require some radical changes if the church in people-poor or poor people areas is to be set free to become autonomous and indigenous.

Can we, however, change those models which are basically hierarchical and dependent on professional, stipendiary clergy? I believe we can. Can we set the church free for renewal in ministry and local responsibility without doing violence to our ecclesiology or to our theology of Holy Orders? I believe we can. Our problems are not theological; they are organizational. I believe our situation is the result — for a variety of understandable historical reasons — of attaching too many functions of ministry to those who exercise the ordained offices, and of "locking up" the sacraments in professional clergy. This has placed the church in a ministerial and sacramental captivity. As a result the local church is seen as a community gathered around a minister, rather than as a ministering community, and the life-giving sacraments are made dependent on the payment of stipends.

We can come out of these captivities to new life and mission to rebuild both "the temple" and the city. That, however, will require more radical changes than merely pouring new money into old methods, or sewing patches on old garments. The church has to be of the people it serves in such a way that *they* carry out the ministries essential for their life and mission, and *they* raise up from *among themselves* priests and deacons. Together, then, as a eucharistic servant community, in the name of Jesus, by the power of the Holy Spirit, *they* will minister and witness to their neighbors, and, together with the rest of the church, call for justice and equity, and shape the life of the city.

Now, sixty years later, the principles Roland Allen set forth as basic New Testament principles are receiving some application and testing in this country and elsewhere in the world. What we call the Total Ministry Program in Nevada is based, at least in part, on some of these principles. The church must be fully indigenous; it is a ministering community in which, potentially, every member shares; every disciple has received gifts for ministry which he or she is called to offer in the life and mission of the church; the offices of priest and deacon can be filled by persons identified and called by and from the congregation; and training opportunities for all members are provided by the diocese serving as the link between congregations and as the basic resource center.

Canon III, 8 (*see Eds. note, page 34*), was originally intended to make sacraments available on a regular basis for special places and situations. Even its limited use in several dioceses has taught us many things.

The most important of these is that unless it is used as part of a total ministry model, as outlined above, it is merely a lesser, cheaper version of the old clergy-dominated, money-dependent ministry model. However, once the church is understood as a ministering community in which each member offers his or her gifts in mutual service, both within the life of the church and in her mission of witness and service, then the ordained offices can take their special place in a different and vital way.

Let us look at those churches which have been able to identify with the poor and with minorities. They have much to teach us. What makes them really indigenous? Perhaps, finally, we'll have to conclude that we cannot adjust the ethos, religious history and culture of the Episcopal Church sufficiently for it to be truly indigenous to the people of the city. But in order to give it a real try, we'll have to go far beyond merely shoring up — with ever-shrinking funds — the old ways of doing things.

In a stimulating article published in the Los Angeles diocesan paper in September, 1979, the Rev. Charles Belknap points out that we have many marginal parishes because an economically stable parish with one employed priest costs $50,000 per year, while one priest attracts, on the average, a congregation of 160 adults. That requires better than average stewardship from an average, upper middle class parish, so it is impossible for a congregation in an economically depressed area. So what are we doing with this heart-sick patient? he asks. Either we give periodic transfusions (support grants) or we prescribe limited activity (part-time clergy) or we do a coronary bypass (rent the facilities) or we slowly squeeze the turnip to death. Belknap concludes his analysis with a call to redesign the heart, "to find new ways to be the church in the urban areas." Right on!!

If nothing else, economics will force us to take a second look at our mission strategy. The future will bring either inflation or depression, the economists tell us. All institutions which are based on voluntary funding will need to face this truth. From experience it is safe to say that no appeal will result in sufficient *sustained* funding to make a significant difference. If the primary strategy of a renewed urban program is based on money, we are likely to fail before we start.

"New occasions teach new duties, time makes ancient good uncouth" (hymn 519).[7] The laos, the people of God, has within itself all the gifts needed for ministry, both for the life and worship of the church and for her mission. "As each has received a gift, employ it for one another, as good stewards of God's varied grace." (1 Peter 4:10)

Once we depend more fully on these gifts, build the self-confidence of the people and provide them with opportunities for ministerial education and training, we will discover the many hidden talents, too long buried, that are present in *every* congregation, no matter of what size or in what place.

In New Testament terms, there is almost no cell of the church too small to be sufficient in ministry for its own life and mission. We ought to be able to take any nucleus of committed, somewhat experienced disciples and, through support and training, enable them for their mission in their place, "to equip the saints for the work of ministry." (Ephesians 4:12) They ought not to be dependent on, or paralyzed by, those models which come from another time and place, and which may still be appropriate and effective in many places and situations — but not all.

For the church in the inner city to become present, to be locally owned and controlled, and thus empowered for mission, it needs first to be free, to be fully indigenous in the life and culture of the people where they are. This calls for change — not really big money, either — but radical change in our understanding and modeling of ministry and the place of Holy Orders within the ministering community.

Notes

1. JSAC, *Grapevine.* 10/79.
2. *To Hear and To Heed,* page 52.
3. Ibid. page 55.
4. Roland Allen, *The Spontaneous Expansion of the Church.* Eerdmans, 1962. Pages 26-27.
5. *To Hear and To Head,* page 47.
6. Ibid., page 51.
7. *The Hymnal, 1940.*

Roger White responds . . .

In "Renewal of the Church in the City" Wes Frensdorff managed to transfer some learnings in the area of indigenous ministry and the development of ministry from the rural, small town scene to that of the urban scene. His transference of these learnings from one environment to another is, I believe, pertinent for those of us who labor in the urban arena.

There is indeed a continuation of dependency, bred by unimaginative approaches to urban ministry, which is both paternalistic and unfruitful. It tends to project the image that ministry is to and for others, with there being little to no possibility of ownership or control by those with whom we minister in our cities. As church we need to redirect our energy to the establishment of indigenous communities which, in turn, can themselves proclaim the gospel and begin to strive for justice and peace in the midst of their own circumstances and communities. Lessons can be learned from the growing experience of our overseas dioceses which verify to us that the development of an indigenous church brings acceptance, fruitfulness and control, in contrast to dependency and a chaplaincy mentality which we often experience in our urban situations.

Bishop Frensdorff holds up the concept that the "heart of urban ministry is found in the worshiping community itself — alive, challenged by the gospel and willing to live it." If a diocese is to enhance its presence in the core urban areas, it must first move to a strong commitment that the church should be of the people, controlled by the people and strongly supported in this conviction through the words and actions of the diocese. Indigenous congregations need to raise up and develop indigenous leadership supported by diocesan program and, in some cases, directed capital investment for economic justice purposes to help make the basics for congregational life and ministry possible. Unfortunately, most of our efforts are from the outside in, and in most cases end up being ineffective as we struggle to establish and maintain an almost "alien presence" in the heart of our urban environment.

The Jesuits in Central America (Jesuit Province of El Salvador) made a commitment to live with the poor — to minister with the poor, to find Christ in the community of the poor — and the presence of the church then becomes an advocate for the poor in addressing issues of justice as the community of faith becomes empowered for mission and ministry and so fulfills its baptismal covenant and calling. This "new kind" of Jesuit presence could be Roland Allen's ideas at work today, and they are certainly applicable in principle to our own urban ministries.

In Milwaukee a base Christian community has emerged from our vast city feeding program. It is a rather large group of street people which is joined by individuals who work with outcasts in our society. It is a community of mainly poor and many disabled in a multitude of ways; in other words, it is reflective of our urban population. This base community now outnumbers the core membership of the local parish where it gathers for prayer, Bible study, fellowship and occasional eucharist. Its members meet for two hours weekly and do not miss! It has grown to be a strong witness, or what we would call a community of faith. It has called for and planned a residential intensified Christian community which will have its own house where people can live and grow in community for six months to a year and move on to a deeper stability; it is a movement from death to life and hope.

The base community I am speaking of has developed its own lay leadership; it does invite bishops and priests to join it on occasion, but for the most part, ministers to itself and to others! It is a congregation which, at present, is very much alive in its worship life and in its ministries, and it is owned by the spiritual community that it has become. It costs the diocese a room on a Monday in an urban parish, support in spirit and little more.

This community epitomizes what Bishop Frensdorff advocated by use of mutual ministry and development of ministry; for us it is a sign of hope and life for the future urban ministry of our church.

My hope is that such indigenous communities will develop and become communities, strengthened and grounded in worship and fellowship, that are advocates for jobs, homes, quality education and the rebuilding of our boarded-up neighborhoods — advocates for justice and peace and for those who seek to serve Christ in others. People power, a people empowered by God's presence, equipping themselves for ministry to one another and to their environment and to the needs of all God's children: that is the goal.

Like Roland Allen, Wes Frensdorff and the Jesuits of Central America, our living, worshiping ministry with the poor of our city has brought us to see an incarnate Christ, for as we "do for the least of these, my brothers," we do it for Christ. Not only have we had an opportunity to experience Christ in doing for others, but in so doing, we have found Christ in that community of faith.

We as church can offer our gifts for the poor to determine how they may best be used. We can offer capital support (few operating expenses are involved), we can offer advocacy and a hands-on physical presence as we are invited to join with them in their living out of the gospel message. This is interdependence: where we both need one another and learn from one another, rather than control by either entity. Together, in the power of Christ, we *can* minister in our urban population centers.

The urban church can be set free — at little risk — for our hierarchical dependency building and non-indigenous model has done little to recognize or enhance the presence of Christ among the poor. It is a new day, for new ways, for the development of indigenous (base) ministry communities grounded in Christ's presence, willing to be Christ, witnessing and ministering to the poor of our cities and offering hope and wholeness of life.

I enthusiastically join Wes Frensdorff in embracing the concept of the "laos of God" in action/total ministry and in looking toward our Lord Jesus Christ fully present in and through his people, the church — Christ's incarnation in the city — a home-owned, self-controlled, enlivened community of indigenous people raising up their own leadership and, pray God, their own clergy in the not-too-distant future.

Enrique Brown responds . . .

In "Renewal of the Church in the City," the late Bishop Wesley Frensdorff issued a call for a "radical change in our understanding and modeling of ministry and the place of Holy Orders within the ministering community."

Ten years later as we stand on the precipice of the "Decade of Evangelism," that call rings equally — if not more urgently — pressing. And, as pertains to the Episcopal Church's ability to genuinely and effectively minister among the diverse and increasingly pluralistic social environment of America's cities at the dawn of the twenty-first century, the call becomes a desperate plea.

The Ven. Hartshorn Murphy, archdeacon of the Diocese of Los Angeles, addressing the 1989 National Conference of the Union of Black Episcopalians (UBE) regarding that organization's concerns about vocations among blacks and declining membership in black churches, urged the UBE,

> *Unless we begin to turn things around, the future will likely see increasing numbers of black congregations merging or closing, their former facilities sold to inde-*

*pendent black congregations that will thrive on the same
spot; or our black churches will be torn down to make
way for redevelopment.*[1]

Archdeacon Murphy continues, pointing out another phenomenon
that causes concern in Los Angeles:

*In many of our urban areas, former strong black parishes
are now being redirected to serve growing Hispanic and
Asian congregations. I know of no new work being envisioned for black people.*[2]

Interestingly, both Bishop Frensdorff and Archdeacon Murphy
quote these lines from that hymn (519) in the 1940 Hymnal: "New occasions teach new duties, time makes ancient good uncouth."

Since the fifties and sixties, many organizations within the Episcopal Church have addressed the need for revitalization of urban ministry
efforts. In more recent times, the Church and City Conference, the Urban
Bishops Coalition and the Episcopal Urban Caucus have organized to
address the myriad social ills that plague life in an increasingly urban
society. We have seen much good come from such national church programs as the Coalition for Human Need, Jubilee Ministry and the 1988
General Convention program for economic development.

What remains for us a challenge, however, is how to be the *church*
among those people who consistently inhabit our cities and who find it so
difficult to believe that we truly take them seriously.

We must examine, therefore, what it is about our ecclesiology and
the way we present ourselves *institutionally* and as persons, lay and ordained, to the communities that surround us in the cities, yet find us *strange*
and alien to their reality. What is it about us that makes us so inadequate
before the task given to us in our baptism, of bringing the life-changing and
people-empowering message of the gospel into the lives of individuals and
communities?

At least part of the problem lies in the systemic arena of the
structures for the ministry and the living out of what it means to be the
church — the "people of God" — in the context of urban society today.
Another problem lies in the language and symbols which we use to communicate the message of the gospel, as well as the instruments — the vessels,
so to speak — which bear the message.

Given these realities, the challenge still before us becomes quite
clear. All around us we can see an increase of the ills that affect human-
kind. We are bombarded daily in many ways with constant reminders of

poverty, violence, drug abuse, racial strife and injustice of every kind. This is the nature of life in the city, and people who inhabit the city are deeply affected by these phenomena. How, then, is the church to respond?

In his book entitled *Ecclesiogenesis*, Brazilian theologian Leonardo Boff, in examining ways of being church offers the following:

> *Before becoming visible through human mediations — those of bishop, priest, deacon, and so on — the risen Christ and the Spirit already possess a presence in the community. There prevails an ongoing, constant immanence of the Spirit and of the risen Lord in humanity, and in a special way in the community of the faithful. It is those who gather to form the church, who constitute it essentially. The hierarchy has the sacramental function of organizing and serving a reality that it has not created but* discovered, *and within which it finds itself.*[3]

It is fundamentally important that we recognize and begin to act out of a realization of what Boff is saying if we are to see our churches in the cities become transformed communities — fully equipped and capable of life-renewing ministry right where they are, with the gifts and resources they presently possess. Part of the task then, is one of *discovery*. We must set out to "discover" the risen Christ and the presence of God's Holy Spirit which dwells in the hearts and minds of God's people and in the community of the faithful. We must call forth this "immanence" of the Spirit with all of its gifts for ministry — affirming and mediating as God would have us; not *suppressing* and *controlling*, but *celebrating* what is offered and channeling it, making it useful for God's purposes.

Bishop Frensdorff reminded us that the "laos, the people of God, has within itself all the gifts needed for ministry, both for the life and worship of the church and for her mission." In my conversations over the years with many of those struggling with the challenge and the need for autonomous, indigenous urban churches, I have encountered, for the most part, a basic and enduring cynicism about the *viability* of the New Testament idea that is so central to the thinking of the English missionary Roland Allen — and cited by Frensdorff as a key point of departure — that "there is no cell of the church too small to be sufficient in ministry for its own life and mission."

That kind of cynicism results in the self-fulfilling of its own prophesy! If, in fact, we organize the church in such a way that we do not affirm the gifts for ministry which are there already in the churches and congregations in our cities — however small and lacking in terms of resources or formal education — it is no wonder that we are unable to do any *new thing* or any really *good thing* on behalf of the God we seek to serve in these communities.

On the other hand, I have seen even small urban congregations come alive and I have seen the beginnings of a hopeful and powerful process of renewal in places and among people where an "encounter" and a "discovery" between *the faith that is in them* and *the God who seeks them* has been engendered. It is here that I find the most exciting prospects for renewal of the church and its ministry in the city. This then is, for me, the task on which all of the support systems for mission and ministry in the city must concentrate some considerable time, effort, energy and resources. This, for me, would be responsible stewardship of the resources that we do possess, in terms of people, buildings and finances.

The Episcopal Church cannot conquer all of the social ills that beset us in the world. We have an obligation to join with other faiths and with secular entities to work for a better world. None of this, however, militates against the dual and equally, if not more important task of empowering all of God's people for ministry.

That task can no longer be avoided if we are to withstand the assaults on God's "little ones," entrusted to the care of the church, as we are reminded by Matthew's Gospel: "And the king will answer them, 'Truly I say to you, as you did it to one of the least of these my brethren, you did it to me.' " (Matthew 25:40)

The renewal of the church and of ministry in the city can only happen as the people of God who dwell in the city are recognized by the church and her agents, having their gifts affirmed. In order for this to happen, we need to take a fresh look at what Bishop Frensdorff refers to as a "radical change in our understanding and modeling of ministry." The need for this "change in our understanding" is so urgent and what lies behind it of such tremendous importance that I am certain God is acting even now to bring this about. We need simply to cooperate, to get out of the way. As Roland Allen said:

> *"We must realize that baptized Christians have rights. What are those rights? They have a right to live as Christians in an organized Christian church where the sacraments of Christ are observed. They have a right to obey Christ's commands, and to receive his Grace. In other words they have a right to be properly organized with their own proper ministers. They have a right to be a church, not a mere congregation. These are the inalienable rights of Christians, and we cannot baptize people*

and then deny their rights, or deprive them of them. When we baptize we take responsibility for seeing that those whom we baptize can so live in the church." [4]

I believe that there is great potential for renewal, growth and strength in the church's ability for ministry in the city if we can learn to take those words seriously. But only if we also take seriously those people and communities who inhabit the city — trusting the power of God's Holy Spirit and calling it forth out of those communities for God's purposes in ministry.

Notes

1. Hartshorn Murphy, *Expanding Our Horizons Through Evangelism.* 1989.
2. Ibid.
3. Leonardo Boff, *Ecclesiogenesis: The Base Communities Reinvent the Church.* (Orbis: 1986), page 26.
4. Roland Allen, *The Spontaneous Expansion of the Church.* 1927. Quoted in *Ministry Development Journal,* No. 15, 1988, page 22.

The concepts presented in this book, their application in various settings and the persisting issues and challenges are not exactly light reading. We thought it likely that many people would appreciate an opportunity to discuss these topics in small group settings. We encourage this, and these notes are our attempt to give you a bit of a head start in designing your sessions.

Setting up

Leadership:

Who is responsible for convening the group, guiding the discussion, designing the formal plan, etc.? Is it one person? Does the leadership rotate, or is it shared in some other way? Remember that you are studying, among other things, church leadership; your small group life will demonstrate some approach to it.

Standards:

Many study groups find it helpful to think through group life standards. Standards are conditions (representing appropriate and desired behavior) that group members strive to maintain out of respect for others. Remember to formulate them as specific conditions. Here are some examples:

If one member thinks the point is relevant, the others at least look at it.

Each member feels that there is an opportunity to speak to the issue — or the freedom not to.

Study plan:

What is your overall plan for covering the material? Sunday morning adult class? Evening sessions (how many?), etc. Presumably, portions of the book will be assigned reading in preparation for the group discussion. How will you divide it up to fit the number of sessions you have planned? Should a schedule be printed so everyone can track progress? Should you give some thought to the question of whether this study might end with some action?

Here are some discussion ideas for Part I.

What concepts in "The Dream" are particularly compelling to you?

"Christians do not ordain to priesthood, they baptize to it." Discuss.

"There is no cell of the church too small to be sufficient in ministry for its own life and mission." (See also I Cor. 1:4-7 and Chapters 12-14.) Discuss:

A) Distinctions in the concepts: "life," "mission" and "ministry."

B) How can we get past the cynicism (p. 54) regarding the claim?

Given the "sacramental and priestly captivity" by professionals, and related job economics, is the Decade of Evangelism likely to go anywhere?

Discuss the relative desirability of these two procedures:

A) A potential leader volunteers, receives training, is ordained and is then assigned to a leadership position somewhere (sacramental leadership is imported).

B) An established leader is recognized, called by the congregation, and is ordained for sacramental functions (sacramental leadership is local).

Note: For congregational leadership we usually follow (A); for episcopal leadership the procedure is more like (B).

If the vision, concepts and challenges of Part I were faithfully and competently addressed by the church in this decade, what would the ministry of the church look like by the year 2000?

Formulate your vision of "Ministry 2000" as a series of conditions that would be desirable and that we might be able to attain by then. Be specific: "By the year 2000, . . . (condition)."

Some possibilities to consider:

* Rewrite Prayer VI (*BCP*, p. 392) as might be appropriate by 2000 (or even next year).

* Will the presiding officer at the eucharist still be called "the celebrant?"

* How many presbyters and deacons might your congregation have in its full range of ministries? What other ministries will be in place?

* Will the salaried "chief executive officer" of your parish (if you have one then) likely be a professionally trained pastor or a professionally trained manager (assuming in either case that s/he is a competent theologian)?

* Consider the composition of your diocesan staff by then: the positions, titles, etc.

* For most dioceses "support of mission congregations" is the largest item in the budget, after "contribution to the general church program." How will this look in 2000?

* What will things be like after a decade of evangelism (assuming the above premise: "that the vision has been faithfully addressed")?

Discuss: What do we in this parish/diocese do to get there?

Part II

THE EXPERIENCE

Chapter 5

NAVAJOLAND:
An Emerging Vision

George Sumner

The Navajoland Area Mission was formed in 1977, by the House of Bishops from portions of the Dioceses of Arizona and Utah encompassing lands of the Navajo Reservation. In 1979, the General Convention accepted the cession of portions of the Diocese of the Rio Grande to be added to the Area Mission. The area totals some 25,000 square miles, and is home for an estimated 160,000 Navajos. The intention was to form "a church in the Episcopal/Anglican tradition, multi-cultured, also expressing Navajo life, culture and tradition, with Navajo leadership at all levels, welcoming and serving all the people in Navajoland; an equal partner with other dioceses of the Episcopal Church."

The Rt. Rev. Frederick Putnam served as bishop from 1980 until his retirement in 1982. The Rt. Rev. Wesley Frensdorff (then bishop of Nevada) was appointed part-time interim bishop and served until his death in May, 1988 —"interim" because the plan was for the Navajos to eventu-

ally elect their own bishop. The Rt. Rev. William Wolfrum (suffragan of Colorado) then took on the part-time interim duties until the ordination of Steven Plummer, March 10, 1990, as bishop of the Episcopal Church in Navajoland — the first Navajo bishop and the first chosen by the Navajo people.

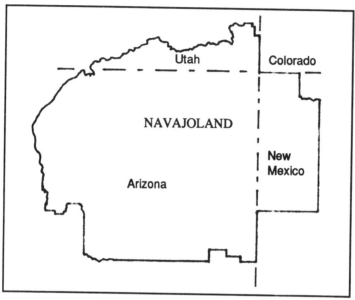

Statistical reports published by the Episcopal Church Center and the Church Pension Fund (as of 1988) do not show the Navajo Area Mission as a separate jurisdiction. (It is, formally, still an "area mission," not a diocese.) Thus, detailed statistics are not readily available. The area mission office, however, reports about 1,500 members, 10 congregations and five house churches. There are three salaried clergy (one locally trained) and six salaried lay pastors. The area mission has two paid staff members in addition to the bishop.

-Eds.

What was the late Bishop Wes Frensdorff's vision of total ministry for the Episcopal Church in Navajoland (ECN)? How has that vision been modified due to the unique historical and cultural circumstances of the Navajo? What aspects of this effort to envision anew the church's mission and ministry have been promising, and what aspects have been problematic? Finally, what role should the Frensdorff vision continue to play for ECN? These are the questions which this essay will tackle. But first several points must be made about my point of view.

Frensdorff's great emphasis, and that of his theological predecessor, the missiologist Roland Allen, was autonomy for the Navajo church, and so it would be painfully ironic for *bilagaana* (Anglos) to presume to speak for the Navajo themselves. The following thoughts claim only to be my own, though they are based on some personal experience among Navajo Christians and spring from a genuine sympathy for ECN. It should also be noted that the more modest claim to be friendly observers brings with it a greater measure of freedom to enumerate and weigh some of the questions posed to the total ministry approach. This is totally in keeping with the spirit of Wes, who used to exhort the clergy of Navajoland to a more "radical honesty" which he believed the struggling life of this young church needed. However I shall not presume to offer solutions to some of the theological debates raised. The period since Wes' death has still been short, and the process of evaluating and revising the vision is ongoing. But however the vision comes to be modified (or retained), Wes would surely have been proud of the legacy of theological ferment itself. Though he was ever an energetic spokesperson for total ministry, he most embodied that vision precisely when he backed away from forcing its implications on the Navajo people, for Wes knew that such a violation of Navajo morés and the principle of self-determination, even for the best theological reasons, would have been highly counterproductive. In the development of ministry Wes was attentive to the process, for there often the Spirit listeth. So the compromises themselves were often consistent with the spirit if not the letter of total ministry. I shall be contending that ECN has entered a stage of "revisionist Frensdorffianism;" now there's a phrase that would have inspired some irreverent joke from the bishop! For him the heart of the search for new (really old) and more serviceable forms of participation in Christ's ministry was creativity; he would have little patience with dedicating some new ministerial structure set in concrete in his name, nor would he have stood for even a whiff of hagiography. He would have known that praise of a past prophet is often in direct proportion to disregard for the bite of his message. I offer this essay in the deepest spirit of thanksgiving to God for the opportunity to have known him as a pastor and friend.

The introduction of the total ministry approach can only be understood against ECN's preceding historical background. The Episcopal Church has had a presence among Navajo people for a little less than a century, but in each of the regions (Arizona, Utah, and New Mexico) medical missionary activity preceded any specifically spiritual ministry. Now, from one perspective, in a culture whose traditional religious attention is so completely dominated by a concern for healing, medical ministry was not a bad place to start (it should be added that the first missionaries were unordained and women). Still it dramatizes the point that at its very root the presence of Anglo missionaries, and thus of the larger church, has involved an inextricable web of care and dependency. Needs were met and good was done, but there has been also a negative legacy which goes deeper than the few thrift shops which remain. Someone — perhaps Roland Allen — described young churches which received at their inception both catechesis and material aid from beyond; Navajoland represents an extreme case in which at first only the latter was offered. Furthermore the way in which worship was introduced to the mission in Fort Defiance is also symbolic of the legacy of dependence. The first services were performed at the Bureau of Indian Affairs (BIA) boarding school located near the site of the old cavalry fort itself, and in subsequent times there was a close cooperation and association between the church and the BIA. Of course moral condemnation is easy in hindsight, but still we need to point out the harsh rejection at that time by the boarding schools of everything culturally Navajo. The hidden wounds of this deeper history must be taken into account in respect to questions of identity, indigeneity, etc. A more mundane but equally important legacy of this earlier era is the existence of mission compounds with numerous expensive, aging buildings, at once a great asset and a great liability.[1]

The more recent history of the relation between these small, isolated missions and their dioceses, as well as the national church is also a mixed one. Some missionaries were pioneers of the training of local leadership, though these efforts were too sporadic to lead very far; someone like Baxter Liebler in Bluff, Utah creatively fused his own sacramental tradition with a deep knowledge of Navajo spiritual heritage, though some of his success may have been too dependent on the strength of his own personality. But the Navajo churches also had burdens to bear. Other clergy were misfits who set the churches back years. Some of the most well-intended help grew out of a romanticism about Native Americans which had more to do with Anglo fantasies and needs. (This remains a matter about which the larger church must be self-reflectively vigilant; on the subject of the harm romanticized views could do, Frensdorff was adamant, for like all fantasies they inhibit real human relationships). Sometimes the missions were viewed as "poor relations," hard to understand and expensive to keep up. When in the early 1970's discussions began about an autonomous ecclesiastical jurisdiction for the disparate Navajo missions, a variety of motives were involved. The dioceses wanted to eliminate point-less duplication of labor. The emphasis on ethnic self-determination has become important in the larger American cultural scene. Real leadership and enthusiasm were shown by Navajo Christians. But in addition there may have been a feeling on the part of some church people that this creative solution also served to unload an expensive problem. An analogy may be found politically around the same time in the employment by the govern-ment of the language of self-determination in what some suspected was a rationalization for the lessening of financial obligations.[2]

Lest I be misunderstood, I am not claiming that this is why the area mission was formed; furthermore I think that this formation was a creative and positive step. But human motives are always complex. I only offer this as the understandable grounds for the wariness some might feel toward the language of self-sufficiency. One of the particular difficulties of a situation like that of the Navajo Nation as a whole, and on a smaller scale but in an analogous way the Navajo church, is its position at once separate but surrounded by the gigantic larger society. Young overseas churches may struggle with many problems in relation to their "parent" church or mission-ary society, but at least they enjoy some distance and operate in a land where their own culture predominates. For the Navajo people this creative distance is harder to find. The difficulties of this relationship will render the whole issue of money and financial self-sufficiency most vexing. This also effects the responsibility of the larger Episcopal Church to ECN; the spirit of diocesan *laissez faire* is not found in the same New Testament which tells us of the collection for Jerusalem. Wes surely was fully supportive of a legitimate sense of Christian mutual responsibility and mutual help; after all ECN is a part of the Episcopal Church. His point was not that there was some moral imperative for Navajoland to support itself. His question was rather, what kind of help was really helpful? What are the ambiguities of assistance? What kind of help can truly be sustained? How can money be kept subservient to the life and ministry of the church rather than vice versa?

When Wes became interim bishop in 1983, he saw that ECN needed to work toward structures of ministry and authority in keeping with the original intent of the separate jurisdiction's creation, autonomy and in-digeneity. It seemed that everyone had counseled caution and patience; after almost a century of Episcopal presence this strategy had produced exactly one Navajo priest still active in ministry, and Bishop Wes liked to say that Steven Plummer was a miracle of perseverance given a system ill-designed to nurture such a vocation. Surely it was time for something more daring, more risky, for on the further horizon Wes saw that not to take risks and so not to develop strong local leadership was the greatest risk of all.

What were Wes' guiding principles for the design of ECN's mission and common life, a project he was fond of likening to the design of an aircraft while in mid-flight? Here I feel that many false criticisms of ECN's approach may be avoided by giving a full and balanced account which avoids caricature. First of all, he stressed the importance of the use of Canon 8 (then) for the ordination of local, sacramental priests, for this would restore the vital connection between community and sacramental leadership. Processes of calling and discernment would enable the Spirit to work through the community itself, and so break down the separate clerical caste. It would make possible the training of sacramental leaders who would be themselves Navajo. But it must be added that for Frensdorff this stress on local ordination had to be balanced by the discernment and utilization of gifts throughout the community. He liked to say that only a community "ordainable" to its ministries could truly discern and ordain a Canon 8 priest. Also, he did not foresee the end of "professional" clergy for Navajoland — clergy with more formal education; as "regional vicars" they would provide encouragement, oversight, and further training to the sacramentalists in the smaller communities. He hoped that in not too many years the appropriate persons could be discerned from among regional pools of functioning Canon 8 priests. From this goal it should be clear that for ECN, which has at present ordained two people through the local process and has another in the "pipeline," the experiment has just begun, and any judgement of success or failure would be premature. It should be added that there is a general agreement that, in spite of some false starts, the persons who have now been identified by the process are highly appropriate. Furthermore Wes was not doctrinaire about the issue of remuneration for such local clergy. It was explained to ordinands that they could not count on a stipend, that the normative situation ought to be voluntary service, but it was also recoginzed that this would have to be considered on a case-by-case basis. It should be remembered that the canon says nothing about non-stipendiary status. Now it would be only fair to mention that the bishop's hope was that non-stipendiary clergy would be possible, for he thought that this would represent a breakthrough from old patterns, but he also recognized how difficult this would be for a variety of reasons which shall be dealt with later. I am only making the point that when ECN decided to remunerate its first Canon 8 presbyter this was not, per se, a contradiction of the stated plan.

Second, the bishop's vision called for a minimum of Anglo staff, all of whom would be sensitive to the need to "take a rear seat," for the obvious reason that otherwise they would get in the way of the raising up of Navajo leadership. ECN has never been conceived of as an exclusive, tribal church. All were welcomed to worship and share in the church's common life, and much emphasis was placed on the development of a web of connections with the wider church. ECN proudly claims its Anglican identity. (ECN's Anglo staff at present is exemplary in respect to commitment and sensitivity.) But Wes was wary of many kinds of aid which would foster dependence, of unscreened volunteers who might bring overly romanticized views to work in ECN, to energy diverted from the central task of ECN's own self-development.

Third, Wes stressed that ECN must not be treated like some exotic flower grown in a pot of Western culture soil, but needed to be transplanted into the good earth of its own Navajo cultural environment. The question of indigenization is a complex one for Navajos, who differ greatly in their own knowledge of and their attitude toward traditional culture, and especially toward the still widely practiced traditional religion. Once again, Wes did not push his own point of view. He advocated dialogue with medicine men and Native American Church roadmen,[3] as well as more conscious adaptation of traditional elements — for instance in liturgical music — but for reasons to be discussed later, these suggestions were not met in ECN with enthusiasm, and the bishop understood that only Navajo Christians themselves could discern the contours of a Navajo church.

Fourth, Frensdorff encouraged ECN to confront the hard issue of money. It should be stressed that he did not advocate the model of total ministry and local ordination because it would save money, though in fact he was convinced that the old way of doing business could not last long in the larger church and was even less feasible for Navajoland.[4] He believed that such a return to a stress on the ministry of the whole people of God was theologically sound and promised renewal for the church, and happened to be financially viable as well. (It must be admitted, however, that the fact that this model has, for the most part, been limited to isolated or ethnic communities makes the convergence of theology and practicality harder to demonstrate). Bishop Wes saw the blessing of considerable resources for ECN at present as a unique opportunity to make progress in autonomy financially as well as communally, for such support would probably not always be present; ECN had to seize the time.

Fifth, Wes encouraged ECN to develop a process of theological education and training for ministry which would be thoroughly planted in the local context and identical whether one was anticipating ordination or not. He met, as one might expect, some understandable resistance from the keener, more able students, who wanted something more. But just the same he resisted an educational plan which would create a separate group of ministerial "gnostics" privileged to know more about the faith than the common run of parishoners. Again, to avoid misrepresentations: it was always understood that certain people with certain gifts might need specialized, more advanced training on a short-term basis. But he did not agree that these persons designated for special training need necessarily be ordinands, and accordingly, available resources were generously allocated to training of the unordained for ministry as youth leader, alcohol counselor, etc.

To return for a moment to theological education, there have admittedly been difficulties with a unified approach. In order to satisfy the able students both the yearlong program and the "imported" speakers have tended to err on the side of rigor, and have left the students with less facility in English behind, but this is a problem of language and diverse educational backgrounds more than a question of training for the ordained as opposed to the unordained. An additional consideration has been Navajoland's desire for an educational program which is seen as "state of the art" and thoroughly Episcopal; some have been wary of specifically Indian-tailored programs as unnecessary "training wheels." While again this may on occasion have resulted in the selection of curricula which left some behind, these motivations too are worthy of consideration.

It may be helpful to point out here that some of the principles reiterated were largely derived from the ecclesiology of Roland Allen, while others are developments moving beyond the thought of that great Anglican missiologist. Allen also stressed the priority of the local community and of course the local discernment, training, and ordination of eucharistic leaders. But the vision of total ministry deemphasized the unique status and sanctity of the priest in a way that Allen did not mention. Someone like Wes would surely have argued that this follows necessarily from the challenge to the historical process of clericalization implied by Roland Allen's thought.[5] Secondly, Allen did not address the issue of clergy pay, though he did advocate that all money in a church be locally derived; again one could respond that the practical implication for a setting like Navajoland is precisely a non-stipendiary approach. Finally, Roland Allen did not address the issue of cultural indigenization; this would be the major concern of a later missiological generation. What he did address consistently and energetically was the issue of the indigenization of decision-making and discipline.[6] He himself believed that once control was in the hands of local Christians, they would know how to address the gospel to their setting. Again the total ministry approach may be seen as an implication of Allen's starting point.

Here it is essential to consider the question of indigenization, both in Roland Allen's sense of control and in terms of theological adaptation, against the wider horizon of religious groups in the highly pluralistic environment of contemporary Navajoland. In fact indigenization may be seen quite successfully at work, first of all in the Native American Church, which by all accounts is growing, is self-supporting and locally controlled, and functions effectively without the encumbrances of buildings, bureacracy, etc. All of this is, of course, highly indigenous to the originally semi-nomadic Navajo. Most importantly, the Native American Church is perceived by its members as indigenous, though in fact it is every bit as much an "import" (in this case from later 19th century plains Indians) as Christianity. The syncretistic use of Indian ceremony and symbol may be partly responsible, and surely local control is even more responsible for the NAC's success. Arguably the most important factor is the answer the peyote cult provided to the desire for spiritual power. A prominent anthropologist has pointed out that the group mushrooomed in Navajo country especially during the painful period of flock reductions mandated by the BIA in the 1930s, a time of desperation and impotence for many Navajo.[7] (Likewise the sings traditional to Navajo culture itself center on the theme of acquisition of spiritual power.[8]) I have come to an unexpected tentative conclusion, that the success of the NAC as a religious community organizationally indigenized may be finally attributable to a deep kind of spiritual indigenization. But in fact this is a sort of adaptation which the church, for its own theological reasons, cannot follow. The gospel transforms human notions of power and religion itself as an instrument of power. The word of the cross tells us of a new understanding of God's power at work through weakness and service, a power not available to human manipulation. Here we must remember that the goal of indigenization in Christian missiology is as much to find the appropriate cultural terms and issues by which to express the scandal of the gospel as to identify the preparatory work of God's word. Clearly the example of the NAC's successful achievment of autonomy and indigenization serves to remind us of what must be universally agreed, that these must always be understood as only means to the promotion of a theologically sound community of the people of God proclaiming the affirming, challenging gospel of Christ. In a sense the NAC is a community with so different a goal and history as to be a problematic analogy.

Much closer to home is the analogy of the movement of tent revivals, camp meetings, itinerant preachers, and pentecostal groups, often centering in particular clans.[9] Here we are dealing with a distinctly Christian movement which is growing, self-supporting, toward which its members feel a sense of ownership. Perhaps the lesson of the revivals, as well as the NAC, for the cause of self-determination in Navajoland is quite simple and practical: mobile, decentralized, clan-based religious groups are most likely to flourish.

Whether or not the Episcopal Church will be able successfully to adopt some of these structural features is still an open question. Historically the Episcopal Church has lagged behind (e.g. the Methodists) in adapting to the logistic challenge of the West. Our history, as has already been described, is a top-heavy burden. But it must be said that the revivals also reveal less desirable features whose correction in an application of this decentralized model would be a further challenge for ECN. They have no oversight of orthodoxy, are less able to provide for ongoing communal nurture, and tend to be divisive. Aren't these the very problems which the threefold ministry was designed in the second century A.D. to combat? We are reminded that even clergy locally discerned and fully identified with the whole community will still need to assist in the vital function of guarding against such errors. Finally the same criticism can be leveled at the revivals that we directed at the NAC. Ironically, however much they may condemn the externals of the traditional culture (calls for the converted to burn fetishes, etc.), in fact they have swallowed whole the deeper indigenous cultural trait of understanding religion as the search for accessible spiritual power. Their pentecostally oriented theology pulls no punches on the matter of offering and delivering tangible blessings to the redeemed. From such a short-cut to numerical success the way for us is theologically barred. However, lest we as Episcopalians become complacent, we must remind ourselves that our historical failure to achieve autonomy and indigenization has much less to do with sacrificial faithfulness to the gospel and the catholicity of the church than to faint-heartedness and cultural myopia. Still we can say that, while the pentecostal revivals remind us that decentralized arrangements might offer benefits to ECN, a sound route to such an end will be much more circuitous.

One other factor, of surpassing importance in the social and cultural situation of Navajoland, must influence how we think about total ministry for ECN: the pervasive problem of alcoholism. For many the goal of sobriety, for even more the goal of serenity, must dominate their attention in a context in which alcoholism is at the root of legions of familial disruptions and the erosion of confidence in cultural identity. So the church must be the community of the ultimate serenity rooted in Christ, a community which fights the evil of alcoholism only by its own non-coercive, prayerful, non-enabling example. This life-and-death struggle must be taken into account by a theology claiming to be contextual.

Having laid out the vision of total ministry which was Wes' gift to Navajoland as well as some of the distinctive factors in the Navajo cultural scene, we need now to turn to some of the questions or challenges which have been or could be raised against such an approach (a number of them from the Native American Episcopal community itself, either implicitly or explicitly). Here we need to reiterate that more important than the "answer" in each case is the creative ferment caused by the question, which must largely be attributed to the Frensdorff contribution. By means of his application of the principles of total ministry to Navajoland he helped to raise anew, even for those who have disagreed with him, the central question of the nature of the Christian community itself. This leads naturally to the first objection, which grows out of the experience of the church's struggle against alcoholism. This scourge cannot be combatted so much by what Christians do as by what they are: sober, serene, sure of their spiritual foundation. Communal identity takes precedence over efforts of individuals. Can the rhetoric of total ministry sound at times too activistic? It would be unfortunate if, for the reality of the harried pastor, were substituted the ideal of the busy parish. It must be remembered that what are most needed in many native communities are just the sorts of things which cannot be achieved by the energetic activism of which Anglos are so fond: progress in the battle against alcoholism, affirmation of cultural identity, etc. These have more to do with the community than the individual, with being than doing. Now this is not to claim that the church should be quietist. The Church of the Good Shepherd, Fort Defiance, was recently proud of a group for pre-teens which combined alcohol awareness education, catechesis, and lessons in traditional culture, most of which were led by lay members of the community, many of them elderly.[10] Concerted efforts can be mounted so long as the primary emphasis is on communal identity in Christ. What is central for ECN is the goal of a community which affirms its own cultural identity and its own serenity as grounded and transformed by Christ. The emphasis on individuals empowered to fulfill their own separate ministries may seem natural to individualistic Anglos but is less appropriate for the Navajo context. Of course such an emphasis is not necessary to the total ministry approach, which most properly stresses the priority of the community as a whole.

Our second question for the total ministry approach for ECN was raised by a national Episcopal Indian leader, the Rev. Philip Allen (who, as a former vicar of the Good Shepherd Mission in Fort Defiance, Arizona, is highly knowledgeable about ECN's situation). In a recent Native American response to the application of the ideas of Roland Allen to native contexts,[11] Allen, speaking from his own Sioux background, is quoted as pointing out that the idea of the holy man, the sacral person, set apart for and supported by the community, is in fact highly indigenous. His point would seem to be that the declericalization of the total ministry approach and indigenization are at loggerheads. Could the criticism be taken a step further to claim that the very goal of the democratization of the church may have an element of cultural imposition?

This argument brings us to the heart of the issue of the particular form total ministry must take among Native Americans. At the outset it should be observed that due to cultural differences the clerical emphasis which Phil Allen suggests is indigenous is one of sacrality while the clerical emphasis which the total ministry camp bemoans is one of professionalism (though there may be an element of this, too, in contemporary Indian thinking about the clergy by analogy to Anglo doctors, bureaucrats, etc.). To some extent we have here a case of clerical apples and oranges. But there still remains a deeper theological conflict; can an intellectual reconciliation be found? It is axiomatic that we are most correct in what we affirm, and in our case both the strength of native communities and the main emphasis in the total ministry vision is the priority of the community. This means in the Christian tradition that the church, God's new people, is the legitimate inheritor of the priestly language which the New Testament applies first of all to Jesus Christ himself: "but you are a chosen race, a royal priesthood, a holy nation, God's own people . . ." (I Peter 2:9).

Now as a corrective to what it perceives as a loss of this perspective, the total ministry approach must be allowed some rhetorical and prophetic leeway. Still the approach is least helpful when it draws its most dramatic conclusions, questioning the idea of priestly character and moving in the direction of functionalism.[12] Could it be that the assumption that we have here a "zero sum game," that emphasis on the community must mean deflation of the idea of the priest, is misconceived?

The goal of the theology of total ministry should be, not to eliminate the idea of priestly character, but rather to expand it radically. Listen to the words of the liturgical theologian Aidan Kavanagh, quoted approvingly by Wes in his "Ministry and Orders: A Tangled Skein":

> *"the vocabulary of priestliness, with which Christian tradition is ingrained, denotes a christic, i.e. a messianic-sacerdotal-royal quality which all the baptized share in the Anointed One himself and is expressed in a vast symphony of charisms, all of which originate from his own spirit given for the life of the world."* [13]

What is required is a more dialectical understanding of the relationship between Christ's sacerdotal community and its sacerdotal examples, the ordained. If real priority is given to the former, a renewed emphasis must be placed on the latter, properly understood. The role of reminding the church of its own nature as priestly becomes all the more important. Clearly the identity of the ordained grows out of that of the community, and clearly the role of the ordained is precisely to remind the church of what it is. The Native American witness, here embodied in Allen's criticism, can help the whole church correct its vision both of the spiritual reality of the community as well as of the legitimate though derivative sacrality of the ordained office. But Anglo society has trouble reclaiming such senses of community and sacrality due to its own cultural history.

Wes points out that our spiritual tradition centers in the eucharist,[14] and so this is the best place to grasp our point. This constitutive act of the church is truly "liturgy," the work of Christ's laos, and yet this is also the definitive event for the bishop/presbyter. In the words of the Lima Text approvingly quoted in "Ministry and Orders . . .,"[15] "it is especially in the eucharistic celebration that the ordained ministry is the visible focus of the deep and all-embracing communion between Christ and the members of his body." Here the true interdependence (to use one of Wes' favorite words) between the priestly community and a "high" view of the ordained eucharistic celebrant as focus and example is clear. We can go a step further and contend that such a theological emphasis may be the proper approach for Navajoland: what it has particularly to offer spiritually among the various Christian groups on the reservation (along with the Roman Catholic Church of course).

The indigenous themes of ordered ceremony, the sacrality of religious officiants, sacramentality, and liturgical recital reinforce the eucharistic spirituality of our Anglican tradition. ECN's strategy must be to "play to our strength" liturgically at the same time that teaching and preaching reinforce the message conveyed so clearly in the total ministry approach, that liturgy is the work of God's whole people through Christ.

However, our dialectical argument cuts in the opposite direction as well. Phil Allen would surely agree that elements of the traditional idea of the holy man must be transformed by Christ. In fact we have claimed above that the holy man as practitioner in matters of spiritual power may be just that indigenous element most in need of challenge by the gospel. Sacral power is concentrated in Jesus Christ, whose glorious wounds constantly remind the Christian that we are talking of a very different sort of power. So total ministry has a prophetic role to play in the evangelization of Native Americans as well.

We have arrived at a real complementarity of emphases rooted in the simultaneous affirmation and challenge of the gospel. Allen implies a second criticism of the total ministry approach, namely that in the situations of intense social and economic crisis we find that on many reservations the emphases on non-stipendiary clergy and local education are misplaced. Scarce secular jobs should not be taken up by the ordained, who need more professional skills, not less. Again Allen's point is well taken, though it is largely answered by the balanced account we have tried to render of the Frensdorff approach. An elimination of professional oversight was never envisioned; the discernment, training and ordination in smaller congregations of appropriate persons, who already presumably have some way of getting along and for whom resources for employment are not available, would not displace people from the workforce, but would provide greater sacramental nourishment to some congregations. Perhaps the suggestion can be put more strongly, that more resources need to be allocated and more positions created to alleviate the crisis. Here some room must be left for discernment of differing local situations, some of which may be socially and economically more critical than Navajoland. Still it is a fair question to ask, as total ministry proponents must, will the help really help? On this question the example of alcoholism is most instructive; while the availability of treatment and professional counseling are necessary, of equal importance is the existence of communities of sobriety and serenity. AA and Al-Anon are, after all, "lay" movements which are largely self-supporting and self-governed. While resources are often called for, both AA and the total ministry approach remind us of the ambiguity of support.

Lurking behind all our discussions has been that old bugaboo, money. It could fairly be observed that for Roland Allen communal discernment of leaders and communal financial independence went hand-in-hand; so long as the missionary controlled the "power of the purse" the relationship would be skewed.[16] This we might call a criticism from the opposite direction, that what is called for is a more radical weaning from outside funding. Of this position and the theological tension which lies behind it Wes was very aware. (It might be added that even Roland Allen himself was aware that one had to take into account the preceding history even of missions whose pattern of financial dependence he disapproved of, though he was insistent about the need to change such a situation promptly.[17])

It must be straightforwardly admitted that this represents an internal tension between Allenesque theory and real-world practice in terms of ECN. I hope that along the way I have already pointed out many of the complexities of this question. ECN's recent emphasis on stewardship education from a Native American perspective is a step in the right direction toward greater self-support, though the road ahead is admittedly long. Frensdorff recognized that this was the great challenge of the future for ECN, but that, given the limited resources of its members, full self-sufficiency might be utopian. We would emphasize the need for clarity about the authentic reason for the push toward greater financial self-sufficiency. While striving after a greater degree of financial self-sufficiency is important for ECN, the reason is that progress toward this goal will help ECN itself grow and help its members see that the faith is not "the white man's religion" but their own. For its part the larger church must be vigilant against the idea that financial aid for ECN or other Native American communities is an imposition, for such a thought is surely a departure from the "mind of Christ."

The final question often asked of the sort of total ministry approach espoused by Wes for ECN has to do with education. Has this really met the need of the church? At the time of the design of ECN's plan of theological education, primarily locally based and primarily equal for all, it was clear that other dioceses involved in Native American ministry were pursuing contrasting approaches (here we have in mind especially South Dakota, which was energetically increasing the number of Sioux ordinands attending seminary). Surely different situations call for different strategies, and equally surely the ECN approach allows for some use of exterior educational resources, just as South Dakota has long had local opportunities for theological education. Yet a difference in emphasis remains. Here we believe it is important to remember that the total ministry experiment in ECN is still young, and that Wes' vision called for the eventual discernment, from among local sacramentalist clergy, of a few who might appropriately receive more formal academic training. (The need for some leaders and theologians with a full theological as well as social bi-culturalism in order to articulate the local community's vision and help tie it to the larger church should not be underestimated.) Still the primacy of local education in ECN's vision must be emphasized.

The truth is that both approaches have hit rough patches in the road. Could it be that, as educational approaches evolve, Native American Episcopalians will behold a process of convergence in which the interdependence of interior and exterior components becomes clearer? This will become especially evident when more of the local training can be taken over by more technically trained Navajo theological teachers. Wes, for his part, was acutely aware of the danger along the way of the alienating effect of theological education outside the local context, and history bears out his concern. Only time and careful discernment will make possible the fruitful training of a few for this specialized ministry. Still the "meat and potatoes" (or should we say "stew and fry bread?") of theological education must remain locally based and open to all. (This, by the way, was essential for Roland Allen too.[18])

We also wonder if in addition to using all the educational options available presently to Native American communities, new experiments might also be desirable. Could an intermediary stage of theological education, more formal and intensive than ECN's local approach, but more specifically tailored to Native American needs than South Dakota's emphasis on seminary training, be envisioned? We should here add that both approaches have had a link with a seminary, Seabury-Western, which in the case of ECN provided mini-courses taught by faculty members in Navajoland. Will the future hold some sort of theological college, Anglican but designed for Native Americans, perhaps affiliated with a seminary such as Seabury-Western, perhaps with a location and schedule designed to reduce the alienation which seminary study in the past has engendered? The memory of Wes Frensdorff encourages us to "dream dreams."[19]

In conclusion, what form might total ministry take in the near future, as ECN strives, by the leading of God's Spirit, to hold on to what is surely true in Wes' challenging vision while adapting its expression according to local cultural circumstances and perhaps compromising on some elements according to the exigencies of real life? First of all Navjoland should celebrate what has been achieved, most dramatically represented in the consecration of Steven Plummer as bishop. In many ways he embodies the goals of a church embedded in the local culture while being deeply committed to Christ. His consecration should encourage much progress in real autonomy. It should be added that his spirit of reconciliation should also make him what a bishop should be and what ECN continues to need, a symbol of unity in Christ. ECN should build confidently on the foundations it already has (for instance the group of ordinands, few but of quality). It should recognize that over the years, through quiet and turbulence, the real backbone of leadership has been its lay pastors, who are female and unordained (though stipendiary).

In respect to the crucial issues of money and education, perhaps a "grand compromise" is called for. The larger church can provide assurance of continuing support at the same time that it encourages gradual and attainable belt-tightening. (In fairness it should be pointed out that support for Navajoland has been generous and consistent in recent years, and this has been laudable). It is essential that such understandings be worked out mutually, openly, deliberately. With respect to education the need for a full spectrum of options for theological training needs to be affirmed.

A word needs to be said about cultural or liturgical indigenization. Frensdorff was, as we have argued, wisest in backing off from deliberate attempts to foster dialogue and adaptation. All such encouragements, certainly on the part of non-Navajos, should be abandoned. It is important here to confront the profound lack of consensus on these matters within Navajoland itself. Also it should be recognized that the resistance which many feel toward self-conscious indigenization, for instance in liturgical matters, arises often for the most indigenous of reasons. By this we mean that respect for tradition and the integrity of a ceremonial system (doing things in this case in the "the Anglican way"), even if experienced only viscerally, is a profoundly Navajo instinct.[20] Here indigeneity may have more to do with the mode of appropriating a tradition than with tinkering with doctrinal formulations or liturgical practices themselves. Issues of self-conscious indigenization should only be addressed as they arise naturally from within the Navajo Christian community itself.

Finally we would lovingly remind all, including all our brothers and sisters of ECN itself, that the experiment of total ministry is still young. (In general of course Navajos have much to teach Anglos about the evils of being in too much of a hurry.) The approach needs to be given a chance, and this means staying on the path. The balance of Wes' understanding of total ministry must be remembered, lest in reaction to its caricature ECN reject the vision itself. Surely the past provides no idyllic ministerial pattern to which ECN should hanker to return. Likewise the hope for great infusions of outside resources is probably illusory, and upon reflection there is a consensus about the ambiguity of assistance. There will be an ongoing need and place for outside help from other parts of this our one church, but the primary source of progress will be the power of the Spirit working from within the whole Navajo Episcopal community. All our scheming should fade to insignificance in the shadow of the mighty wings of that hovering divine Presence.

Notes

1. My information about the early history of the missions which would eventually become ECN is derived from Owanah Anderson's *The Jamestown Commitment: The Episcopal Church and the American Indian,* Cincinnati: Forward Movement, 1988), especially pp.84-86. I gained valuable information from conversations with Mr. Howard McKinley of the Church of the Good Shepherd, Fort Defiance, Arizona.

2. Suspicion about the motives behind governmental use of the rhetoric of self-determination is described well in Francis Paul Prucha's *The Indians in American Society: From the Revolutionary War to the Present,* (Berkeley: University of California, 1985).

3. "Medicine men" are religious practitioners of ceremonies of healing called "sings" or "chants" in traditional Navajo religion. "Roadmen" are spiritual leaders in the Native American Church, a syncretistic, pan-Indian religious cult centering in the consumption of peyote. The group spread especially among plains Indians since 1870 and soon included groups espousing a quasi-Christianized version. For more

information, see Weston LaBarre's *The Peyote Cult,* (New York: Schocken, 1969).

4. Wesley Frensdorff and Charles R. Wilson, *Challenge for Change: Clergy and Congregations* (Arvada: Jethro, 1987), *passim.*
5. Frensdorff, "Ministry and Orders: A Tangled Skein," Chapter 3, p. 17 ff.
6. See, for instance, David Paton and Charles H. Long's *The Compulsion of the Spirit: A Roland Allen Reader,* (Grand Rapids: William B. Eerdmans, 1983), pp. 28 ff.
7. David Aberle, *The Peyote Cult Among the Navajo* (Chicago: University of Chicago, 1983), Part II.
8. Gladys Reichard, *The Navajo Religion: A Study in Symbolism* (Tucson: The University of Arizona, 1983), Chapter 9.
9. These groups are described by David Scates' *Why Navajo Churches Are Growing: The Cultural Dynamics of Navajo Religious Change* (Grand Junction:1981), pp.131-135.
10. This group, it should be noted, received funding assistance from the national Church through the help and advocacy of Mrs. Owanah Anderson.
11. He is quoted in Owanah Anderson's "Native Americans Question Roland Allen Model as Currently Applied," in *Ministry Development Journal,* published by the Episcopal Church Center, No. 15, 1988, pp.47-48.
12. Frensdorff, "Ministry and Orders . . .," p. 29 ff.
13. Ibid., p. 31.
14. Ibid., p. 19.
15. *Creeds of the Church,* John H. Leith, ed. (Atlanta: John Knox, 1982), p. 637.
16. Paton & Long, op.cit., p. 10.
17. Ibid., p. 45.
18. Ibid., p. 38.
19. See Chapter 1, "The Dream."
20. The core of this idea comes from Philip Turner's article "The Wisdom of the Fathers and the Gospel of Christ: some notes on the question of Christian adaptation in Africa," in *Journal of Religion in Africa,* IV, 1971-1972, pp.45-68.

Chapter 6

WINDS OF CHANGE:
A Honduran Strategy

Leo Frade

The Episcopal Church in Honduras is part of Province IX of the Episcopal Church, U.S.A. Province IX is comprised of the dioceses of Colombia, Dominican Republic and Ecuador; the four dioceses of Mexico and five of Central America, and other area Episcopal Church work.   *-Eds.*

The best time to fly a kite is when the wind blows. I still remember my grandfather telling me that if the prize is good enough, it's worth the risk to try to win. There are also times when your best incentive to do something is when you don't have any other choice *but* to do it.

That about sums up the situation when, in January 1984, I first arrived in Honduras as the brand new bishop. For many years the diocese had been almost entirely dependent on professionally trained missionary clergy from other countries: people, for the most part, educated in the traditional seminaries. It also became quite clear to me early on that the Episcopal Church U.S.A. was no longer committed to footing the bill for large numbers of clergy in the mission field. That was a strategy of a bygone era. Furthermore, we had inherited from our "mother church" models and structures of ministry in which full-time, seminary-educated clergy were the ideal. But mother church somehow forgot to leave us the money to pay for it.

There had been several attempts, prior to my arrival, to get a traditional seminary program going in Honduras. But with fiscal constraints and lack of staff, it had proven impossible. Something short of a miracle would be needed to get us up and running.

But the winds of change were indeed blowing. While the risk of failure was great, I had one advantage: an inherited model and associated policy that had failed to produce native clergy. Something different *had* to be risked.

I had been educated at the University of the South, Sewanee, Tennessee, and spent most of my ministry in Province IV (southeastern U.S.A.), working with minority groups, mainly Hispanic. It was while working with Joe Morris Doss at Grace Church, New Orleans, and through his friendship with Wes Frensdorff that I was introduced to new approaches in parochial work. I discovered that it was possible for minorities to have access to theological education without having to earn a Ph.D. or taking the full three-year seminary course, and that properly trained clergy could thus be provided to meet local church needs.

At the time I also chaired our national church's Commission on Hispanic Ministries and I was familiar with the plea from many quarters frustrated with the lack of indigenous clergy. I was also familiar with the practice of many U.S. bishops when they needed a cleric for Hispanic ministry: the practice of shopping in Latin America and importing someone. This was not a practice appreciated by the Latin American bishops, to say the least, and it had the effect of stifling any attempts to raise up local Hispanic vocations in the U.S.

So, like Philip, I was translated to a new area where, in my case, I ended up with a purple shirt, a ring, a miter and a staff, but no native clergy and no money to train anyone. Actually, there was one native Honduran priest in the diocese at the time. Others were from the U.S., Belgium, Guatemala, Nicaragua and Chile — something like a micro-council of the United Nations.

It didn't take me long to remember Wes and his ideas, and I wasn't shy about asking him into the diocese to help us launch a program that would lead to the ordination of Honduran personnel. To our good fortune, he agreed. In late 1984, we had our first training session and laid the ground work that resulted in the ordination of seven deacons in 1989 — the first Hondurans ordained in the Episcopal Church in over 15 years.

As I said, we did not have much to lose. Our financial resources were very limited. The most we could have done in pursuing the traditional model of ministry would have been to send one or two students to the U.S. or to seminary in a Spanish-speaking country. Financial constraints were not the only ones. Educational entrance requirements were simply beyond what our students could have met. The people coming through our local program would not have been accepted into a traditional seminary — or even a not-so-traditional seminary. In Honduras the ministry of the church places us in some very geographically isolated areas, areas neglected by the public education system.

Church growth in Honduras has been extraordinary and exciting. To hear stories about how the Episcopal Church is not growing is amusing in this setting where the church is strong, dynamic and growing by leaps and bounds. In 1980 the Episcopal Church in Honduras consisted of nine con- gregations with a total membership of about 1,000. Today (1990) we have 45 congregations with over 10,000 members. Our challenge is keeping up with ministry training to serve the needs of the many congregations we have.

The first step was "conscientizar" (consciousness-raising) of the existing clergy. It did not take Wesley Frensdorff long to do that and set the challenge before us. He shared with us the experiences of Nevada, Alaska, New Zealand and others. He provided many ideas, but the plans had to be ours. There was some initial hesitation on the part of our clergy: fear of a corps of "uneducated" co-workers, or fear of creating a new caste of clergy. But we enlisted the aid of existing clergy in the design of training programs and the training of candidates. It became clear that the new clergy would be as effective as the training clergy could make them. Most importantly, we were blessed in having been given a vision of how it looked on the other side of the mountain, and with that vision, found the courage to begin the journey.

We issued the call across the diocese in the form of a pastoral letter challenging Honduran Episcopalians to end their dependency on foreign missionaries. The call downplayed the obstacles and pressed the challenge on anyone who might feel called by God to rise up and respond. Those so called were invited to a meeting in Siguatepeque (a city of central Hondu- ras) to learn more of the program. No promises were made and the limitations of funding were fully recognized.

The call was heard. We were amazed at the response, as several groups were formed in our parishes. At first there was a severe shortage of educational resources in Spanish. We were able to get some of the material that the "Seminario Biblico" of Costa Rica had available. Later, when Sewanee's Education for Ministry (EFM) course was translated into Spanish, we used that material. The scope of the work turned out to be much greater than expected. A new deacon Volunteer for Mission just out of Sewanee came on board to help. On loan from the Diocese of West Texas, the Rev. Carmen Guerrero was the first to head the theological education program. Once into the educational program, and with her help we began to identify those students who could handle an academic load. The commission on ministry and the standing committee were determined that we would end up with a quality product. We were not going to ordain anyone simply on the basis of *their* sense of the call. Those identified as able students and as responsible and productive ministers were given special assistance with their studies and eventually, for their final year of preparation, were enrolled in a full-time residential diocesan program. During this year they spent four days a week in residence, then three days back home in their places of work. Upon the return of Carmen Guerrero to her home diocese, our companion diocese of Central Florida sent the Rev. Robert Sanders to direct the program for another two years. After his departure the work continued under the supervision of two clergy from Guatemala, the Revs. Leonel Blanco and Rolando Segura.

What we actually did was not exactly what we had set out to do from the beginning. Things seemed to go very slowly at times. To speed up the process we eventually got people on designated tracks. Of those who participated in the meeting at Siguatepeque, some found their way into a program designed to prepare people for various lay ministries. The more able students, mentioned above, were in a parallel, more intensive program. Some of these would be destined for ordination. We also found the means to place a couple of students, clearly headed for ordination, in traditional residential seminary preparation at Sewanee and Austin, Texas. We were surprised to see that the results of traditional seminary preparation were similar to those we were getting in our own residential program, not considering the more advanced educational background of those students, and the advantages one gains from the experience of travel.

The advantage we had was that we were not uprooting people. At the same time our local students continued in the political processes of the nation and they could participate as educated Christians. (Actually, most of our students are involved marginally in politics. It appears that the more humble the origins and the more limited the financial resources, the less likely it is that one will be politically active. However, we do have some middle class people who can afford to be involved, and they are — both sides, left and right. One student in particular was very involved in helping young Nicaraguans escape from their country. Repression has not been as serious here as in some parts of Central America. There is an escape valve for frustration in that we have freedom of the press, the right to strike and a quasi-social democratic government.) On January 6, 1989, we ordained the first five people to the diaconate and on October 6 of the same year, two more — direct results of Wes' ministry with us.

It may be that our experiences do not apply to all dioceses and certainly we do not presume to teach others something that we are still learning. Today we have over 20 postulants and candidates, including some women. We are now moving into our original plan of making training available through an extension program by combining the Sewanee EFM program with material produced in Costa Rica, and we are cooperating regionally with other dioceses. Our program has been approved by the Ninth Province Theological Commission, and the province provides some financial aid. Outside teachers are occasionally brought it for short term courses, and our students sometimes participate in courses offered in Guatamala.

Our initial emphasis was on preparing people to fill our desperate need for ordained personnel. However, we soon discovered that there were others interested in improving their theological knowledge and our original program spun off three more: a continuing education program in support of the ongoing needs of our deacons, short theological programs (a few months) open to all lay people, and special Christian education courses for lay people to enable them to take on a variety of teaching ministries.

In processing people for ordination, we still adhere to the canons of the Episcopal Church. In some cases I have approached certain individuals, suggesting that they should consider a call to serve in an ordained capacity, but generally people are identified for ordination through our training programs; the Lord has given us a good supply and I have been able to pick and choose. Only a few of those called can come into church employment. We encourage volunteer vocations and have had some success, but the demands are many on such people. We have five lay ministers leading congregations as volunteers and nine others in charge of congregations, who receive some financial assistance to supplement their job incomes, now reduced because of time devoted to church work.

It is true that the realities pressing us into new ways of thinking of ministry have been mostly financial realities. But the changes are opening the doors of the church in many places and making us more responsive to educational needs in everyone's ministry. One has only to examine the seminary catalogs to be reminded of how expensive seminary-based theological education has become. I hope that there will always be enough money to keep our seminaries open. But I also hope that alternatives in preparation for ministry will be found acceptable and given the green light by our men and women in purple.

We are now, in Honduras, able to have university-trained clergy working side by side with clergy presently taking their high school equivalency tests. In rural Honduras a college and seminary degree are not all that important. We are determined not to become the church of the elite. If we claim to have a commitment of ministry to the poor, we need clergy who can live and work with the poor, and with the wisdom to recognize that our Lord Jesus Christ is calling the poor to ministry. Too bad, maybe, for bishops, deans and administrators that the poor generally have neither the education nor the money to *get* an education (especially in a traditional seminary). But they *do* have a call to ministry and we *do* have our commitment to serve with them.

Our work continues; the quest has not ended. There is still a long way to go. However, for the time being we have managed to alleviate the need for native clergy and we still have strength to continue down that road. Both the missionary church abroad and the missionary church in the United States need to take a good look at what Wesley Frensdorff represented. The best time to fly a kite is when the wind is blowing. It's blowing now.

Chapter 7

THE MINYERRI VISION:
Roland Allen in Australia

Clyde M. Wood

N athaniel Farrell is married to Debra and they have eleven children. Nathaniel has been a stockman in the general area of Hodgson Downs, Hodgson River, which is approximately 300 kilometres south, southeast of Katherine in north central Australia. Nathaniel, like many Aboriginal men, has not always known full employment, has frequently lived on unemployment benefit and has occasionally drunk far too much alcohol. In the early years of the decade of the 1980s, the community of Hodgson Downs, which has now been named Minyerri, was visited by Canon Barry Butler of the Church Missionary Society and also occasionally by the Rev. Gumbuli Wurramara, the rector of the parish of Ngukurr. Consequently, there was a small number of Christian people who occasionally met for fellowship, and two or three times a year received the stimulus of a visit either by Canon Butler or the rector of Ngukurr or the bishop of the Northern Territory.

Early in 1984, God warned Nathaniel to stop his drinking and some time later he determined to find out if God were true. Early one morning Nathaniel Farrell took himself off to spend the day alone on the top of a large rocky outcrop which overlooks the community of Minyerri. There he prayed for God to show his power. During the day he became aware that God had a special plan for him.

There are many Aboriginal people whose Christian lives began, either through a dream or through a vision. And so it was to be this day, when a stockman of Minyerri had an experience that would change his life. Like Moses, Nathaniel Farrell came down from the mountain and shared with his family the vision of God's call for him to be pastor to the people of Minyerri.

* * * * *

Arnhem Land is an area of approximately 100,000 square miles situated in the tropical north of Australia, on the eastern side of the Northern Territory adjoining the Gulf of Carpentaria. It is primarily an area set aside for Aboriginal people who have been in that region for up to 40,000 years. This part of Australia was first settled by white people in the middle of the 19th century. Long after the first incursions by white settlers, Aboriginal people in many parts of Arnhem Land continued to live in their traditional ways. It was not until the early part of the 20th century that the dislocation of the traditional way of life of Arnhem Land Aboriginal people began to take place. By the 1920s their nomadic hunter/gatherer style of life was slowly being broken down by the establishment of a range of settlements created and maintained by both government and church mission organizations.

The Anglican Church's involvement in this process was primarily on the southeastern side of Arnhem Land through the agency of the Church Missionary Society. The first settlement established by the Society was near the mouth of the Roper River where it enters the Gulf of Carpentaria. That was in 1909. Between that time and the last of the Anglican settlements to be administered, Umbakumba in the mid-1960s, the following settlements were established: Umbakumba, on Groote Eylandt at Anguruga; Numbulwar and Roper River, now called Ngukurr, on the mainland; and Oenpelli on the western side of Arnhem Land. In the 1980s the community now known as Minyerri, Nathaniel's home, grew in numbers and has become a sphere of influence of the Anglican Church in the Northern

Territory. Until 1968, the work was administered by the bishop of the Diocese of Carpentaria, situated some thousand miles away on the tip of Cape York Peninsula. In 1968 the Diocese of the Northern Territory was created and its first bishop, the Rt. Rev. Kenneth Mason, took up residence in Darwin.

The work of the church in the various settlements covered nearly every aspect of life. In extremely difficult conditions because of isolation, distance, lack of roads and communication, missionaries virtually created settlements out of nothing. In some instances they lived in extraordinarily primitive conditions, isolated for many months at a time, and endured considerable physical privation and hardship. Naturally, therefore, a great deal of the work of the early missions was the provision of adequate places in which to live, of educational opportunities for Aboriginal people and their own children, and of health and welfare services. In latter times the actual building of hospitals, creation of roads, building of stores and provision of adequate water supplies has occupied them. In effect the early missionaries were involved in the establishment of the equivalent of small towns and fulfilled the roles of missionary, educator, healer and local government administrator. Although all who went to work in these places went there primarily with the intention of spreading the good news of salvation through Jesus Christ, the majority found that for most of their time they were involved in the establishment of a local community. Hence, for example, although it was a major policy of the Church Missionary Society for mission staff to become fluent in the use of the language of the people with whom they worked, in fact very few ever managed to achieve it. There were, however, some instances where missionaries took very seriously to learning the language and diligently worked at translating parts of the New Testament. In a couple of notable occasions their works

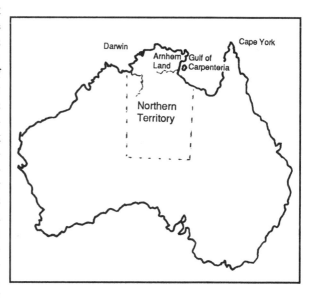

were published. Still, little use was made of what was translated. Many missionaries openly discouraged the use of local language by the indigenous people. Few missionaries knew the language and so in most settlements in Arnhem Land the work of mission, preaching and teaching was in English.

Early attempts or desires to fulfill the sort of vision of ministry represented by Roland Allen's writings (the development of local ministry and handing it over to indigenous people) were, in most instances, thwarted by the belief that preparation for ordination must conform to the normal standards appropriate to the preparation of white priests in other dioceses in Australia. Hence, in the early 1950s, Aboriginal men who showed some interest in ordination would have been required to leave their homes and families for a period of up to six years to fulfill the requirements then in force in their own diocese. It probably comes as no surprise to learn that the men were not prepared to fulfill such requirements. So it was not until 1972, that the first Aboriginal person was ordained priest: the Rev. Michael Gumbuli Wurramara, who continues to be priest and rector of the parish of Ngukurr, formerly Roper River. This was an instance where the bishop, Kenneth Mason, proceeded to ordain a man who was recognised by all concerned to be a satisfactory leader of his people. About this time a group known as the "Arnhem Land Seven" began to be encouraged to be trained for ordination. For a variety of reasons most were not eventually to proceed. The exception was the now rector of the parish of Angurugu, a brother of Gumbuli Wurramara, the Rev. Aringari Wurramara.

In the late 1960s those with a vision of Aboriginal ministry began to work towards a training centre specifically designed to meet the needs of Aboriginal people. The vision was shaped during joint discussions between members of the Anglican and United Churches. In 1973, Nungalinya College in Darwin was opened. Over the past sixteen years it has grown into one of the most significant educational institutions for Aboriginal people in Australia. It now provides education for Aboriginal Christian people of most churches and from every state in Australia. The college has been most innovative in designing education specifically for Aboriginal people and has provided theological education by extension courses, community development courses, residential theology courses and other courses for skill enrichment of Aboriginal women.

In 1983, the author of this paper, much influenced by the Roland Allen conference in July of that year, was elected bishop of the Northern Territory, succeeding Kenneth Mason. In November of 1983, a meeting was held at Numbulwar in Arnhem Land. There a representative group of leaders from each of the six communities in which the Anglican Communion is involved in Arnhem Land discussed the future of the faith in their communities. In particular, the conference focused on the development of ministry, local leadership and indigenisation of the gospel. As a result of that meeting, three communities identified people for training in 1984. (Some of our communities were either not together in their agreement with the plan or simply not ready, at that point, to begin.) In early 1985, three men were ordained deacon, priested within ten days, and have since become leaders in their own communities. They experienced one full year of training in Nungalinya College and are now required, as far as possible, to be involved in two three-week courses each year.

I have chosen not to attempt to describe at great length the writing and thinking of Roland Allen; the material is readily available these days. I will quote here a summary of Allen's basic principles taken from an interview recorded by Gerald Davis with the Rev. Canon David Paton of Gloucester, England, at the time of the Pacific Basin Conference in Hawaii in 1983. This summary is found on page 21 of *Setting Free the Ministry of the People of God,* a report prepared by Gerald Davis with the assistance of Eric Cheong and H. Boone Porter, printed by Forward Movement.[1]

The summary highlights the major criteria of Roland Allen's work to describe the movement from mission to church.

1. *A Christian community which has come into being as the result of the preaching of the Gospel should have 'handed over to it' the Bible, creed, ministry and sacraments.*

2. *It is then responsible, with the bishop, for recognising the spiritual gifts and needs in its membership and for calling into service priests or presbyters to preside at the Eucharist and to be responsible for the word and for pastoral care.*

3. *It is also required to share the message and the life with its neighbouring communities not yet evangelised.*

4. *The Holy Spirit working on the human endowment of the community's leaders are sufficient for its life. Don't 'train' them too much! Don't import from outside.*

5. *A Christian community that cannot do these things is not yet a CHURCH; it is a mission field.*

6. *The bishop and his staff (cf. Timothy, Titus, etc.) are crucial.*

I will take these six points as a summary of Allen's basic principles and endeavour to interpret them in the light of what is now happening in Arnhem Land. The interpretation is, naturally, quite subjective and, of necessity, brief.

1. "Handing over" the Bible, creed, ministry and sacraments

As an introduction I would suggest that the most crucial element in Allen's basic approach hinges on the question of language. For a whole variety of reasons, the handing over of the gospel in Arnhem Land was not accompanied by the use of local language. In the early years some very competent teaching of English was accomplished by mission educators and, as a result, it was assumed by many — if not most — that it was sufficient to proclaim the gospel in English. It is also quite true that most of the native languages in this part of Australia are very complex and require many years of dedicated effort to master. Hence, when one turns to point one, the handing over was confined to those who were fluent in the English language.

As has already been pointed out, although it was official policy for missionaries to learn and use the local language, few did so. However, in the late 60s and especially from the 70s this began to change. Some missionaries were freed from other duties and encouraged to do language work. In the last twenty years there has been a growing program of translation work, and we are now beginning to see the fruits of those labours. In one place the New Testament has been completed and, in three others significant portions of the New Testament will be available by early 1990 in local language. However, the use by local people of what has been translated has not been easy.

There are a number of reasons for this. One has been the apparent belief that ceremony must be done in the proper way. Worship is seen as a ceremony; all experience of worship has been in English and therefore the proper way to offer worship is in English. Secondly, there is the matter of power amongst local people. Some leaders, fluent in English, have perhaps unconsciously recognised that language is power. Wishing, perhaps not intentionally, to retain their capacity to direct what happens in the life of the congregation, they stay with the use of English. A further factor has been that Aboriginal people are an oral people. Their capacity to memorise large quantities of material is prodigious and many of the older people have learnt by heart the English hymns and services of their childhood. Translating hymns into local language is also retarded by the ownership of local tunes and words by particular groups and the need to gain permission for these to be used in different ways and at different times. Another vital factor has been the great difficulty of local people being able to read their own language. Some of the languages have words with 20 or 30 letters. When people attempt to read these by sounding each of the letters and syllables, it makes reading an extremely difficult procedure. Creative work is now being done in helping people learn to read using tapes. The practice is growing and, slowly, progress is being made.

It is more and more apparent that handing over is a process, not an event, and it is a long term process, especially when a range of languages is involved. The process requires learning another language — ideally by both the indigenous people and by the missionaries. It requires the lengthy process of translation, not only of scriptures, but liturgy, hymnology, commentary and materials for use in theological education. With regard to worship, there is the need to try to understand the basic ingredients of Christian liturgy and allow incorporation of traditional material and forms while retaining some degree of, in our case, Anglican heritage. There are few manuals outlining how one does this.

Not only is it a long term process, but it is a process that is not happening in a vacuum. With regard to handing over of ministry, there is the problem of appropriate models. New indigenous leaders have had perhaps a lengthy exposure to models of ministry which are of another age and another experience. From whence do Arnhem Land people, becoming responsible for ministerial leadership in their own communities, draw their model of ministry? This problem is further exacerbated when we consider that members of their congregations — both white and Aboriginal — also carry with them expectations and models of leadership which may not ultimately be ideal for ministry in the emerging indigenous context.

A further difficulty in this whole area is one of finance. The communities of Arnhem Land have, in the past, experienced a full-time ministry supported from the outside. Worship takes place in buildings which were erected by the use of outside finance. In some of these communities the total population numbers only 200. It is not realistic to expect that such small communities, where maybe only a percentage are practicing Christians, where unemployment rates are high and most members of the parish on government benefit, can support a stipendiary ministry. This is especially so when one considers other outside responsibilities, diocesan relationships, travel, etc. Aboriginal people need to come to terms, not only with a style of ministry which can be gradually oriented toward the life of their own community, but one which will be affordable in their context by their own people. It is not possible to consider that ministry has been "handed over" if that ministry must be supported financially by an outside group.

2. Calling into service those who will preside at the eucharist

It is understood in Aboriginal communities that the only group capable of recognising who its leaders should be is, in fact, the local congregation. It is very difficult, if not impossible, for an outsider to be

fully aware of the variety of tribal responsibilities and interlocking clan relationships which may determine who will be able to fully exercise a
Christian ministry in such a context. In at least one of our communities this
has been made even more difficult because of a major division within that
community between local traditional land owners and those who have
moved in to be part of the settlement during the last 50 years. In another, it
is further complicated because those who show the most promise are not
members of the group which holds sway as local traditional land owners. In
one community it has taken five years to get agreement allowing one from
"the wrong side of the tracks" to be accorded recognition of gifts. It was
finally accomplished by including someone from the traditional land-own-
ing group and proceeding with two leaders. (In fact, it would be ideal, in
most of the Arnhem Land communities, to have at least two leaders, as
Aboriginal people have, as part of their normal life, avoidance relationships. This means that in any community where there is only one person
responsible for ministry, there are at least some people with whom that
person is not able to talk.) It has been the practice over the last five years
for the bishop to request the local community to identify the person or
persons they believe would be right and for the bishop to accept that
recommendation. The present bishop would be loath to deny the person put
forward by the community to become their new priest or preacher.

3. Sharing with neighboring communities

In Arnhem Land opportunities for sharing the good news with
other communities are limited. Because of distances, the cost of travel and
the amount of time involved, sharing the message has not been easy, nor is
that likely to change in the future. One of the communities has engaged in
several very long distance forays, in one instance covering probably 4,000
miles in a journey using newly translated New Testament material and a
team of singers and musicians. Another journey was carried out in the latter
part of 1989 in an entirely different direction, partially as a process of
evangelisation and secondly as an evaluation of the usefulness of the Kriol
translation of the New Testament and significant portions of the Old Testament. In journeys undertaken so far, Aboriginal people, serving as evangelists and using their own languages, have been very successful. This has
been of great importance on two counts. First, the very acceptance of
Aboriginal people serving in this capacity, that "one of our own is able to do
this sort of thing" and the boosting of self-esteem that results. Secondly,
the proven effectiveness of using the language and affirming the culture of
the people.

4. Trusting the Holy Spirit and resisting the temptation to import too much

This is probably the most difficult for white leaders. How much training is too much? What are the criteria — for diocese and congregation — to indicate that a congregation has moved from dependency to interdependency? How much general exchange should there be between Aboriginal congregations and the wider church? Perhaps the most difficult thing for white leaders to accept is the patience required. The second most difficult element is to come to the point of being able to believe in Aboriginal people. The third difficulty for white church leaders is their inability to predict the directions that indigenous ministry, worship and every other facet of its life will take. Westerners have a penchant for organisation, control and manipulation. All this means that the teaching of Jesus about the Holy Spirit that blows where it wills, requires a capacity to be willing to let go and allow the Spirit to endow the community leaders for the life that God intends for them.

5. When a mission field becomes a CHURCH

One of the unfortunate characteristics of the congregations in Arnhem Land has been the scarcity of men in the life of the church, especially in leadership positions. In one of our churches only one man has been involved; in others, perhaps two or three. In a culture in which no major community decision is made except by a group of male elders, and where the male half of the population is not part of the church, one can hardly claim that the church has become indigenous. We have been striving to get beyond the popular notion that "Christianity is women's business" by engaging men in the proclamation of the gospel in their native language. With great joy we are now seeing significant numbers of tribal elders beginning to take their part in the life of the local church.

"When a mission field becomes a church" suggests that one can distinguish between the two, or that there is some point where a transition occurs. It suggests that there is a terminus to the handing over of Bible, creed, ministry and sacraments. That when a local community, in conjunction with the bishop is able to call into service priests and deacons and has begun to share the message with neighbouring communities, and community leaders are sufficient for the local life, then, in a way, our process is complete. Surely church history would teach us that whenever we believe that the process is complete, we are reaching the point where the whole process really has to be begun all over again. Surely the state of Christianity in western societies (certainly in urban Australia) would suggest that this is so. The process is always one of becoming, and of developing human endowment so that the fulness of the stature of Christ will always remain a goal for any Christian community.

6. The bishop and his staff are crucial.

In Arnhem Land we have endeavoured to have, along with the bishop, two members of staff who, while they have other responsibilities, are free to visit and play a supportive, listening, teaching role with Aboriginal communities. One of these, the Rev. Canon Norman Barry Butler, is now a member of the staff of Nungalinya College. He, along with other members of the staff, visits each of these communities at least twice a year. It is common for these visits to last a week, and for as many members of the local community as can, to gather together in an educational experience. In one area there is a white priest who has the responsibility of caring for a mining community congregation, but who also has provided a listening backup support for Aboriginal ministers and congregations. These two positions are quite critical as they require people with the capacity for a non-directive, listening, supporting, counselling type of ministry. The bishop's role, too, has mainly been one of listening, counselling and encouragement. Only on rare occasions has he found it necessary to intervene in the interest of compliance with this or that diocesan policy. In one particular community the bishop resolutely refused over a period of three years to agree to a desire for further white leadership to be imported from the outside. It has also been necessary in one or two cases for the bishop to step in and deprive a priest of a license to operate for a period of months in an effort to bring a difficult situation under control.

* * * * *

As time went by, Nathaniel Farrell shared his vision with Canon Butler and also with the Rev. Gumbuli Wurramara. Later that year he was confirmed and discussions were held about his coming to Darwin to spend a year at Nungalinya College. This, however, was to pose a number of problems. The first was that he wanted to bring his family. While this was in accord with policy of the Diocese of the Northern Territory — that men cannot come to Nungalinya for a whole year without their families — Nathaniel had not only a wife and eleven children, but also the husband of one daughter and a grandchild. The second major difficulty was that Nathaniel was basically illiterate.

So provision was made for the whole Farrell clan to spend the year in college. For the family it was a very fruitful year and Nathaniel worked with great diligence. *Owing to the patient care of the staff and, in particular, Terry Hume, a CMS-supported teacher of English as a second language, Nathaniel made great progress in learning to read and write, as well as learning a considerable amount of biblical theology. After his year in Nungalinya in 1986, Nathaniel received his certificate of theology and was made a deacon in the church of God at Minyerri in May of 1987.*

During his deacon's year (1987) the practice was for either Nathaniel's children or other members of the congregation to read the lessons. The prayers and hymns were normally led by Nathaniel and he preached the sermon. His preparation for preaching involved listening to the New Testament on tape. In 1988 he was ordained a priest and by that time was able to read the gospel from the Kriol Bible and to read the service of Holy Communion in the Kriol translation.

So over a period of four years, one who began with a day apart with God, during which he believed that God spoke to him clearly about the need for him to be the pastor of his people, Nathaniel has now moved to the point where he is a priest of the Anglican Church of Australia, an able and effective pastor and teacher of his people, and one who has, on occasion, been used by God to heal the sick. He will continue to spend three to six weeks a year in residence at Nungalinya College, continuing his more formal education, and there will be occasions in which the members of the staff at Nugalinya will be in residence at Minyerri for theological education by extension programmes, not only for Nathaniel, but also for anyone else who wants to participate.

Other ministries contribute to the life of the parish of Minyerri. Lance and Gwen Tremlett, supported by the Church Missionary Society as literacy workers, serve the whole Roper Valley area and indeed, beyond. They regularly visit Minyerri to sit for days at a time and tutor people who are not able to read. They use the Kriol translation of the Bible and other materials developed for the purpose, to teach those who, for whatever reason have failed to learn to read during their childhood. Thus the Tremletts are a very important part of a team of people who are involved in the encouragement and enabling of people in this part of the Diocese of the Northern Territory to grow in their understanding of the nature of the gospel and in their capacity to share it with others.

* * * * *

Somewhere Roland Allen writes of the "three selves." A church should be *self*-supporting, *self*-governing and *self*-propagating. The work in Arnhem Land over the past five years has been an endeavour to make this real. Local communities are, insofar as possible, responsible for the selection and support of their own leadership. Outside financial assistance has been provided for education, for non-local travel and for the maintenance of buildings which the Aboriginal people did not ask for and probably didn't need.

In any case, our experience suggests that the real core of the other selves is a fourth self — self-esteem. We have embarked upon a process in which people believe in themselves, believe in their own culture and believe that their way of doing things will make a major contribution to the life of the wider church in Australia. It will be a long, drawn out process as the people of Arnhem Land are strengthened in these beliefs, people who not long ago heard missionaries describe their ways as the ways of the devil. Ways which can now, in fact, be used to the glory of God and for the proclamation of the good news of Jesus. Our journey can hardly be called a success story. Progress has been slow and difficult to measure. Sometimes great leaps forward appear to be made, but then, on occasion, a big slide backwards seems to follow.

* * * * *

It is most unlikely that a priest like Nathaniel will ever move from his home and so his training has been devised for him: a person of tribal background, well fitted to work with his own people. The preparation of Nathaniel and the circumstances under which the people of Minyerri worship should not be considered by urban Anglicans as an oddity. They are part of the rich fabric of the Anglican Church in Australia. We must appreciate that worship, experienced by urban Anglicans in Gothic type buildings, is not exclusively "the proper way" and that the simple worship of an Aboriginal community gathered round two forty-four gallon drums covered with a slab of three-ply is equally "proper." For such an altar is not an unfortunate aberration, but an expression of Anglican incarnational theology. It is important that non-Aboriginal and urban Anglicans know something of the way of life of the people of Minyerri, and be enriched by it.

Note

1.   Gerald Davis, *Setting Free the Ministry of the People of God.* (Cincinnati: Forward Movement, 1984).

Chapter 8

BECAUSE OF PEOPLE
Every person is a person because of people.
- Zulu proverb

Richard A. Kraft

In the Diocese of Pretoria, Republic of South Africa, "Every parish a school for ministries" is a kind of rallying cry or slogan; it is a challenge to the faithful and a call to action. In South Africa, however, a "parish" is often like a mini-diocese, with one strong central congregation surrounded by 20 or so "local" congregations. The slogan has to do with the intention of making the primary congregation a center for theological education in ministry for the whole parish.

More on that from Richard Kraft. As a graduate of General Seminary, he had learned of Roland Allen from Allen devoteé, Boone Porter. In June, 1976 — the month when the Soweto riots erupted in South Africa — Wes Frensdorff visited Zululand, and he and Richard enjoyed some time together, comparing notes and sharing experiences in total ministry. Kraft became bishop of Pretoria in 1982, and began total ministry development as a diocesan-wide strategy. -Eds.

In December, 1981 when I was elected Anglican bishop of Pretoria in the Church of the Province of Southern Africa, I could not help asking, "Lord, why me? Why me, a white, an American, here in Pretoria, the capital city of South Africa?" It is always dangerous to ask the Lord questions, because he has a way of answering. Clearly, from that time until now, the answer has been consistent: "All these years you have been teaching and training others; now I want you to get on and implement the vision of ministry that I have given you in this diocese." To understand the Lord's response requires some background as to what he had been teaching me during my years in Africa.

An indigenous South African church

When I arrived in South Africa in 1961 as a newly ordained deacon I was excited by the prospect of living in a society and working in a church very different from that of my upbringing. What surprised me, however, in those early years was finding myself in a predominantly English church rather than an indigenous South African church.

The church architecture was overwhelmingly like that found throughout England. We suffered through the hot weather in churches with small windows, often unopenable stained glass, meant to keep the cold and damp out. I had come from the "beretta-belt" of the Episcopal Church into a predominantly high church Anglican province. With that background we never thought twice about wearing the heavy, brocaded eucharistic vestments which we put on over alb, amice and girdle, and that over the cassock which we always wore, again over a plastic clerical collar and black shirt — at least one lost weight in that portable sauna during the long summer months! It was as though our predecessors had indeed found the proverbial "sky-hook," and had picked up completely equipped old churches in the U.K. and plunked them down in the dorps and veld of Africa. I began to discover that it went much further.

Only a few years before, Bill Burnett had been elected the first South African born bishop, and the year before I arrived Alphaeus Zulu was consecrated the first black bishop, a suffragan. Church finance was just beginning to climb out of the hole created by a mentality of an endowed state church with a bit of sustentation fund thrown in to make it work in the colonies. We were beginning to cut the umbilical cord of dependency on the mother church, and to establish the "Wells scheme" of planned giving and stewardship teaching.

I could go on to give other examples, but perhaps what I found can best be illustrated by the use of the *English Hymnal* or *Hymns Ancient and Modern*. Somehow it has always seemed ludicrous to sing "In the bleak midwinter" at Christmas time in southern Africa. I had grown up on an indigenous American (U.S.A. to be more specific) hymnal which could cope with "midwinter" hymns even better than England, but which also included such contributions as Negro spirituals and lively Methodist evangelical songs. The soul and suffering of the black Americans and the missionary zeal of the Wesleyan circuit riders were part of our North American Christian history and culture. I had difficulty discovering the roots of South African history and culture in the Anglican tradition here.

When, a few years later, I was plunged into ministry in the black community, I encountered a Zulu Anglican hymnal which had only one hymn out of 278 written by an African; all the rest were tunes from the *English Hymnal* or *Ancient and Modern* with usually badly translated words from the same two sources crammed in to fit the notes and cadence foreign to the poetic and musical beauty of Zulu. I was to discover in the all-night revival meetings, called iMvuselelo, the power of African song and dance expressing the deep things of the Spirit. However, these nights ended at dawn with a solemn, sung high mass in which we reverted to the westernised Zulu hymn book. Both parts were profoundly moving experiences of Christian worship. However, they were kept hermetically sealed from one another — an underground, indigenous African Christianity at night, an authorised, formal western Christianity by day.

I must say that I am grateful for my time as a curate in this English church tradition. Many of my fellow students at seminary in the U.S.A. went out on their own to so called "mission" congregations or out-of-the-way, isolated parishes. Granted, our seminary training did more to try to prepare us for taking full responsibility from the beginning than did the English system operating in South Africa as well as the U.K. at that time. In the U.S.A. there was always a scramble in our final year of seminary to try to get an appointment as an assistant in one of the big city or eastern seaboard parishes, but there were only a small number of such places available. The foundations that were laid through two and an half years of priestly formation in my first parish, followed by another year as an assistant priest in a vast, rural, Zulu-speaking parish, have proved invaluable.

I was a deacon in name only because the whole focus was on the priestly ministry, so that even as a deacon I was trained to do everything that a priest could do, barring celebrating the eucharist and other sacraments, and pronouncing absolution or blessing. The church had no concept of what the diaconate was all about; it was just a stepping-stone to the priesthood. I should actually have been called a sub-priest (like the word sub-deacon). I mention this, not only to show the model of ministry that we were operating with, but also because this experience was the beginning of my thinking about the ministry of the deacon.

The rector of my first parish, Mervyn Sweet, was a Mirfield-trained priest, in the best of the Community of Resurrection, Anglo-Catholic tradition. He was a thoroughly dedicated parish priest. He was a good teacher and a very powerful preacher. He had a strong sense of social justice and was willing to stand up for the kingdom of God in the face of the evil of apartheid. He was disciplined himself and was therefore able to develop a lively, large and disciplined parish. We had a daily mass, morning and evening prayer — and some people came! We had scheduled times for confessions, healing services, even a few public anointings, and baptism only at the Sunday eucharist. Not only did we prepare the parents of children for baptism, and, of course, young people for confirmation, but we had some adults whom we prepared for baptism and confirmation. Those ill or shut-in, either at home, in hospital, or in some other institution were visited on a regular basis and the full range of sacramental ministry was available to them. At the heart of our pastoral programme was a systematic and extensive pattern of visiting.

Given the model of ministry on which we were operating, it was an effective and vital parish. The rector was a hard taskmaster and a good trainer of priests. It has often been said that the liturgical tradition of the Prayer Book and the worship that flows from it is one of the main strengths of the Anglican Church; we certain made full use of this strength. He taught me to appreciate the real treasure that we have in a pastoral approach centred on the sacraments. An added plus, and by-and-large a rather un-Anglican asset, was the powerful preaching ministry. The only problem of which I very gradually became aware, was that we could have been in Chicago or London as easily as in Pietermaritzburg, Natal in the early 1960s. Only much later, with considerably more and wider experience in Southern Africa did I come to realise, that even at its best this model of ministry was too restrictive if real growth in the body of Christ was to take place and be sustained.

I had been plunged into an exciting church with a vital ministry in this new country, but it was not a South African church. The next chapter of my ministry was to make this rather vague and largely unarticulated impression abundantly clear.

A model of ministry for Africa

After two years as a deacon and assistant priest at St. Alphege's, Pietermaritzburg, I went to my diocesan bishop, Vernon Inman, to discuss my future. I told him how grateful I was for his invitation to come to serve in the Diocese of Natal and for his wisdom in appointing me to work under

Mervyn Sweet in St. Alphege's Parish. I knew already that I had received a very solid grounding in the priestly ministry and I said that I would be very happy to stay there for some years. However, I told him that I was afraid that if I stayed too long at St. Alphege's there would inevitably come a very strong pull to return to the U.S.A., as the white suburb of Scottsville was not all that different from the one in which I had lived in Chicago. I felt that if I were going to remain in Africa I needed an opportunity to get involved in the kind of "mission" work that I had come to do; my idea of mission was still not big enough. I asked him for an opportunity to learn Zulu and to minister in the black community.

The bishop understood immediately and was most sympathetic to my plea. His only problem was that he did not have a place for me to do this in the Diocese of Natal — or so he thought. Some years before he had embarked on a process of appointing black priests as rectors of parishes; he contended that had he not done this as a conscious policy, his black priests would still be assistants to white rectors. As a consequence, he only had two older and very experienced white missionaries working in black parishes within that diocese. Graciously, he offered to write to the bishop of Zululand to introduce me. Bishop Tom Savage was overjoyed as he had a difficult time attracting clergy to his diocese. We began corresponding; he invited me to come to see him and to look at a particular parish. Just as we were about to tie up the remaining loose ends, one of our mission priests, Tommy Hopkins, got wind of what was happening from his friend Mervyn Sweet. He telephoned me, and although we did not know each other well, he immediately challenged me: "Why are you going to Zululand?" I explained and his response was, "That is nonsense," or words to that effect.

Tommy was a tough, red-headed Scot who had grown up in Glasgow. He was anything but a diplomat when he thought he was right, which made him forthright and blunt — even to bishops! He phoned the bishop of Natal and gave him a piece of his mind. The bishop, also a tough and practical man, simply shot back that he had no place to house me and my family while I was learning Zulu and training for mission work, as it was then called. Tommy had obviously anticipated this: "What about right here with me at St. Chad's Mission? There is a staff house between me and the girl's hostel which the Bantu Education Department is not using because it is too near the hostel." The government did not want whites living next-door to a black school hostel and they would not think of putting one of their black staff members in such a nice house. Tommy had to fight hard with the Bantu Education Department to get this house back in our control and in the end we had to erect an eight foot high, split-pole fence because we as a white family were going to live so close to the hostel.

That is how we came to St. Chad's Mission — still in the Diocese of Natal. The Bishop of Zululand was bewildered by the sudden, last minute withdrawal of my name for appointment by the bishop of Natal. However, Bishop Inmann and Tommy Hopkins were delighted and so, in the end, were we.

The parish of St. Chad's, Klip River was really a mini-diocese. It covered two and a half magisterial districts, an area about 130 miles wide and 80 miles tall. It had 33 congregations. Some of them were large, such as the one at the central mission station where we lived, with over 300 communicants at a Sunday eucharist and about 900 members altogether. Others were small, like the one at Bethany where we met in the rondavel of a family who produced four communicants and with a few of their neighbours usually had about 20 worshipers at a service. Five years later they built their own mud and thatched roofed church and had over 80 communicant members.

We visited these congregations by Land Rover and later a pick-up truck — when the mud or flooded rivers permitted. One of the assistant priests travelled around by bus and at one stage we also had a motor cycle. Some of our congregations were up in the Drakensberg Mountains; in their case we would drive about 65 miles, leave the car and proceed for the next 5, 10 or 15 miles on foot with back-pack, or on horseback. The local people would supply the horse. Before the government took away our church schools, one parish had nine primary schools which were also used for worship, a girls' boarding high school and on the central mission station a boarding teacher training college and high school for boys and girls, as well as a higher primary which was also used as a test school by the teachers college. The central mission station was a six thousand acre farm which the church had originally acquired to settle Zulu converts for whom it was too dangerous to stay in their tribal setting because of persecution. Many of the mission stations of all the dominations were established to give refuge to new Christians in the early days of Christian mission. By the time I got there the government had declared that only 100 families could stay and even they were considered squatters in what had been proclaimed a white farming area. These families were the descendants of the original converts the Anglican Church had made in that area over the years.

I was to live at the mission station along side Tommy Hopkins for the next two years to learn Zulu and "mission" work. If that went well then I would be made rector of another large Zulu-speaking parish like St. Chad's, Klip River — in fact, the bishop indicated that he already had one in mind. In my experience, the Anglican Church in Southern Africa has never taken language study very seriously as did the Lutheran, Roman Catholic and even the small Congregational Church. I had to get on with it myself. I found a tutor, a simple language course on records, some text books and reading books used in the schools. Starting at the beginning, I gradually worked my way up through the grades. I set up my own discipline and schedule, for it was really up to me. After I had learned some of the basics, I found it most helpful to visit the homes of the people on the mission, where I would sit for hours with (especially) the old people and the children, listening and trying to converse. The old people had infinite patience and were delighted to teach someone their language. The children played it like any other game; they helped me to laugh at myself and not worry about damaging my self image. It was they who taught me the meaning of Jesus' saying, "that unless you become like a little child you will not enter the Kingdom of God." That was also true for the kingdom of the Zulus and their language: unless I was willing, like a little child, to play with the language, which really meant I had to be willing to make a fool of myself a lot of the time, I would never ever be able to speak it. As I learned and acquired more courage, I began to spend time with other adults: when they were working in their fields, or up on top of their roofs thatching, or sitting around the beer pot talking. Gradually I began to learn something not only of the language but also of their culture and history. Unfortunately, my progress was cut short when, after five months, Tommy and his wife decided that with an assistant like me they could take long leave and visit Scotland where they had not been for 12 years. So I was left in charge for four-and-a-half months and shortly after they returned, Tommy decided it was time for a move. So as the first year drew to a close, I found my self rector. From the time that I had been left in charge, I had continued studying Zulu, as they say about learning to fly an airplane, "by the seat of my pants."

Tommy like Mervyn Sweet was a tough disciplinarian — on himself first, then on others. He was a hardened missionary priest who had cut his teeth in the Transkei among the Xhosa people. What he had learned from the old missionaries he passed on to me. He had been used to itinerant work, mainly on horseback — and he had a bad back to prove it. In the Transkei he would ride a circuit of part of a vast parish for ten days or two weeks, visiting four to six congregations during that period and staying a day or two in each place. With a Land Rover, motor cycles and buses now available, he had adapted this itinerant ministry at St. Chad's. There were never more than three priests and for most of my five years there, only two. We would try to visit each congregation once a month, a few of the bigger ones twice a month. So Sunday was not the only "Sunday" in a week. After I became rector, my normal monthly schedule was two congregations on Saturday and two on Sunday for three out of four weekends. On the fourth weekend I added two more congregations on Friday. This would usually be in the most remote area from the mission station. When there was a fifth

Sunday in a month we tried to use that weekend to visit some of the congregations that were neglected or in special need, or in some other creative way.

During some of the weekdays we would have what today might be called a house church; we would organise and announce a eucharist in the home of an elderly, infirm or sick parishioner and encourage neighbours to attend. Any number from about 15 up to 40 or 50 adults and children used to cram into the room in someone's house, with some sitting in an adjacent room or looking through a window. When you sit on mats on the floor many more people can fit into a room than when chairs are used. The Holy Communion would be celebrated on the same table we would later use for tea or even a meal. The sermon and prayers would be more a time of sharing than of just listening to the priest. After the service we would visit and talk, sometimes discuss important issues and even do more teaching. If there were sick persons present we had prayer, laying on of hands and sometimes anointing with oil. We normally shared food together, either a simple tea and biscuit or a hearty, usually chicken, dinner. We could easily spend two or three hours in this way and so we scheduled only one such gathering a day. Often when we dispersed we would then go to visit other nearby parishioners, especially the sick. Or our own members would take us to neighbours who were not Christians, and so an evangelistic contact would be made. It was not unusual to leave between 5 and 6 in the morning and to get back in the late afternoon. These were invaluable contacts with our people and their local communities, and served to demonstrate the importance of the house church and spending quality time with people in their own grass-root situations.

When I was made rector and left in charge I continued this pattern faithfully. In fact, in a modified form which I will explain, I continued this pattern for the whole of the remaining five years I was at St. Chad's. Given the model of ministry I had inherited, it was a very responsible way to handle the challenges of pastoring so many people spread over such a large area. And the people responded! "When is uMfundisi coming again?" "Can we have more services in the month?" "Please come to my home next time." "I would like you to visit my neighbour." When such requests are coming from people in 33 congregations it doesn't take long to be overwhelmed. I was running around like a chicken with its head cut off. In later years, when I was training clergy or preparing people for the ordained ministry, I used to tell them that it is better to be a lazy priest than a successful one, because the whole world will queue up at your door and finally both you and your family will be eaten up alive. Of course, I wanted them to be successful, or perhaps a better word would be effective. But I was trying to make them aware of the limitations of this model of ministry centred on the church-supported, seminary-trained priest.

As I travelled around visiting my vast parish, I began to realise that ministry would often move into a community when the priest arrived and then move out of that community when he left. We did have some wonderful and faithful catechists and evangelists in a few of the congregations or areas of the parish — and I praise God for them. However, once again I became aware that the bulk of the preaching and teaching had fallen to them by default. We seemed to have something back to front. Those who had received little or no training and theological education were doing most of the training/education ministry, while the person whom the church had trained the most — the rector — was often engaged in what might be called the mechanical part of the ministry: driving a vehicle and presiding at the Holy Eucharist. Of far, greater consequence, the congregations and the parishioners were on a starvation diet because the availability of the sacraments had been locked into my ministry and the two, or at best three, priests who were available to that parish and other parishes like it.

If I looked at the South African Prayer Book and the eucharistic lectionary in the *front* of the book, it was clear that the church's expectation was that the people should make their communion every Sunday and on the other great festivals and saints days. If, however, I looked at the eucharistic lectionary in the *back* of the same book, it indicated that they should be gathering around the table of the Lord daily! I came to the realisation that no where in the Prayer Book or the Canons and Rules of the Church did it require me to visit my congregations monthly or quarterly — far more was expected as the norm, and this not only of the eucharist, but all the other sacraments and pastoral ministrations. It was the beginning of my realisation that we had tied the sacraments and the resultant pastoral ministry to the priest rather than to the body of Christ as it manifests itself in the local church. This starvation diet produced dependent, forever "baby" Christians, and a stunted, defective church that had no way to grow and expand or produce mature Christians.

So I began to stop running around all the time, and to break the pattern. I began using the fifth Sunday weekends and sometimes other weekends in the course of the year to gather the people, especially the leaders, so that we could spend quality time together learning and growing as Christians and as ministers. We would gather in one of the local churches on a Friday afternoon to spend the whole weekend together until late Sunday afternoon. The meetings rotated from church to church. We would join in the daily offices and the eucharist, spending time over the word of God and singing a lot. We had Bible studies, discussion groups, teaching sessions. At night I would hook up a filmstrip projector to the battery of my truck to show teaching films. We would write up our findings on blackboards or newsprint sheets, which I would later have transcribed into notes; thus we created our own resources. We ate together, slept together and played together, and over the years we came to know, trust and love one another. Christian community was developing. Christians began growing and maturing. Ministries were discovered and encouraged.

In the beginning these weekends were intended only for the leaders gathered from the parish's congregations or from a particular geographical area of the parish. However, most of the members of the congregation where we were meeting would also show up. In Africa where the community, and not just the individual, is so important, it was impossible to keep them away. So it was my African Christian brothers and sisters who taught me the value and power of the church as a community of God's people. From that we developed Congregational Life Conferences. We had other conferences for the youth, or the women (Mothers Union) and the men. We introduced vacation Bible school during the summer school holidays. We would also arrange great eucharistic celebrations followed by a feast, for example at Easter, so that all the congregations could gather.

It was this experience that plunged me into an approach to Christian education which emphasised leadership training and the nurture of every member of the body of Christ. As director of christian education, first for the Diocese of Zululand and then for the Church of the Province of Southern Africa, these formative experiences and experiments were to be taken much further.

I only wish that at that time in the Diocese of Natal we had embarked upon the development of the self-supporting, ordained ministry, for it was exactly what we needed in the parish of St. Chad's and similar parishes in that diocese. But such a development was still ten years away. What God had taught me was the importance of "equipping the saints for the work of ministry," and during my five years as rector we made a significant start in that at St. Chad's and in some of the neighboring parishes. I also discovered the important distinction between the itinerant and settled ministries of the New Testament church, which had become blurred in the modern church. The model of ministry on which I had been raised and trained emphasised almost exclusively the settled ministry. Thus, when I visited my scattered congregations I carried on my ministry in them as though I were the settled minister living among them. This is why, by and large, the ministry of Christ moved in and out of those congregations whenever I or some other priest visited them. I had to come to terms with the fact that I was an itinerant minister and therefore what I did when I visited a congregation had to be quite different from what I had been trained to do. I had been trained to do the ministry of Christ — all of it! I came to see that what I had to do as an itinerant was to equip and enable the ministry of the local church. I did not stop leading worship and celebrating the eucharist when I visited my congregations, but I started concentrating on other things during such visits. Not only were the weekend conferences that I have described an important part of this process, but every regular visit to a congregation was an opportunity to share the vision of an every-member ministry, to teach and train, to follow up the conferences, to give encouragement and oversight to those discovering new ministries, and to those who had exercised a ministry for years but were now growing and learning more. I discovered that both the settled and the itinerant ministries are essential to the life and growth of the church.

Human relations and leadership training

During the time I was at St. Chad's, a development was taking place in which I was to become deeply involved and which would relate significantly to what I was discovering in my parish. It was also to move me into the next chapter of my ministry.

In 1963 Bishop Tom Savage of Zululand asked the Episcopal Church, U.S.A. to help him develop youth work in his diocese, which resulted in the Rev. Don Griswold coming to be rector of the parish of Empangeni. Don took his time, as he was trained to do, getting a feel for the situation and doing his homework. He came to the conclusion that both the church and the South African society had such a tight authoritarian structure, that if he started the kind of youth work in which he had been engaged in the Diocese of Oklahoma, he would do one of two things, or possible both. He would either blow the lid off the authoritarian structure of the church, or he would build up so much frustration among the youth that they would become more alienated rather than more involved. Don shared his analysis with the bishop who, when he heard it, was in despair, thinking that nothing could be done. However, Don, claimed that it would be possible to start a vital programme for youth, but only if the clerical and lay leadership of the diocese were themselves re-orientated and trained so that they would both understand and be able to support such a ministry. He was recommending what came to be known as the Human Relations and Leadership Training Programme.

First, Don asked the bishop to appoint various clergy and lay leaders in the diocese to be responsible for various portfolios, such as youth, Sunday school, stewardship, post-ordination training, etc. Don, as I was to learn later, had a theory that people learn best when they are dissatisfied with their performance. For nine months these leaders were allowed to struggle with their task. Then Don had the bishop invite them all to a training course at KwaNzimela, the diocesan conference and training centre.

Needless to say, they were eager to attend so that they could obtain help for the tasks they had been given.

Don discovered that a priest from my diocese of Natal, the Rev. David Poynton and his wife Jean, had had some involvement in such training while on a sabbatical in the U.S.A. Together they launched this effort which was to included Bishop Savage and key leaders in the Diocese of Zululand. Then Don and David went to see the bishop of Natal and convince him that such training would benefit his leaders. The next thing I knew I received a letter from the bishop, as did a number of other clergy and lay leaders in the Diocese of Natal, inviting us to attend a course at KwaNzimela Centre. Well, in those days, when the bishop invited you to do something, you did it!

We learned about interpersonal communication, about giving and receiving feedback, about what helps and hinders such communication. We explored personal dynamics: self-image and the masks we wear; the part emotions and feelings play, for good and ill; how to read body language as well as the words we use; to encourage the growth of others and enable them to contribute their unique gifts. The field of group dynamics opened up for us: the shape, "personality" and development of a group; the factors at work in a group that impede or stimulate its life and growth; driving forces or restraining forces as they effect change. All this and more was equipping us with new resources for working more creatively and effectively with God's people in the church, but the most powerful impact on the model of ministry which we were then using came from new insights into leadership. We were introduced to the concept of shared leadership; that leadership skills could be learned; that there were distinctions among authority, role, title and leadership; that leadership was a function or provided a function that helped the group to live its life or do its work; that such leadership functions could be provided by any member of the group at any particular time; that good leadership enabled other members of the group to provide such functions, or in other words, released their gifts for the benefit of the group.

This was called "Phase I," and only five months later, in September, 1965, I was asked to be a co-trainer for the third such course which now involved many of our ecumenical partners in the Methodist, Congregational, Presbyterian and Roman Catholic Churches. In the same month I attended a "Phase II: Designing Educational Events," at the newly acquired Diocese of Natal training and conference centre called Koinonia. Koinonia came into being as the result of the vision of David Poynton (who was soon to become the first director of Christian education for the Church of the Province of Southern Africa) and Philip Russell (then archdeacon of Kloof but soon to go on to a long episcopate in three dioceses, concluding as archbishop). I mention this because both KwaNzimela and Koinonia have played a seminal role in the renewal of ministries in the life of the CPSA, and set the pattern for the creation of similar centres in dioceses throughout that province.

"Designing Educational Events" was another watershed coming fast on the heels of "Phase 1," and gave us tools for implementing what we had begun to learn there: experiential learning instead of depending on the teacher-tell method; the use of the action-reflection model — do-look-think-change; education in its original meaning, as drawing insights out of the learners rather than merely pouring in lots of information. There was orientation design which could deal with the attitudes, feelings and the emotions; skill training which could deal with behavioural change. Even when communicating content (information and data) we discovered methods whereby the learner could be more pro-active in its acquisition and inter-active with what needed to be learned. At the heart of it all was learning the discipline of listening to and gathering data from the target group; determining the goal and subsidiary objectives for the plan; then designing the educational format to which are attached the various methods and resources for implementing it; executing the design, normally with a team of trainers who had been part of the whole process from the beginning; and finally, the humbling step of evaluation whereby the trainers learned as much if not more than the trainees.

So during my last two years at St. Chad's (1966-67), in a situation crying out for a fresh approach and fertile for experimentation — one which had challenged me to reconsider the model of ministry which I had inherited — I was given new tools for doing the job. Existing educational resources and programmes were not only translated into Zulu, but radically adapted for that cultural situation. Even more exciting, we began developing our own indigenous training programmes and accompanying resources thanks to the designing tools that we had been given. I say "we" because now, as a result of this training programme, I was not alone. Alfred Mkhize, who was later to become suffragan bishop of the Diocese of Natal, was then rector of the neighbouring parish which, like my own, spread over a vast area with many congregations. We began working together in the training of our laity. With other priests from Zululand we developed Phase I and II training in Zulu so that our training was not limited to members with a command of English. We began to discover all sorts of gifts among the people of God as they grew in confidence, became more effective in ministry and developed the leadership base of our parishes.

Training for ministries in Zululand

During this period I was increasingly involved in training courses at KwaNzimela, Koinonia, and even farther afield, as well as in other parishes. Although I took a number of my own parish leaders with me and invited others to come help me in my parish, the tension between my responsibility to my own parish and family at home base, and the expanding training programme throughout Southern Africa began to weigh upon me. Before returning to the U.S.A., Don Griswold recommended to Bishop Alphaeus Zulu, who had become bishop of Zululand in 1967, that he needed a director of Christian education to follow up the training programme that he and David Poynton had initiated. Some friends and colleagues in Zululand suggested my name, and Bishop Alphaeus asked me to visit in order to discuss the possibility. I remember the meeting clearly. He explained that throughout his ministry he had been involved in the training of lay people for ministry and leadership in church and society. But he knew that as bishop he would not have the time to continue. He said, "Rich, if you come to do this job you will be my right hand, doing this work on my behalf." In fact, although he did not have time to be involved in the planning and organisation of courses, he participated whenever he was able and would spend quality time with clergy and lay leaders — listening, discussing and teaching. It was in him that I saw the bishop of the early church as pastor of the pastors, teacher of the faith, and instrument of unity, building up the family of God in that diocese. It was from him that I first came to see the importance of the role of the bishop in setting the pattern of ministry and mission in a diocese.

So it was that, at the beginning of 1968, I found myself in Zululand with a free hand to develop the work in ways the Spirit led me; the bishop was always available for consultation and he was wonderful at encouraging my efforts. There were some things, however, on his agenda that he asked me to attend to which, because I was his "right hand," I felt deserved the best that I could give. He asked me to take over the training of lay ministers which he himself had started the previous year. He was deeply committed to the ongoing training of the ordained and asked me to organise an annual clergy school as well as post-ordination training for clergy in their first five years of ministry. He was delighted with the other continuing education opportunities that were organised for the clergy. The most exciting request which came from him and his chapter, was to research the growth of the self-supporting ordained ministry throughout the Anglican Communion, together with the training programmes that were being developed for this ministry, and to report back to chapter with recommendations. After my experience at St. Chad's, this opened up for me the most exciting and relevant development of the ordained ministry for our situation in Southern Africa. My books by Roland Allen, whom I had first encountered in seminary, came out again to be re-read then and many times since. I discovered that here and there throughout the Anglican Communion others were exploring and pioneering in similar ways. Even in the CPSA Bishop Edward Knapp-Fisher, formerly the head of a theological college in the U.K., had embarked upon the training and ordination of self-supporting priests in the Diocese of Pretoria.

I do not know what I would have done if the Zululand diocesan chapter had turned down my recommendations, for by now my parish experience, education involvement and this research had committed me to the development of a model of ministry that would equip each local church with the fullness of Christ's life and work. Not only did the chapter agree to proceed, largely because Bishop Alphaeus had already caught the vision, but they gave me the job of developing the whole programme, including the training and theological education.

I was fortunate that as director of Christian education for the diocese I was responsible for the whole spectrum of ministries: various lay ministries from Sunday school teachers to community developers; licensed lay ministries; elected leaders such as church wardens and parish councilors; post-ordination training and continuing clergy education, as well as the training and development of the self-supporting priesthood. As the years went by we were confirmed in our belief that it was total ministry that really equipped the local church. The inter-relatedness of all these aspects of the ministry of Christ on a continuum was essential to release the gifts that the church and the world needed. The healthiest ordained ministries, whether self-supporting or church supported, came out of the flow of this process. It was the Ephesians 4 model all over again — a passage of scripture which, among others, was essential in guiding our strategies.

My research showed that overwhelmingly the seminary or theological college model was the model in use elsewhere to develop the training for the self-supporting priesthood. Since that had been my own experience it was the easiest way to start. It soon became obvious that there were some essential flaws in this model when training people for the self-supporting ordained ministry. Also, my involvement in the Human Relations and Leadership Training Programme had given me an educational approach very different from that traditionally used in theological education. In most of the programmes I had reviewed, the students were taking a multiplicity of courses and subjects at the same time, even if these were fewer in number than at a residential seminary — Old Testament, New Testament, church history, liturgics, pastoral studies, etc. Even for those few students in our programme who had an academic background, it was tough going when one was trying to study, care for one's family, earn a living and carry on a full ministry in the local church. Also, modern learning theories (as apposed to teaching theories) stressed that a person learns best when the focus is singular and learning takes place in a series of manageable steps or digestible bites. Preferably, whatever is learned should be used in practice to make it stick. Since our students were already involved in ministry in their local church and community, it was easy to use the action-reflection model of learning. With regard to course and subject organisation, we made at least the first year a time of laying a solid biblical foundation with the student. Although biblical studies continued, once we felt that this foundation was solidly established, the next stage was to weave these biblical themes into theology and church history. At the third stage, we made the application of this foundation and its development in pastoral studies, ethics, worship (liturgics), missiology, etc.

The pace in which any particular student moved through this pattern depended upon that person. There were numerous factors to be considered: educational backround, language ability, age (and how long it had been since they were last involved in a formal learning situation) motivation and discipline and commitments to family, work, church or community (which for some were constant, but for others changed from time to time; for example, the end of the year exam period was a very difficult time for teachers). The most important principle we learned from all of this was that theological education and training could not be "store bought off the coat hanger;" it had to be "tailor made" for each individual. This was a lot harder to provide and administer, but it paid dividends in the quality of growth and learning. It also meant that those who would never have been able to get into a seminary (possibly because their English was too poor, or their academic qualifications too low) and yet felt called by God, were not only trained, but often became effective priests and leaders of their communities.

Another element in the mix was the creation of a community of learning, a discipleship group, a school of ministries. Community and the extended family are very important in Africa. There is a saying in Zulu, "a person is a person because of people." In that rural diocese where distances were great we met once a month for a weekend from February through November and for ten days (two weekends and the five days in between) in January; in December we took a break. We met at KwaNzimela Centre where we studied together, ate, slept, played, worshiped, and ministered together. Those who had been in the programme for a few years would take responsibility for certain aspects of the learning of other newer members. Everyone was encouraged to take responsibilty for the group and for the learning of others. There was lots of discussion and sharing. In fact we stumbled upon a very simple method of building faith and fellowship. One January as we commenced our annual ten-day course, to which quite a number of candidates came for the first time, I asked everyone to introduce themselves to one another by telling the group how God had called them to ministry. I had expected to do this on the first Friday evening as we started the course, but we only finished some time on Monday morning. In fact, when we did finally finish we were all so deeply moved that I suggested we go into chapel to give thanks to God and to pray for one another; that took another two hours. We ate a late lunch that day! Thereafter, every month when we gathered, I would ask two or three members of the group to share what God had been doing in their lives and ministry since we last met — two or three because we really did want to get through this step on the Friday evening. Often what came out of this sharing influenced how and what we studied for the rest of the weekend; sometimes the whole programme would change to deal with an issue that emerged as the concern of many in the group. Not only did this bind us together as a community of learning in the Lord, but sometimes our deepest insights came out of these sessions. I might note here that many years later in the context of a city where the distances were not so great we learned that weekly or at the least bi-weekly gatherings for a Saturday morning or afternoon had the same effect of building this kind of Christian learning community. So powerful was this community, that even when a student found that the pressures of other commitments were squeezing out study time, assignments, and the like, we would insist that they not miss these gatherings for we discovered that this is what kept them going and growing. When the pressure was off they could always pick up on their studies again.

This training for ministry was an ongoing process which did not cease when one was ordained, and that was part of the commitment that people made when they were accepted as ordination candidates. It meant that ordination was based on readiness as discerned by the local church, the candidate and the wider church of the diocese, and particularly the bishop and the director of training. Sometimes, when a person had a clearly recognisable ministry in the local church which he had been exercising for some considerable time, we would proceed early to ordain him deacon and then embark upon the training.

After some years' experience and when our numbers of trainees had grown to the point where "tailor made" training was becoming difficult to administer, another very effective way of handling subject matter emerged. We began selecting a particular focus for our weekend gatherings: for example, the healing ministry, or evangelism, or preaching. For that weekend all our biblical studies, church history, theology, liturgy and other appropriate fields of study would centre on the focus chosen, with practical assignments, homework and preparations tied into that focus. Sometimes the trainees would go back to their local churches to do the practical work and then report back at our next gathering. Not only did they learn their various subjects at far greater depth, but they were learning to use these resources of the faith in practical ministry.

When I started this training programme for the self-supporting ordained priesthood in 1968, I felt like a one-man seminary. Over the years I involved others from the diocese and the wider church as trainers and resource persons, especially in the annual ten-day course. I also had the great advantage of using an educational approach that depended on learning rather than teaching theories, so that the resources of the trainees and the training group were available. Still there was a need to communicate to the trainees the content of the faith, and at that time virtually nothing suitable was available. I adapted the Episcopal Church's (U.S.A.) Teaching Series, the original version. Some years into the programme I discovered some workbooks for this series produced by the Diocese of Michigan. During the nine-year period I was director of Christian education of the Diocese of Zululand, the Theological Education Fund (WCC), of which Archbishop Desmond Tutu had at one time been director, began to produce their series of text books. This was an extremely valuable resource because they were written for those countries in the developing world — Asia, South America and Africa — as well as for those whose first language was not English. They used examples, framed questions and included pictures from the developing world countries rather than from the western world. Some of these are used as text books for the South African TEE College courses (theological education by extension).

However, because of our special circumstances and needs, I had to begin developing my own indigenous resources, especially if they were to relate to Zulu cultural experience. Some of my colleagues and I started writing and developing courses under the banner of Khanya Theological Education by Extension —"khanya" is the Zulu word "to light." Some of the other dioceses and the Roman Catholic Church were also trying to develop similar courses. My dean, Robin Briggs, was at that time head of St. Bede's Theological College in the Transkei, and he took the initiative to sponsor a consultation of all those similarly involved. This was the initial step towards the establishment of the TEE College, an ecumenical venture sponsored by a number of the major denominations in South Africa. The courses of the TEE College are offered on three levels: award, certificate and diploma. Some of the courses on the award level have been and are being translated into some of the major vernacular languages of South Africa. The TEE College has proved to be an invaluable resource in our ongoing work since it is flexible and contributes to a "tailor-made" training programme. It is also part of an ongoing process of developing theological resources with the participating churches.

A vision of ministry for Pretoria

In January, 1977 I was appointed director of Christian education for the Church of the Province of Southern Africa and moved from Zululand to Johannesburg where our CPSA offices were situated. Since the founding of that department in 1966, I had been an active board member. I had thus participated in many of its programmes in diocese and denominations beyond Zululand. Although my time as CPSA Director was too short, it did give me an opportunity to help other dioceses consider a new approach to Christian education and another model of developing ministry. Among the dioceses which used me as a consultant was the Diocese of Pretoria.

Bishop Michael Nuttall invited me to come to Pretoria and in July, 1979 I became dean of St. Alban's Cathedral. Over the preceding years I had participated in a number of training courses and had worked with some of those involved in Christian education in that diocese. Robin and Margaret Briggs from St. Bede's Theological College had preceded me to the diocese and were already working with TEE students, some of whom were preparing for the self-supporting ordained ministry. Bishop Michael did a wonderful job of beginning to weld a very diverse diocese into a family. We had ten different languages that were used liturgically. We had been very high church; then from 1975 many were deeply touched by the charismatic movement. We had vast, scattered rural parishes, many small towns, and a dynamically growing industrial-urban complex centred on Pretoria. There were the divisions of rich and poor, black and white, and numerous tribal affiliations. Pretoria is the administrative capital of South Africa and represents the power base of the evil apartheid system. Indeed, the separation of people into "their own" group areas had been well implemented in and around the city of Pretoria, and in the many "homelands" throughout the diocese, which threatened not only the unity of the nation but the church as well.

Bishop Michael was elected Bishop of Natal in 1981, and I suddenly found myself plunged into the Episcopal leadership of the Diocese of Pretoria. God made it very clear to me that he wanted me to implement in that diocese all that I had experienced and learned about the life and work of his church. He had given me a vision for the ministry and mission of his church which had its roots deep in the New Testament and early church. He had also drawn together a significant number of colleagues in Pretoria who shared that vision or were at least open to it. God had prepared the ground wonderfully by my predecessors, especially the last two bishops: Bishop Edward Knapp-Fisher who had initiated the self-supporting priesthood in the CPSA and as a former head of a theological college in the U.K. had set high standards; and Bishop Michael Nuttall, a man of the Spirit and a teacher of God's word, who took the ministry of all God's people seriously and began the process of building unity in the diocese. I am presently working on a book detailing our Pretoria experience. For our purposes here, however, I will touch on a few key pointers out of that experience.

We have learned that it is helpful, in trying to share vision and goals with the people of God in a diocese, to capture the essence of the vision in a slogan which is short and concrete so that people can really get a hold of it. Then we have done a lot of teaching and communication, especially in face to face contexts, around the slogan. At the very beginning of my episcopate, in order to pick up on the work of building unity in the diocese under the leadership of Bishop Michael, we adopted the diocesan theme, "Becoming the Family of God." The slogan has been so important to us in trying to find creative ways to consciously build bridges and combat the unhappy divisions that are the result of apartheid, let alone other forms of human sin. This has led us to commit ourselves to the "ministry of reconciliation" which was so important in the New Testament church (cf. II Cor. 5). In recent years we have added the theme, "Reaching out as the Family of God" which has implications as to how we engage in mission through evangelism, service, prophetic witness, and socio-political transformation.

The implementation of such a diocesan theme has also had implications for the model of ministry that we have been trying to adopt. We emphasise that it is Christ's ministry in his body, the church, of which we are members by virtue of baptism, and that the risen Christ gives ministries (always in the plural) to the church. Thus, the leadership he provides to enable this to happen, to order and coordinate its functioning, needs to be expressed in a community or college of ministers at every level. In some parts of the world they have also called this "team ministry." This is seen as another expression of family in Christ. Thus, the bishop, together with the chapter, archdeacons and canons, as well as diocesan resource persons such as the director of training for ministries and the diocesan administrator, seek to model this corporate, shared leadership. This we try to reproduce at the archdeaconry level (or what in some parts of the Anglican Communion would be called the deanery level). We try to have all the church-supported clergy, and those self-supporting clergy who are available, meeting together weekly. At the parish or even congregational level we challenge the rector or priest-in-charge to develop a similar college of ministers composed of the elected lay leaders, the licensed lay ministers and the self-supporting ordained personnel. It means spending quality time together regularly and frequently for worship, prayer, sharing, planning, encouraging, learning, eating and playing. We find that this pattern reproduced at every level releases and makes available the plethora of gifts that the Holy Spirit has given to the church.

In December, 1981, two weeks after I had been elected bishop of Pretoria, I was invited to the final meeting the Joint Boundaries Commission of the Dioceses of Johannnesburg and Pretoria. Given the fact that just over half the total population of the Republic of South Africa lives in the Transvaal which had only two dioceses, the Commission recommended that both dioceses consider division. The Commission suggested a process whereby suffragan bishops would be used in regional episcopal areas to test out the viability of new dioceses. The goal was to create dioceses that were more pastorally manageable and could focus more sharply on the ministry and mission challenges of their area. Given the timing of these recommendations I have always taken them as one of the mandates laid upon me for my episcopate. Although people in the two dioceses could grasp the reasons for division intellectually, emotionally they were finding it difficult to "break up the family." So the whole thing started to bog down. Literally, in a time of prayer, God gave me the word 'multiplication' to replace the idea of division. This was a positive idea: creative, life-giving; we started talking about it in terms of giving birth to children. We even applied it to over-large, multiple-congregation parishes; to evangelism; to reproducing ministries in the local church. So another slogan was born.

In going through this process of multiplying dioceses we have had to re-examine the role and model of the bishop. We discovered that the people wanted and the church needed a chief shepherd who was much closer to them — not just one who visited once a year for a few hours to confirm. If he was to be pastor of the pastors and a teacher of the faith, then he needed to spend quality time in all parts of his diocese, which in turn relates to the size, numbers and focus of ministry and mission in an area called a diocese. We also discovered that it is important for the bishop to be the receiver and bearer of the vision God has for his church. Sometimes the tension between the traditional role of the bishop with the expectations that accompany it and this new, emergent role is overwhelming and quite exhausting, but along the way there have been enough creative breakthroughs to show that the effort is worthwhile.

The most important slogan for moving the diocese into this new model of ministry has been "Every Parish a School of Ministries." We have a wonderful Diocesan Department of Training for Ministries which, when I became bishop, was headed up by an inspired retired priest, Canon Ian Carrick, who thought up this slogan. That department continues to develop in exciting ways as this new model of ministry has caught on and spread under the professional and creative leadership of Margaret Briggs, the wife of our dean. Despite the financial constraints on our diocese, as on other South African dioceses at this time, year after year we have invested a sizeable amount of our budget to support this work. Yet the key is the local church, and, good as our diocesan department is, we know that we fail wherever we have to keep pumping ministries and resources in from the outside. The purpose of our diocesan department is to assist the local church with the resources it needs to do the job of raising up and equipping people for ministry, and to help the parishes do together what they would struggle to do separately. In fact, our slogan, "Every Parish a School of Ministries" is that of our department, which it uses to promote and teach the concept of total ministry.

The goal is to equip each local church with ministries. Many of the learnings that I have already described have been built into this process — and God is still teaching us new things. Initially, our licensed lay ministers, as with other South African dioceses, were essentially liturgical assistants. The CPSA was one of the first provinces in the Anglican Communion to involve such lay people in the distribution of Holy Communion, reading the word of God and leading prayers. However, we realised that there were many other lay ministries that did not involve wearing vestments and being up front in the sanctuary. So we started developing other categories of licensed lay ministers: pastors, teachers, healers, preachers, evangelists, church musicians, administrators, as well as worship leaders. Although this is an ongoing process, we have worked out guidelines for the exercise of each of these ministries, and we continue to develop training programmes and educational resources for each of these categories, as well as for all lay ministries whether licensed or those being exercised by any baptised person.

We have also been moved to restore the diaconate as a full ministry within the church of God, rather than just a stepping-stone to the priesthood. We would prefer to be able to ordain people to be priests without going through the step of being made deacon so as not to confuse the issue, but our Canons and Prayer Book do not permit this. We believe that this is an issue that the Anglican Communion needs to address if the ministry of the deacon is to be restored to the modern church. Over the years we have developed the practice of having the ordination of deacons separate from that of priests, and in normal circumstances those whom we discern are called to the priesthood we try to move through their diaconal period as quickly as is advisable. I praise God, for some of the men and women whom God has called to be deacons in our diocese, because we are really learning from them what the ministry of deacons is all about and what we have been missing. When our diocesan chapter was considering the establishment of the diaconate in our diocese, the late Canon Trevor Verryn said, "If we do this, please let us not put the training of deacons into the hands of priests, for we will only make them into our own image." We took that to heart, and have predominantly kept their training and formation in the hands of the laity and now fellow deacons. In a situation like South Africa, where first world and developing world exist side by side, where affluence and poverty are "cheek by jowl," where so many are hurting and wounded, the ministry of the servant Jesus who washes the feet of his own disciples and friends is revolutionary. My own simple definition of the diaconate is, "all the practical acts that makes love go around within the body of Christ and in the world God so loved that he sent his son." I have a vision of each local church being led into this serving ministry by a band of deacons, and we are beginning to see this happen here and there.

We have also been experiencing the contribution and gifts that women have to offer to the ministry of Christ's church. While the CPSA does not ordain women to the priesthood, we have women involved as elected leaders, licensed lay ministers and deacons; in fact, the whole of our Department of Training for Ministries is staffed by women. Total ministry is not only being expressed in our diocese in terms of every member ministry, but also in a wholistic quality of ministry when female and male, young and old, black and white, schooled and unschooled, rich and poor are drawn in.

At the time of writing we have 38 church-supported parochial clergy while altogether we have 119 priests and deacons in the diocese. This means that the self-supporting ordained ministry predominates. When I became bishop the biggest parish in the diocese, Rustenburg West, which covers a vast area of Bophuthatswana, had 38 congregations and was ministered to by a priest over the age of retirement who was finding it difficult to travel. Now, eight years later, that same parish has a vital church-supported priest in his 40's who started his ministry as a self-supporting priest. He has four other priests working with him, others in training and a number of licensed lay ministers in each congregation. The parish now has 42 congregations and is still growing. Archdeacon Itumeleng Moseki still says that they are not touching sides (coping) in terms of the developmental potential of that "mini diocese," but at least they are on the way. I could give numerous examples both rural and urban.

We have called our self-supporting clergy by many names as we have learned more about this ministry, but we now call them community priests and deacons *(the same terms used in New Zealand -Eds.).* They are raised up and rooted in the local church and community, and are set aside by God to share in the leadership of his people in their community. They are on the cutting edge of the church's mission to the world in a way that the church-supported clergy can never be because they have one foot firmly planted in their community and the other in the church. They are part of the settled ministry, together with the other lay ministers of their local church, while the church-supported clergy are seen as part of the itinerant ministry, the apostolic band, sharing in the episcopal oversight of this college or school of ministries. In fact, in the early church what we now call a rector in many of our parishes would have been called a bishop. In our experience, the church-supported priest also comes into his own. He is the one who usually has had more extensive training and experience in the wider church and thus brings this catholic dimension to the life of the local church. He becomes the team leader, the enabler, the coordinator, the trainer. Of course, this process also sorts out those who are meant to be part of the settled, local church ministry from those who are meant to be part of the itinerant, wider church ministry; we must admit that this has been mixed up in the past when we were operating on a different model of ministry.

I have been criticised at times, by some of my fellow bishops, for having so many licensed lay ministers, community deacons and priests. "Surely you are killing the ministry of lay persons generally. If you ordain some deacons in a congregation, aren't you taking away the servant ministry of Christ from others who may also be exercising it?" And so on. I can understand the fear, in theory. But it does not hold up in fact. I usually challenge the critic to come with me to visit parishes where there are many such licensed and ordained ministers, and those where there are only one or two or none. In every case in my own diocese those parishes which have become schools of ministry have all sorts of lay people exercising a great variety of ministries both in the church and in the world. However, the parishes that are depending on "the minister" — and we still have both kinds in our diocese — struggle to get Sunday school teachers, are always asking for volunteers, have a small overburdened leadership core that is "trying to support the rector," as they say. There is just no comparison in our experience. Also, it is a failure to understand the representational and incarnational nature of set apart and authorised ministries, be they licensed or ordained. When ministry is focused in a person, such as it was in Jesus, we can best understand it. When a man or a woman from one's own community is raised up and used by God in particular ways the other baptised members say, "well if so-and-so can do it, maybe God could use me too."

In the Diocese of Pretoria we have consciously embarked upon this process of moving into a new model of ministry for a number of reasons:

1. VISION: God has told us to do it. He has given this vision of ministry to the bishop and a number of others whom he raised up in or

brought to our diocese.

2. THEOLOGY: We see this model as rooted in scripture and expressed in the life of the New Testament and early church. We believe that ministry is the work of our risen Lord Jesus by the power of the Holy Spirit in the body of Christ, the church. We believe that the sacraments flowing out into pastoral care belong to the local church — not just to the one ordained priest. For this to happen, each local church must be equipped with ministries.

3. PRACTICALITY: It works! With all the good will in the world, even a highly gifted priest cannot be in two places at one time, and does not have enough energy to keep going twenty-four hours a day. When the local church begins to be equipped with the plenary gifts of the Holy Spirit, then we begin to see the real needs of the people in the church and in the world around them begin to be met.

4. GROWTH: I have often had rectors bemoan the lack of growth in their parish. My reply has been, "God is being good to you. He knows that if you received several hundred new members tomorrow there is no way you could cope with discipling and pastoring them. You need more helpers." Growth in numbers becomes possible when you are equipped with ministries. People growing in ministry are growing in Christian vitality. This creates excitement and is, in turn, attractive.

5. FINANCE: For all sorts of reasons we do not have, and I believe never will have, the financial resources to support a paid ministry to the extent we would need it in the traditional model of ministry. Africa and a number of other places in the developing world are among those parts of the world where Christianity is growing rapidly. Yet we have been saddled with a model of ministry we cannot afford.

6. CRISIS: We believe that it is the only model of ministry that can take us through the wilderness experience of South Africa. Already, in the chaos and violence of socio-political change and resistance to it, we have discovered that the church as presently organised is too vulnerable. All it takes is a bishop or priest being detained, a church headquarters blown up, or endemic civil strife in an area, for the work of the church to be seriously disrupted. On the other hand, wherever the local church is equipped with ministries, it not only survives, but has made a creative contribution under these difficult circumstances. We are trying to order the ministry of the church so that it can make its contribution as we go through our crisis, and in any kind of new dispensation that may emerge.

This is an ongoing process in which God continues to teach us new lessons and causes us to grow in new ways.

Chapter 9

A KILLAM'S POINT DIARY

David W. Brown

Perhaps 30 years ago, here and there around the church, we began to hear talk of a new approach to small town church leadership called "cluster ministry." "Cluster" referred to a group, or cluster, of congregations in a county or region. Recognizing that most small congregations work better together than separately, three to seven small congregations in a region might depart from the expensive "one priest, one parish" model and have some good people team up to provide clergy leadership cooperatively for the lot. It was a time when dozens of small churches were simply being closed down as "not viable" — 80 in the Diocese of Albany alone in the early 1940s. (The exception was the Adirondack Mission which is still going: an early venture in team ministry.) At first critics belittled the cluster idea. It was nothing but the old "circuit rider" form of ministry being resurrected — a reinvention of an old wheel. But the visionaries saw it differently. In the old circuit rider model the ministry of the church was present when the rider was in town. Otherwise it was not. If "church" is embodied in the visiting pastor, it has no staying power as local Christian community. George Gilbert of 40 Years a Country Preacher fame, rode herd single-handedly on seven churches in Middlesex County, Connecticut, was chaplain to the state legislature, and managed a family farm as well! A photograph exists of the Epiphany, Durham choir in 1940, labeled "Mr. Gilbert's choir." When Mr. Gilbert died in 1948, all but three of those stations were closed. In the cluster ministry model, according to the vision, the ministry of the church would be continuous — not dependent on the actual presence of the professional leader. The new model was, accordingly, out of sync with at least two traditional models the local church folk might be familiar with: the church as a visiting parson and the church as a subsidized pastor on location. Gaining acceptance of the new model locally would be one of the challenges.

Pioneers in cluster ministry development, at least early on, also found themselves out of sync with traditional diocesan methods of doing business, in which something probably called the Department of Missions had oversight of subsidized "mission" congregations, and in which most of the missions had become permanently dependent, second class congregations. The problem becomes acute when a non-communicating triangle develops: assigned diocesan staff/bishop/cluster head. The solution is for all three to sit down and develop policy together. Getting such conversations going in the diocese would be another of the challenges.

In the early '80s, two such cluster ministry teams out of two dioceses found each other and began a series of annual meetings for mutual support and sharing. This is a diary of those meetings.

- Eds.

We first met at Port Jervis in September, 1982. Port Jervis, New York, is in the Poconos on the Delaware River, some 40 miles north of where the river cuts through Blue Mountain, a deep gash known as the Delaware Water Gap. Port Jervis is also one of the small towns involved in the Tricounty Episcopal Area Ministry (TEAM), led by the Rev. J. David Stanway and his associate, the Rev. Steve Kelsey. The Rev. Tom Ely and I represented the Middlesex Area Cluster Ministry (MACM) of Connecticut. TEAM and MACM were, at that time, experimenting in "cluster ministry." MACM was started in 1980; TEAM, a year later. Both were five-point clusters and each of the ten small rural congregations had been drawn through some kind of a knothole several times over. Few members were happy about being pioneers and the four of us were already tired and worn. We came because some of us had worked together before. The trust level was good. The need was great. We shared joys and sorrows and learned from each other, bound up each other's wounds. We were all "building the airplane as we flew it." To sit together for a while and just talk about it made all the difference in the world. What follows here are notes of some of that talk during the first seven of these annual gatherings.

1982: Notes

What a good thing, the supports of a team ministry! No comparison with working alone — frustrated, underutilized, often bewildered by the contradictions with official church routine which seemed to have no down-to-earth relation to who we were. What a good thing, mutual encouragement and sharing. Pioneering is stimulating for those who acquire a taste: participation in a new chapter of church life. David and I were delighted with our staffs. What a bountiful support! Everyone agreed that weekly staff meetings were essential. We always suffered if one got dropped. Some good seminarian field workers brought gifts and variety to the enterprise — their joy in discovering the rightness of the small church, the new/old way of regional ministry. Few seminaries give much, if any, attention to regional ministry. One ordinand expressed his happiness, "I came out of seminary to a place I would like to be at." This meant a place where he had a fully collegial role in planning, opportunity to preach each week, and, upon ordination, officiate weekly. He also had the freedom to get beyond the chores and do what he could do best and experiment as well. This contrasted sharply with his classmates who had been assigned to conventional posts.

We were also cheered to see a visible increase in order and responsibility in the congregations. We emphasized the well known goals of competence, collegiality, and accountability in total ministry. This meant that people needed to outgrow the "stained glass window" mentality and realize that their particular call to ministry was a serious, adult responsibility. The local spirits and self-images were better after two years. But with the joys, we shared the sorrows. The fears and insecurities of parishioners. Silly carping about the cluster — more transference of ghosts than reality. False expectations of the clergy. Yet apathy and indifference. Some with no vision yet, others who had it but were unwilling to invest the energy needed to support it. Lip service Christianity. A seeming immobility in getting the vision beyond the leadership to the grassroots. The usual promises made and not kept: keeping up the vicarage, getting the audit done, beginning (whatever) work on time. And with all of this which reflects normal parish life, an unexpected obstacle for some of us: a continuing struggle with a diocese on a different track and with different agenda and goals. Sand in the gears.

We shared practical detail as well. The value of a (flexible) liturgical customary for a cluster with Sunday clergy rotation. Comparing the procedures for funding team ministry. For example, in TEAM it worked this way. Each congregation had a "staff" line item in its budget and the New York diocese pledged a support amount. That was meant to cover the cluster budget. The first year the total fell 10% below what was needed. So each — congregations and diocese — upped the ante by 10%. The diocesan portion was to diminish by $5,000 each year, although that was not understood to be absolute. As MACM got under way in April, 1980, the understanding was not that clear. Each congregation agreed to do "what it thought it could." This led to considerable Yankee horsetrading. The Diocese of Connecticut provided a grant covering about half of the staff budget. And MACM would try to diminish the grant annually by an unspecified amount. It was said that some congregations in one of these clusters had been kept vacant until there was enough money to begin.

As this kind of sorting out brought on a measure of strain and stress, we found it helpful to see a five-stage process at work: innovation, reaction, confrontation or "shake down the grate," reintegration, and motion into a new chapter.

The MACM stated goal was stability in mission. We described mission in a paradigm: offering the prayer of Christ (public and personal), learning the mind of Christ (learning and social concerns), and doing the deeds of Christ (caring and administration). These three dimensions, of course, interlock and inform one another. And each has an evangelical, that is, both altar and cosmic, thrust to it — *altar axis mundi*. We noted that events in this schema were the *innovations* in the process mentioned above. Specific issues were eucharistic orientation, outreach program, challenge to lay popery and powergrab. These congregations had not been accustomed to seasoned pastors who were prepared to deal with brouhahas. At first it was rocky indeed.

1983: Notes

Now it was Connecticut's turn to host. We met in September at Killam's Point. There is an old house built on rock ledging out into the sea at Branford. Around a fire we talked again of what was near and dear. TEAM had brought a new staff member, so there were five of us. MACM had had women on their staff from the start; TEAM was pleased that a woman had been chosen as their new staff member, as it had appeared unlikely that any of those small, conventional congregations would have called a woman for years. It seemed that the cluster arrangement encouraged innovative, forward-moving actions where timidity had been more the norm before.

MACM was pleased (having run the gauntlet of the five parish meetings) that there was mostly approval for another five years. One congregation had been bulldozed by a lay pope into merely a two-year extension. Curmudgeons never seem to let a good thing by unscathed. But we were all happy that when one parish is down for some reason, another springs up and things balance out. From the outset we all recognized that total ministry was our primary goal and that building a cluster was but a practical way in that direction. TEAM thought that MACM had done well in gradually working to one Sunday morning liturgy in each place. To split a congregation of forty in half seems counterproductive, but habits die hard. We explored linkage methods of outreach and ways to encourage this process. We recognized the verger to be a key officer. In MACM the verger coordinates five liturgical ministries: lectors, servers, altar guild, music and clergy. Each has a head who reports to the verger.

With some important high school graduations, the Connecticut youth group was not as strong as in 1980, and the program seemed less. But we recognized the normal undulations graphing every parish program. In TEAM youth groups were, at the time, the heart of area celebrations and people rallied behind the youth. They, in fact, were the first to connect across parish lines in TEAM and led the way in forming friendships throughout the cluster. They also led the way in "mutual ministry" that summer, having provided a cluster-wide vacation Bible school at the congregation whose church school had died out. Within a year that church school was revived and, in later years, when other TEAM congregations were in a "slump," they returned the favor, helping to revive *their* church schools! The young people understood their leadership role. Lectors at celebrations were often young people. In strange contrast, adults in the TEAM cluster were resisting sharing leadership in liturgy. The priest-ridden years are reflected here. Kelsey and sidekicks reported disappointment in that the people had not carried through with a lay reader school. I was grieving that many years of work in another diocese were being dismantled by a reactionary and short-sighted administration. So we leaned on each other and shared the grieving.

We examined some of the differences between the two clusters.

The TEAM clergy are each parish-oriented and the MACM staff a floating team. The greater distances between the New York parishes have something to do with this. The Connecticut clergy officiate for three or four Sundays in a place, then move to other congregations. Advent-Christmas and mid-Lent through Easter 2 are exceptions, as are July-August vacation units which tend to be longer. The MACM missioner is vicar of each congregation and chairs most vestry meetings. The TEAM coordinator provides a different presence as "priest in charge" of all TEAM congregations: present at all, but chair of none of their vestry meetings. TEAM finds its unity in certain things which the congregations regularly do together: learning events, for example, and celebration of the great days in the Christian year, such as All Saints Day, the Great Vigil of Easter and Ascension. The content of TEAM's education program is formed substantially from the materials of their liturgies and their implications. The MACM missioner is the chief liaison with Diocesan House, but in New York the regional archdeacon, Robert Willing, is given this role: running interference for and advocating TEAM's concerns to New York's mammoth diocesan bureaucracy. In fact, with the efforts of their archdeacon, TEAM has to do little battle beyond her borders, which frees the leadership to focus on internal concerns. The TEAM staff is very grateful for this support. The New York grant (initial grant period, five years) diminishes by specific annual amounts; the Connecticut grant (initial grant period, three years), by annual negotiation between cluster council and the diocesan Department of Congregational Development and the bishop.

An education and lay training program in Connecticut sponsored by Diocesan House (not the Department of Congregational Development) seemed to be a breakthrough in collegiality. Rather than topdown directives, the program was constructed by members of the cluster and other congregations working with members of the diocesan staff to develop a program with strength and depth, yet flexibility and adaptability. Could this be a straw in the wind? We were cheered!

In MACM an orchestration process brought a long overdue grief therapy process to four congregations. Using the mission paradigm outlined above, the participants in special parish meetings identified the ministries which the people were actually doing, usually 35-40 ministries in each congregation. Acknowledgement, affirmation and praise of this "treasure" provided a sturdy basis for looking to "where we might do better." In one congregation eight (!) tumultuous sessions were needed until the boiling wrath, accumulated and unrelieved for decades, could be dissipated. This wrath seemed to have generated through both a sense of powerlessness in a large diocese by the congregational and personal issues transferred into the congregation by prominent lay leaders. These were the "confrontation" points from which the congregations moved to synthesis and growth stages. We noted that a seasoned leader was needed to enable this work. Younger people — even very good ones — do not have the objectivity or sense of context to do it. The superintendent of a regional ministry needs to be "a tough old bird."

1984: Notes

A gentle autumnal sea lapped the ledges of Killam's Point and a bright October sky greeted nine of us that year. There were two from Vermont, four from New York and three from Connecticut.

Frustration and discouragement had the newcomers chewing two-penny nails. Promises had been made and encouragement given. "We thought we had something and then . . . . Is the opposition greater than warrants our efforts? We need help from this gathering to put flesh back on bones." Some thought that the Connecticut and New York experience and data could help. But Connecticut was having its own troubles with mixed messages from the establishment. Perhaps the best thing to do was follow the advice of the industrialist Henry J. Kaiser, back in World War II, who said, "Figure out what you ought to have happen and then just *lean*."

In Connecticut the Roland Allen forum had grown up to review and discuss that "saint of the movement" and other new/old ecclesial thinking. Here was brightening in the night for those who prayed for response to crying needs: group ministries, total common ministry, authentically collegial style, decentralization, and the development of planning regions. People came to these gatherings from six or seven dioceses.

In contrast, the local scene improved slowly. The "golden fantasy" hung on tenaciously, that if each congregation had the right full-time resident priest all their troubles would be over. We recognized that this did not mean that the people felt uncared for, but they had somehow been led over the years through the tortuous ways of clericalism to think that they were owed a "sugar daddy." Somehow a congregation had less — so the fantasy read — if they did not "own" a charming and omnicompetent cleric, no matter how much more practical service they might be getting now from a capable and effective clergy team. Someone put it clearly, "We need to move from parent-child games to being the body of Christ." Overlooked by the complainers was the loyal work of the saving remnant who had held these small congregations together for generations despite inept clergy and inappropriate choices by absentee landlords. Much of this illustrates the maxim, "Do not teach what you later have to unteach." But we believed that time was on our side. Stability for a few years would disperse local distrust.

We talked of practical detail: making job descriptions (focus and limits): for example, that a parish treasury department ought to have a treasurer to pay the bills, a comptroller to keep the cash journal, a corresponding treasurer to send out information and a head counter. This design keeps any one of the four from cornering the money market. We asked what was a parish's share toward a cluster staffing budget? There seem to be several answers and they change with experience and situations. For example, the TEAM formula was based solely on income; in MACM, on several factors. The best hard data for a formula seem to be three things: number of legal voters (determined by a selection method in common), attendance (average of the four Sundays of Advent and the six of Lent less the high and the low; i.e., an average of eight), and the previous year's operating expense (items mutually agreed on). We (MACM) discovered that our quarterly review had become redundant with the reportage now expected by Diocesan House. We spoke of the freelancers who provided care without participating in a care team. And this seemed appropriate as long as communications were open and the pastor in each instance knew what was happening. The deepening and broadening of total ministry seemed to correlate with diminution of an old fable: that the impetus for new ways of ministry was a short money supply.

Some of the "dripping cloud" spirit in two or three places seemed to originate in the "critical mass" theories of the 1950s — that a parish was only "viable" which had such and such a number of dollars and bodies. We recast this viability theory in terms of mission, total ministry and management (in the sense of stewardship). Exercises were invented to turn parishes around in thinking about viability and vocation. All of this related to our insight that the medieval quest for "the *minimum* validity which bore salvation" needed to be converted into a quest now for *maximization*, "the life more abundant." In one diocese a participant had answered a long record of closing parishes by opening some new ones!

1985: Notes

Hurricane Gloria brought chaos to the Connecticut shoreline. So 14 of us were graciously made welcome at Camp Washington, the diocesan camp at Morris, Connecticut. This was the largest gathering yet, with participants from five dioceses and the national church center.

Quite a bit of time was spent bringing up to speed newcomers who had just begun in regional ministries. We reviewed several models of finance. Discussed the fears of small churches. Reviewed planning methods and the importance of identifying indicators that goals had or had not been achieved, "standards which have previously been agreed upon." This, of course, must be done in the planning before the project is begun. These and other matters were related to the opening of the Down East Cluster in Maine and the Bridgeport Episcopal Partnership (BEP) in Connecticut.

BEP, incorporating strong Hispanic components, introduced the findings of the Gonzales study undertaken by Trinity Church, New York. How can the popular goal norms of the Episcopal Church — the swank suburban church which is building a new education wing, beginning to look for a second curate and thriving in a "bread and circuses" climate — how can this matrix of norms make sense to Hispanic, Appalachian, or any typical rural/urban small church setting? What are new and appropriate norms and goals? Our mission model (see 1982, last paragragh) moves toward the answer.

TEAM and MACM began where they had left off the year before. The Connecticut cluster was searching for ways to move from routine toward enrichment of the mission components. There is continuous need to emphasize mission as the sustaining work of the church. TEAM was celebrating their success at cultivating among lay leaders the same dynamics which were strengthening the ministry of their clergy team: collegiality and accountability (fostered by their weekly staff meetings). Lay leaders sharing ministry roles (e.g., church school teachers, wardens, musicians, etc.) were gathering across the cluster every few months to share learnings, provide mutual support, and plan for some mutual programs and celebrations. Far more mission and outreach, for example, were emerging in these places than anyone could remember before, as they discovered themselves challenging and inspiring one another to reach beyond survival to mission concerns. We all recognized that some program is appropriately short term. New York and Connecticut had different evaluation procedures: TEAM, by annual conference; MACM by peer review every two or three years with other aided congregations.

Suddenly and unexpectedly, the tiny parish at Ellenville, New York, had received a legacy of over half a million dollars, "the interest to go for the expenses of the father in charge." That church could now revert to the conventional model. But their vestry saw the value of TEAM and voted 9-1 to stay with the cluster. This gave an enormous boost and vote of confidence to what we were all doing.

An alternative to the five phases of innovation described above might be infancy (an interlock of dependence), adolescence (counter-dependence), early adult (independence) and adult (interdependency). Reflecting on both models is freeing for lay and clergy leaders, especially when applied to local situations and cases.

Several other topics were reviewed: telecommunication systems, care team procedures, a strange and inept book issued by the Standing Commission on the Church in Small Communities, nationwide small church work, the Leadership Academy for New Directions in Ministry (LAND), and a letter to the Presiding Bishop reviewing our interests and concerns.

The experience of this larger, more diverse, yet very successful conference led the founders in looking ahead to plan limits. In the future the first 24 hours would be for TEAM and MACM, since their sharing had been long-term and their understanding close. Then any others could participate and be welcome for a second 24 hours.

1986: Notes

Next September found us back at a repaired Killam's Point. There were five the first day, joined by three more from new clusters in New York on the second day. Discussion ran the gamut from computers and office equipment to ascetic, a basic need in all program. The faces, but for the senior priests and one junior priest, had changed. Turnover rate of part-time clergy was greater. To provide work in a stable and varied church community for clergy in transition is a valuable regional ministry contribution, a vocation. But this reinforces the import of long terms for persons in superintendent/coordinator roles. We were sad to learn that a young couple who had been with us the year before had left the cluster of which they had been in charge. They were now in secular work. The lesson was clear that only very experienced, seasoned persons should be asked to head up clusters.

Special objectives for MACM at this time included clarifying in the popular mind the difference between social concerns (prophecy) and care (pastoralia), work on ascetic (spiritual growth) as the basis for better performance by lay and clergy leaders, and upgrading parish music. MACM was broadening opportunities for social service, partly through a companion relationship which had grown up with a large town parish. They helped each other when the supply of available clergy was thin and in programs such as youth, the elderly and education. This mutual support system between large and small congregations is also illustrated in the Paris Cluster, Diocese of Central New York. (See 1987 Notes, ¶ 8.)

We compared the organization of TEAM and MACM again. TEAM has two tracks: local program-administration and the "church life team" which functions as a unifying council in developing program and mutual support. MACM has one council which administers the staffing budget and various coordinative functions; the council has several standing committees. After five years Connecticut can show that cost in aid from the diocese is about one-fourth per parish that of the conventional model aided parish. This ratio has continued year after year. The phrase "getting more for less" is more than a slogan. TEAM's three-year experimental period had ended with a thorough review process, resulting in the formal adoption by all member congregations of a new set of bylaws which made the cluster arrangement permanent, while providing a process for congregations to join or leave TEAM if they so chose. MACM and TEAM had, in turn, come to the same conclusion in this! Was cluster ministry becoming a new norm?

By now there was so much going well that the sorrows seemed less wearing. Nonetheless, we asked, "Why do some places always choose to seem down?" We were glad that signs indicated that Diocesan House in Connecticut was more tolerant of the claim that non-preferential pluralism in ecclesial models was the appropriate stance today, in contrast with making the one priest/one parish model the expected and "normal" goal. It is *all right* that there can be choices in ministry models. This would soon prove to be an over-optimistic assessment.

1987: Notes

An angry November sea gnashed against the foundation of the old house on Killam's Point as five of us came at night and three more at noon the next day. The wind was raw and the gratefire felt very good.

I had just returned from a four-month sabbatical which had tested a new model positively. A *lay vicar* was in charge of the five parishes and the cluster council through that time. Highly collegial work, as usual, by the whole team made this experiment effective (with hard work). The junior priest covered administration and by November was ready for well deserved time away. A new but experienced seminarian helped through the summer. The large companion parish mentioned earlier was now sharing a priest half and half with MACM, and this strengthened the staff greatly.

But this was the year that the Connecticut Diocesan House announced a compensation ceiling for aided parish vicars. In effect this policy, arrived at unilaterally and clearly without much thought, cut the MACM senior priest's compensation. Diocesan House's response to MACM's expressed concern was that "the missioner's sabbatical allowance will make up the difference." Lay leaders were furious that Diocesan House seemed unable to recognize the policy implications and tended to read the episode as a "shabby" attempt to undermine. It took two months to right this matter, with recognition that the superintendent of a cluster was a rather different job from vicar of a single aided parish. We could not understand why this had not been thought through.

TEAM was beginning to explore the values of MACM's Sunday rota — about three or four Sundays in a place. This admits fresh air and a variety of styles and voices. We talked at length about the myriad factors in calling persons to a cluster team and about the relationships between paid and volunteer members of the team. Connecticut and New York were fortunate to have many worker priests looking for Sunday jobs. Vermont's situation was quite different. As did Connecticut in the Hispanic community, Vermont ordained several local clergypersons. It was agreed that the cluster arrangement with its regular clericus and evaluation process provides a wonderful setting for training and supervision of emerging leaders (lay and those to be ordained locally). Increasingly, need was being expressed for those trained and experienced in cluster ministry to lead such efforts. We recognized our responsibility and opportunity to train future missioners, believing that this would be accomplished most effectively in the field rather than at seminaries.

Part of all Killam's Point conferences turned to some form of the question, "How do you get Nicodemus to take the leap?" Someone told of the lump of coal, cold and wet, which, nudged against a fire after a while, glows and burns. The saving remnant and a right climate of expectation are that fire. And these both need feeding and tending.

How does a deacon fit into an area ministry? We thought this was a case-by-case matter. The people who head up ministries — the local strawbosses — are the *de facto* deacons right now. But they are asked to make bricks without the straw of ordinal grace. How can our cluster life relate to the tedious, constricted and convoluted programs for deacons currently fielded by many dioceses? The people of the Acts of the Apostles would gape and stretch their eyes!

MACM's budget process was described. It begins in the winter with the new vestries. A preliminary budget is prepared by the cluster council finance committee and is reviewed by a council meeting in April, to which all local officers are invited — wardens, vestry, etc. A share formula and proposed staffing budget are hammered out. (See 1984 Notes, ¶ 5.) The vestries, in due time, report back to the finance committee. If there is no need to begin all over again, the proposed budget is presented to the quarterly meeting of the council in May. Sometimes this is not accomplished until the August meeting. The grant is prepared and sent to Diocesan House in September and the grant amount is announced in mid-December, giving the missioner *two weeks* for negotiation with staff members and preparation of the working budget which is to take effect 1 January!

This year members of the Paris Cluster in Central New York joined

us. This seven-congregation federation is not tied together programmati-
cally, but all staff are paid by the cluster. Five of the seven have resident
priests. This federation grew out of the head being rural dean of 26
congregations, 19 of which probably will never have full-time resident
clergy. Three of the seven have large budgets and extensive program. A
cluster to the immediate north provides neighborly cooperation and, sometimes for practical reasons, congregations move between clusters.

We talked, as we often had over the years, of the flexible relation
between the local and cluster levels, that focus is always on the local, the
cluster itself being skeletal and as minimally burdensome as possible. The
cluster serves the local, and grassroots spontaneity is encouraged. Again, it
should be emphasized that the regional ministry is the handmaid of total
ministry, and not the reverse.

1988: Notes

November at Killam's Point was warm and welcoming this year,
as nine of us from four dioceses met around the fire in the old house. There
was much talk of transition. I was retiring. Others had moved to new posts.
And some had adopted new roles. We felt good about all of this, that it was
an appropriate change with growth. Again we were heartfelt in affirming
the nourishment which these gatherings with their mutual support gave us.
We talked about similar gatherings — Sindicators and New Directions
Northeast — the benefits of centering and exchange of information. We
were always learning from the experience of places where similar work was
being done — Nevada, Northern Michigan and Oklahoma, for instance.

We reviewed the developments in the Allegheny County Episcopal
Ministry and the Oneida Episcopal Consortium. There appear to be about
thirty regional ministries now in Provinces I and II, no two alike. A thaw in
the Connecticut Diocesan House was cheering, and the small rural church
experience of the new bishop in New York was appreciated.

The Connecticut parishes had voted in January to continue MACM
indefinitely and we laughed, remembering that the parish which had de-
layed its vote some years ago registered, when the time came, only one
negative vote and that because any time restrictions at all were retained.
The parishioners were bored with these periodic reviews. The cluster had
proven itself. And a sixth congregation was on the edge of coming in. (By
1990 it was fully incorporated.)

Of course the usual nuts and bolts: the organist drought, a shower
of new Christian education resources. A Connecticut actuary discovered
that if the MACM congregations had followed the conventional congrega-

tional development model, it would have cost that diocese an additional $600,000 in the past eight years. By now the Connecticut grant had diminished to about 14% of the staffing budget (from 50%). And the budget had kept up with inflation — and doubled! TEAM's grant from the diocese went from 53% of their budget in 1982, to 16% in 1988, while staff grew concurrently from two full-time clerics to three.

In looking at some more abstract studies, we thought Arlin Rothauge's life-death cycle a helpful tool which should not become a frozen pattern or agent of a self-fulfilling prophecy. We explored Carl Dudley's formal/ informal membership concept and recognized its importance in the Episcopal Church, especially in small rural family-size parishes which are often rather less than judicatory-oriented. In reflecting upon different cluster designs, we found Anthony Russell's distinction between groups and teams helpful.

* * * * *

Here, then, is a review of some things we talked about at the first seven Killam's Point conferences. Much more information, detail and perspective could be brought to this sketch by the twenty or so other participants. Stephen Kelsey has helped me greatly with some of the details about TEAM and in other ways. The human issues of mutual support and information seem to tower over the content of our discussions. What we have come to mean to one another as companions in the struggle is immeasurable. Of the four who began the journey, not one is where he began.

One of the abiding challenges of our work was to get the local grassroots leadership beyond equating "cluster ministry" with "the clergy team" — to understand total ministry development, not clustering, as our goal. The focus of our discussion thus broadened over the years from clergy issues (related to how a team of clergy can better work together) to how emerging leadership (lay and ordained) can best be supported through the clerical presence. Clearly, sustained public verbal support from the episcopate is essential in all of this.

Today the Diocese of New York has seven or eight regional efforts in various degrees of settlement. In fact, spurred by a movement toward decentralization by a "block grant" process initiated by the new diocesan bishop of New York, regional ministries have been blossoming in New York. By 1990, two-thirds of the 60 congregations of the Mid-Hudson region of the Diocese of New York have chosen to become involved in some form of area ministry. Several of the others have asked for assistance in exploring it. Connecticut is birthing six or seven now. The honest, collegial trust which has developed in doing total ministry together has made the difference by God's grace. We have always made eucharist at Killam's Point.

Chapter 10

A CHURCH WITH A TRACK RECORD

Charles R. Wilson

In May 1982 I accompanied Wes Frensdorff in his Accord (custom license plate, "AMEN") on a tour of the diocese. I don't remember what was on his agenda, but I was doing research for a book. The research had to do with models of effective small churches. Lynne (my wife) and I would eventually visit ten carefully selected congregations from Vermont to Hawaii for on-site study. Realizing that "diocesan climate" — the general attitude of the diocese regarding ministry forms and formation — had a lot to do with what kinds of innovations a small congregation might be inclined to consider, or to pursue, or find moral and professional support for, we wanted to include at least one where we knew the diocesan environment was positive. That one would be Christ Church, Pioche, Nevada's most isolated and one of its smallest congregations.

We drove north on highway 93 out of Las Vegas, up into the high desert country, through the little town of Caliente — stopped briefly to enjoy the view at Cathedral Gorge State Park — over a ridge and down into Patterson Wash and the mining town of Pioche, population 600 or so, elevation 6,060 feet. I had worked with Wes on and off for many years and was well aware of what he was up to in Nevada. Along the way he told me about Pioche (PEE otch). Christ Church had been one of the first Nevada congregations back in 1974 to get involved in a new diocesan program of ministry development. The idea was to affirm everyone's ministry — in the world and in managing the affairs of the congregation. If everyone is a minister, then the priest ceases to be the minister, and a true sharing of the functions of ministry becomes thinkable. In this context the presbyters and deacons would be signs and liturgical functionaries of the priesthood and diaconate of all. Priest would no longer be equated with rector, and shared volunteer ministries, including ordained ones, would seem normal, viable and proper.

So the congregation was supported by the diocese in an intensive and extensive program of study, dialogue and planning, and in translating the vision into specific ministry roles for members. In late 1976, Jean Orr was unanimously called by her congregation and commended to their bishop to be Christ Church's local priest. Following further study and preparation by Jean and the congregation, she was ordained deacon in 1979 and priest in 1980 — six years from start up.

Wes showed me around town. In the late 1800s Pioche had been one of those wild, lawless mining towns with a population of some 10,000. Millions of dollars' worth of lead, zinc, silver and gold were taken from the nearby hills. With an evolving national economy, mining gradually ceased to be profitable. Today Pioche is surrounded on three sides by reminders of its history: mountains of mine tailings and rusting hulks of once functional heavy equipment. Yet there is a certain beauty about the place and evident pride in the maintenance of the quaint shops and homes. To the northeast Patterson Wash opens on to the broad expanse of Meadow Valley 300 feet below and the Wilson Creek Range 30 miles across the plains. Quite a view.

After our brief tour we pulled up to the church, freshly painted and with well kept grounds, and went in to meet the people. Later that year Jethro Publications released the book, Against All Odds: Ten Stories of Vitality in Small Congregations.[1] *Chapter 8 is the story of Christ Church, Pioche. Since it came out of Frensdorff territory, a pun seemed appropriate for the title: we called it "Orr in the Tailings." It is, in a sense, a story within a story — the story of one small church's experience within the story of a diocesan strategy of total ministry development.*

In our planning for this new volume, it seemed important that we include a story of a situation in which total ministry had been in place and functioning for some time — a church with a track record, so to speak — and we were still interested in the "diocesan environment" angle: not just

*a story of a positive parish experience, but one of creative diocesan strate-
gizing that sets the stage and makes it possible. In November 1989, Phina
Borgeson, former diocesan staff member, and certainly no stranger to these
people, visited Pioche. She met with many of the folk I had visited with in
1982. Later she met with the current diocesan, the Rt. Rev. Stewart
Zabriskie, for an update on diocesan strategizing. She took notes, taped
conversations, sent them to me and we talked on the phone. This, then, is an
update of Christ Church, Pioche —a church with a track record.*

CRW

There are no physicians in Pioche. When I was there the closest
was in Ely, 110 miles away. Felix Murrin was the local volunteer emergency medical technician (EMT), at that time the individual
people turned to for most of their needs.
He was trained and kept up on his
field. He was formally recognized by
the professionals, accepted in this capacity by his community and backed
up by the total system when necessary. He consulted with the doctors
by phone any time he needed to. And,
as appropriate, he referred people to
the more professional or technically
sophisticated services available in Ely.
(Today there are two doctors within a
25-mile radius and Felix no longer
serves as EMT.) By profession Felix
was and is the local telephone company's expert in high tech. He is also
a volunteer fireman and is usually
exercising some leadership function as
a member of Christ Church. In a small

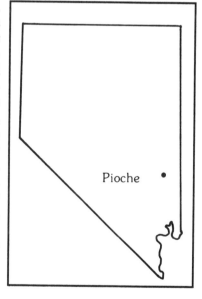

town competent people tend to assume numerous community leadership
roles. It's true of quite a few of the saints of Christ Church.

I was, at the time, especially intrigued by Felix as EMT. Here was
a story of how an isolated community, far too small to support the services
of a full-time doctor, had, with the support of the system, provided for ef-

fective, adequate and locally acceptable health care services. And here was an isolated Episcopal parish, far too small to support a full-time cleric, at work with the diocese developing an effective, recognized and accepted local ministry that would be an integral part of the larger diocesan system and backed up by professional services as needed. The parallel, it seemed to me, had not been noticed by the local folk.

Pioche, after its wild boom and bust era, gradually settled down to its present size of some 600 souls, which has more or less held steady these past 50 or 60 years. It is the county seat. Government and the pensions of retired people contribute to the local economy. There is some farming and ranching, and a somewhat uncertain tourist business. Sue Hutchings, who owns a small motel, reports that she has placed it on the "honor system." When someone phones for a room, she assigns them a room number, tells them where to find the key, and asks them to leave the money in the Gideon Bible. (They often leave personal notes as well.) Unemployment is high in Pioche. But the cost of living is not, and with neighbor helping neighbor the community hangs together.

Christ Church has also stabilized in recent years. While some members can recall having a "full-time priest," a lay vicar or a deaconess, they mostly remember having to rely on someone from outside for sacramental services: very occasional eucharists and weddings or baptisms scheduled far in advance to suit someone else's calendar. Otherwise they looked after things themselves — lay reader services, classes, pastoral support — but in those days these duties were not "ministries;" they were temporary, necessary substitutes or compromises. The parish now consists of about 45 households with 30 or so people on hand each Sunday: like the town population, figures that don't vary much over the years. In conversations with Phina about the larger church's current emphasis on evangelism, members concluded that if they did everything exactly as the church growth professionals prescribed to get Christ Church membership "up to its potential for the area" (calculated as a percent of population), they would lose members. The parish already claims a higher proportion of the population as members than any other Nevada Episcopal church. Pioche is overwhelmingly Mormon. So the witness of even a small mainline Christian communion is important. For example, Ken Adams, a lineman with the power company and another Episcopalian with many community roles (senior warden at Christ Church now) is a scoutmaster in the Mormon scout program. It's a strategy for keeping the program denominationally neutral and open to all. It has become a tradition at Christ Church to host a well attended annual community Christmas eve service, and in cooperation with the Southern Baptists (another tiny Christian group), to provide the community with a vacation Bible school each summer. In these and many other ways, a handful of Episcopalians help keep the Christian faith alive and vital in an isolated desert community.

Christ Church is the only Episcopal church in Lincoln County. The whole county has fewer than 4,000 citizens. There used to be a church in Caliente, 20 or so miles to the south. But it, like hundreds of small Episcopal churches, faded away during the '60s and '70s, too small to be "viable," according to somebody's criteria of viability. (The Caliente church was formally closed in 1980.) However, there are still a few Episcopalians there, now associated with Christ Church, and the parish continues a ministry in Caliente. Some half dozen women — not all Episcopalians — travel by bus each Thursday to Caliente to visit the elderly and the ill in the hospital's extended care facility, and a local version of "meals on wheels" gets a hot lunch to some of the shut-ins on occasion.

The bus is another story. Mary Bradshaw lives in Caliente and administers the county-subsidized bus service, primarily, but not exclusively for seniors. The service consists of two 14-passenger buses. Mary, too, is a senior citizen. She was ordained deaconess in 1937 in Chicago and was one who had served Christ Church in those early years of memory noted above. She had to give up that ministry when she married, in accordance with the standards of that less enlightened age, and settled in Caliente, attending the old St. Matthias Church. So, with the closing of St. Matthias, Mary once more became a part of Christ Church. She has since been reinstated deacon by Bishop Stewart Zabriskie. Thus Christ Church is now served by a local deacon and a local priest. There is more than one way to raise up local ordained ministry. Mary's diaconal ministry, besides coordinating the bus service, includes training acolytes at Christ Church.

I've searched Phina's notes and taped conversations for changes that have occurred since my visit in 1982. There is an "honor camp" nearby, a minimum security institution administered by the state prison in Carson City. It provides prisoners nearing parole an opportunity to gradually become acclimated to normal community living. They constitute a substantial pool of talent and skill, and prisoners are farmed out here and there around the county to contribute to various community work projects. Christ Church keeps in touch with these folk, and prisoners know who they can call on for toiletries or someone to talk to. That was and still is a ministry of the parish. AA and ACOA groups are currently meeting in the church. There are other places they could meet, but, it seems that meeting in a church facility has special meaning for them. This is an on-and-off service of the parish, depending on current community needs. No change there. Someone noted that the ministry of music had slipped several notches. This was the consequence of the out-migration of a family that had made substantial contributions in this area. But it is a characteristic, particularly of small churches, that the current strength and weakness in overall ministry is largely a function of the skills at hand. So, with the inevitable turnover in membership, you win some and you lose some.

There is, however, one substantial change that has taken place over the past eight or nine years. . . . In 1982 the congregation had just come through a "developmental" phase of getting a vision of total ministry in place. By 1989 the system had clearly become "operational." It is accepted, considered normative, and there is no hint of a desire to go back to some earlier model. One of the things of note in '82 was the new interdependency of this congregation with the larger church. The reason I was particularly interested in this phenomenon is that the skeptics were saying at the time, that becoming self-sufficient in ministry would make a small isolated church even more isolated. The implication was "keep them dependent so they will continue to have ties with the larger church," meaning, probably, "so we will continue to have the power." Yet precisely the opposite actually occurred.

At first parish-diocesan mutual involvement centered on the training for ministry so important during the developmental period. But soon other things began to happen. For the first time members managed to get their young people off to church camp (Camp Galilee on Lake Tahoe, 10 hours away), then to take more interest in the leadership of the diocese. After all, the major diocesan strategy of total ministry development was a key element in their life. But the diocese was doing other things too: Cursillo, a prison ministry, etc. The point here is that sustained and imposed dependency will lead to resentment, counterdependency and more isolation. But recognized self-sufficiency and independence opens the door for interdependency. The theory is a good one. Christ Church is a thousand times more involved in the larger church now than in the days before total ministry. Jean has been a deputy to General Convention a couple of times (and is for 1991). Bill, her husband, served on the diocesan commission on ministry for several years. The group proudly reported to Phina that many of their youth had gone to church camp last year — and that they had sent five youth representatives to the diocesan convention "since it was so close — the next town" (110 miles away). A few years ago a whole troupe of members attended a "tiny church conference" in North Dakota where they were key resource people for the program. (The printed resource was *Against All Odds*.) It was an experience they would like to repeat. All of this sort of makes one wonder what "isolated" means.

In the Nevada lexicon a "regional vicar" is a professionally trained, paid deacon or presbyter reporting to the bishop and serving a region which might include something like 6-8 congregations. The job is a Nevada innovation. When Christ Church was first persuaded to take on total ministry training, the diocese arranged for a retired priest, Hunt Parsons in Las Vegas, to come in to teach courses in scripture, theology and pastoral work. Later a diocesan-wide training program directed by Deacon Phina Borgeson was begun and provided the educational services. (Ely was then the study center where Jean, often accompanied by one or two others from Christ Church, participated in classes and workshops.) Shortly after Jean's ordination, the idea of regional vicars surfaced, and Phina became Christ Church's regional vicar, providing consultant services, personal support of local leadership, training and organizational ideas, etc. (In 1987 the parish requested a planning day, which Phina led — a sign of maturing local leadership; *they* were identifying the needs.)

During those early years when the exact nature of the regional vicar's job was being conceptualized, I was serving as consultant to the diocese. It was clear early on that the regional vicar's primary accountability was to the bishop and that the diocese paid the salary. The question was, what is the nature of the relationship between this individual and the congregations of his/her region? There were some who were inclined to think of the regional vicar as supervisor. They were probably thinking of a clinical model of supervision where the relationship is more or less collegial and the supervisor coaches an intern. Most people, however, think of supervisor as boss. A supervisor delegates and attempts to elicit accountability, and might even do some coaching as necessary. But the key characteristic of supervision is that if someone drops the ball or messes up, the accountability is, in the final analysis, the supervisor's. (See my *Under Authority*.[2])

Now, if the objective is to gain a high degree of ministry self-sufficiency and ownership within the congregation, then accountability, in the final analysis, has to be with the congregation. Accordingly, I made a strong case against calling the regional vicar a supervisor. The regional vicar would be a resource person, a consultant, a friend, a direct link with the diocese, but not finally responsible for the life of the congregation. The regional vicar would be accountable to the congregation for whatever the congregation and regional vicar mutually agreed to. But the vestry did not supervise the regional vicar, nor the regional vicar, the parish. This was the attitude that finally prevailed.

The job of the regional vicar was also in a developmental phase in those days. Now it is operational. Richard Henry is the new regional vicar for the territory that includes Pioche. Today there is no confusion whatever about the nature of accountabilities of parish and regional vicar. There is a lot of agenda before Christ Church right now: a need for some serious theological education for the young people; as age creeps up on Jean and Mary, a need to raise up a new generation of ordained leadership; probably a need to recycle total ministry training for all — a booster shot to keep it alive. As the Christ Church folk explore these matters with Richard, there isn't the slightest hint that the diocese or the regional vicar is expected to own the problem, provide the solution or take the initiative. It's Christ Church's agenda. They are interpreting the needs and looking for resources. And they will pass on to the next generation their understanding of and accountability for ministry.

That doesn't mean that the diocese is passive. Christ Church has had its finger on Ken — to become a local deacon — for a long time. "My heart wants to say 'yes,'" says Ken, "but my mind says 'you don't have time.'" Ken has a family to raise and a lot of other community responsibilities, not to mention his job. The time bind has to do with the fact that training for ordination, for someone in Pioche, means a lot of time traveling. The diocese is working on that one. Perhaps a way can be found to export the training so that members of Christ Church can study together in Pioche and continue the process of calling forth from among themselves people to cover all the ministries. Richard is there to listen, to interpret to the diocese and to help identify resources. Jean feels that getting new ordained leadership in place is crucial. Phina says that the leadership will surface when the community calls forth one who can't say "no." No one is claiming that the diocese is the party with the problem, and no one is asking, "When is the bishop going to send us a priest?" It's simply not in the model that is operational today.

There is evidence that the diocese, too, has shifted from developmental to operational status. A diocese or bishop with total ministry in mind can't just sit there and wait for the grassroots to generate something. One has to be pro-active, prophetic. The vision, concepts and models have to be shared and taught, the support services created and matters of policy worked out. One of my pet peeves with usual diocesan structures is that commissions and committees are set up with such frequent and required rotation of membership that one would almost think they were deliberately designed to keep them powerless. One of Wes Frensdorff's big assets during Nevada's developmental phase was a commission on ministry in which there was scarcely any turnover throughout this crucial period. The commission tended to be more conservative than Wes. So while Wes energetically pressed his agenda, the commission probed every angle. Wes' unusual ability to love, respect and listen to his adversaries, and his humor have already been noted by others in this volume. His style was contagious. Out of this dynamic of patience and urgency in Wes, caution and continuity on the part of the commission, and plain old fun that characterized the developmental process throughout, the ongoing hammering out of policy was exceptionally fruitful. (A lot of this is recorded in Nevada's *Total Ministry*

Notebook.[3]) However, once the total ministry model is operational in the field — as in Pioche — the diocese itself can be less pro-active. No need to create new models or provide all the answers and solutions. One can back off, see how the new organism develops and set up to be more of a provider of resources and back-up services than an initiator and visionary. This seems to be where the diocese is today.

What difference has all this made in the diocese as a whole? Statistics tell part of the story. In 1974 there were 22 salaried ministry positions: 19 full-time parochial priests, two lay vicars and the bishop. Today the diocese is covering the field with 14-15 salaried professional positions. The salaried jobs include the bishop, three regional vicars and 10-11 parochial clergy. However, there are also 22 active local deacons and presbyters. In 1974, the diocese received a national church subsidy of $81,000, and it, in turn, was subsidizing local church budgets to the tune of $63,000. (In most dioceses the subsidy to mission congregations is the largest program item in the diocesan budget apart from its contribution to the general church program.)

As the total ministry strategy began to pay off economically, both the national church subsidy to the diocese and the diocesan subsidy to congregations were gradually diminished: to zero by 1984. Over the period, '74-'88, plate and pledge income, all Nevada congregations, increased 195% (nationally, all U.S. dioceses, 184%). Average Sunday attendance increased 11% (nationally, 22%). A measure of member giving levels is the plate and pledge income per attendee. On this indicator Nevada Episcopalians lag seriously behind national norms, but there are gains. The annual plate and pledge income per attendee nationally went from $244 in '74, to $569 in '88, an increase of 133%. In Nevada it went from $163 to $437, an increase of 168%. The median clergy salary in Nevada (adjusted to reflect local cost of living) in '74-'76, was trailing the national median salary. From '75 through '83, it exceeded the national median. It has more recently again slipped behind. The differences are not great, however, throughout the period.

One might suspect that with all this attention on reforming the ministry, a diocese might tend to lose ground somewhere else. The stats do not support the suspicion. While all this developmental effort was going on and while national church support was diminished, local income and attendance trends generally followed national church patterns, and local salaries kept the diocese handsomely in the job market.

Furthermore, the scope and significance of local paid positions was being enhanced. In 1974, with the 22 paid positions, there were, on average, about 120 people in church on Sunday per position. The figure is now about 200 per position, an increase of 67% in scope of the average job as measured by active members associated with the job. Nationally the figures are 126 and 174, a 38% increase. Plate and pledge income per job is another measure of scope. In Nevada this went from $22,700 to $86,300 over the period, a 280% increase. Nationally, from $30,800 to $99,100, a 222% increase.

Of course, that is just the statistical story. What it doesn't show, but perhaps implies, is that paid professionally trained people in Nevada are now in responsible, challenging and fulfilling positions: no more underemployment. The jobs today are not the same kinds of jobs as those of the '60s and early '70s. The *total* number of clergy — of course, most of them "local clergy" — is much greater than before, sacraments much more readily available everywhere, ministries in the church widely shared and locally owned, and ministries in the world much more appreciated. This isn't true everywhere, of course, and the diocese is in no position to simply rest on its laurels or celebrate total "success." But it is an amazing story of reshaping ministry and redeploying professional personnel. In 1983 we (CRW Management Services), working with the diocesan commission on ministry, did an evaluation of the Nevada program. It was published as *Living Out the Vision: Nevada's Experience in Total Ministry.*[4] At that point areas still needing attention were identified:

> * In Nevada's approach to total ministry development, it was seen that in order for volunteer ordained ministries to work, nearly everyone would need to have a pretty good grasp of what the ministry of all baptized people meant. Otherwise a local priest would be raised up and immediately cast in the model of rector — the only model then known. This would be the inclination of the one ordained as well as the rest of the congregation. Of course, this wasn't the only reason for broad-based training in total ministry, but it did indicate that the training must precede the call. So it was that general training in total ministry went on for several years before anybody was ordained. By 1983, however, there were some dozen local presbyters and deacons in place, and commanding most of the more recent attention. The diocese would have to reinforce the vision of total ministry — validation of "Monday morning ministries" and more consciousness about the offering of these ministries in the action of the eucharist. And renewed attention to congregational outreach ministries was called for — the diaconal ministry of the congregation and the diaconate as the sign and reminder. The original vision of total ministry had been pulled askew a bit by the successful launching of the new volunteer ordained ministries. Adjustment needed!

Since then the diocese has re-emphasized the ministry of all the baptized. The big challenge today, says Bishop Zabriskie, is constantly affirming the ministries of the laity in the world. The tendency to associate ministry primarily with church work is not easily overcome.

    *   Congregational theological reflection was seen to be weak. With local priests functioning here and there, the "sacramental captivity" by professionals was broken. But local church members were too cautious about theologizing and becoming too dependent on professionals. There was a suspicion that the diocese might be creating a new "theological captivity" in career people: in other words, a sort of unconscious fall-back position for turf guarded by professionals. Somehow the whole theological enterprise must be kept open.

The TEAM (Teach Each a Ministry) Academy is Nevada's diocesan ministry training unit. Now that the first generation of ordained people is in place, TEAM has been moving toward more broadly based education: trying to do theology in the local vocabulary and help people see that they have been theologizing all along. Two new regional vicars have brought some fresh ideas into the mix: contextual education, right-brain education, etc. Under recent changes in the national church canons, the diocesan commission on ministry has developed guidelines for the office of catechist. The bishop: "We hear a lot about the catechumenate around the church, but nothing about catechists as an important lay ministry." It is hoped that the new guidelines will hold up a model for the importance of gifted lay leaders in the ministry of teaching.

Here we have an example of changes in national church standards opening the possibilities for dioceses. The point has already been made that the local church interested in ministry innovation or experimentation operates within a diocesan environment which might be positive and supportive of such efforts, or negative and constraining. The diocese, too, operates within an environment of national church norms, standards and policies.

    *   In the Nevada vision of total ministry the local priest was seen as sacramentalist — period. Not pastor, not administrator, not preacher — at least not necessarily. The *functions* of ministry were to be spread around, but the function of the priest was administration of the sacraments. Thus Jean Orr, for example, was ordained to administer the sacraments, but not (originally) licensed to preach the word. On the other hand, the senior warden would be the local overseer or manager, but not necessarily preacher, teacher, pastor or sacramentalist. George Sumner, in his article on Navajoland (Chapter 5) took note of some resistence to this idea on the part of Philip Allen (Oglala Sioux), archdeacon in Minnesota and a national leader in Indian ministries. Alaska has identified the same issue in the raising up of sacramentalists in its native congregations. Can sacerdotal leadership be separated from other leadership functions in a given culture or context? Or is that question itself simply more evidence of the need to defend an outmoded "omnicompetent" leadership model? In any case, by 1983 Nevada was taking a hard look at the question, "Can word and sacrament be separated in leadership functions?" More reflection needed!

Studies have shown[5] that the most satisfying situations are not those in which the local priest is restricted to the sacramentalist functions or those in which the priest struggles to fill a traditional omnicompetent leadership role. They are situations in which, in addition to sacramental leadership, the local priest also has one or two additional roles according to his or her own gifts. Nevada's experience has borne this out. Accordingly, diocesan pre-ordination preparation now takes this into account. The individual called to ordained ministry goes through a procedure of identifying gifts and possible auxillary ministerial roles; the specific ministries of others in the congregation are also identified. Jean Orr, for example, did complete the requirements for a preaching license, but in Pioche this is not understood to be her ministry exclusively, nor to accrue automatically to the person ordained.

While these issues, identified in 1983, have been receiving appropriate attention over the years, they persist on the diocesan agenda.

During the period of this report, the Episcopal Church at large was going through some other changes: getting used to new liturgies and ceremonial, and coming to terms with the ordination of women, to mention a couple. Those transitions were part and parcel of Nevada's total developmental period. And, I think it is safe to say, Nevada made these adjustments with much less stress than many places. It may be that because total ministry development was so important these other adjustments were simply experienced as part of it and in this perspective, found to be natural and necessary. In any case, Christ Church, Pioche, was not insulated from them. Early on there was some opposition to women's ordination. But after all that preparation, when it came time for members of one tiny congregation to decide for themselves who would be raised up to be their priest, the question of gender ceased to be a factor; Jean Orr was clearly the one.

While some places were (and still are) trying to (or trying not to) depart from eucharist the first Sunday, or first and third Sundays, or celebrating the eucharist while looking at the priest's back, Pioche had been accustomed to an almost steady diet of Morning Prayer and had never heard of a free-standing altar. The changes didn't come overnight. When Jean was finally ordained, eucharist once or twice a month was a big change — welcome, but sufficient. Since then Christ Church has gradually come to follow the practice of most Episcopal churches. Jean says that there is still some tendency for folk to think of pastoral work as part of the priest's ministry; a remnant of the old cloth persists. Actually, a lot of the pastoral work is, in fact, carried on by others, but the "ministry" clings to the priest. (Jean doesn't disclaim *any* role in pastoral work, just that of being its sign and central figure.) Well, nobody claims that the job of ministry formation is — or ever will be — finished in Pioche. During the operational phase of the past several years, Christ Church has seen the resignation of their pioneer bishop and of Phina who, as diocesan ministry development coordinator, had strongly influenced the spirit and substance of the developmental period. Now they have settled in with new episcopal leadership and are getting acquainted with a new regional vicar. These, too, are big transitions for a little congregation, maybe not so much for small *isolated* congregations, but for Pioche, significant transitions.

Phina, commenting on her visit, said, "It gave me a lot of hope; I saw that Christ Church, Pioche, has the confidence and skills to identify new needs as they emerge and to organize to meet them. They don't ask much from the diocese except a regional vicar they like and who will help them meet their goals. They've become active partners in ministry with the diocese. It is especially evident now in their developing youth ministry: sending them out to Camp Galilee, taking them to diocesan convention, connecting with the diocesan youth commission, raising money to send them to winter retreat . . . . They own total ministry and are able to model it and to teach it to their children."

And that's the track record to date.

Notes

1. Charles R. Wilson and Lynne Davenport, *Against All Odds: Ten Stories of Vitality in Small Churches.* (Arvada, CO: Jethro Publications, 1982).
2. Charles R. Wilson, *Under Authority.* (Arvada, CO: Jethro Publications, 1989).

3. The Diocese of Nevada, *The Total Ministry Notebook* (Reno, 1979, 1982, 1986; full revision, 1990).
4. CRW Management Services, *Living Out the Vision.* (Arvada, CO: Jethro Publications, 1983). The title comes from Nevada's (then) statement of diocesan mission which reads in part, "We commit ourselves to explore and live out the vision of total ministry."
5. John T. Docker, *From Survival to Renewal.* (New York: 1988).

Here are some ideas for Part II.
(Numbered items could be used with the corresponding chapter.)

5)   In Navajoland the bishop's miter is beaded. At Trinity Church by the Sea (Kihei, Hawaii) the call to worship is made on a conch shell. At St. Stephen's (Fort Yukon, Alaska) the "fair white linen" is a beautiful bleached beaded moosehide. Lloyd Gressle, retired bishop of Bethlehem (eastern Pennsylvania) has a pectoral cross made of stainless steel and decorated with anthracite. What does "indigenous" mean in your church?

6)   How have financial realities in your parish over the past 20 years affected the way you do ministry? What are the positive factors and the negative factors in the evolving shape of ministry?

7)   Compare and contrast the ministry development strategies reported in Chapters 5 (Navajoland) and 7 (Australia).

8)   What would a ministry education program in your parish (or diocese) look like if Richard Kraft were to come on board as your consultant? Be specific, detailed.

   "Growth in numbers becomes possible when you are equipped with ministries," says Kraft. Discuss this in light of the Decade of Evangelism.

9)   Chapter 9 (Killam's Point) is the only story in this series where the initiatives came from someone other than the bishop(s). Discuss the implications of this for MACM and TEAM.

10)   Compare and contrast the ministry development strategies reported in Chapters 9 (Killam's Point) and 10 (Pioche).

The prophetic voice of Roland Allen resonates throughout this book. Why did it take the church so long to hear that voice? Is it widely heard today?

Grade each of these six cases (scale of 1-10) on the basis of the extent to which each incarnates the vision of Part I of this book. Discuss the reasoning behind your grading.

Divide your group in half and have a debate.
   Side 1 proposition: "All six of these stories reflect a narrow view of

ministry since they deal mainly with church work and little with mission."

Side 2 proposition: "The stories illustrate the old maxium that one has to have one's own house in order before tackling the issues of the world."

Divide your group in half and have a debate.

Side 1 proposition: "If God has called the individual to a particular ministry, who are we (the congregation) to stand in the way?"

Side 2 proposition: "If God is calling some individual to a particular ministry, that call will issue through the community to the individual, not to the individual alone."

Part III

SYNTHESIS
AND
UNFINISHED BUSINESS

Chapter 11

BAPTISM, ORDINATION, AND DEACONS

Ormonde Plater

One of Wes Frensdorff's concerns in ministry development was the recovery of the diaconate as a vital office of servanthood for today's church. On the occasion of the 25th anniversary of his ordination to the diaconate in 1976, he held a symposium on that order in Las Vegas. Papers from the symposium were widely disseminated by the Diocese of Nevada, and later reprinted in Open, *the newsletter of Associated Parishes. In Nevada, and through his service as president of what was to become the North American Association for the Diaconate, Wes encouraged deacons as a part of total ministry development, always seen in the context of the ministry of all the baptized.*

Here, in an excerpt from a forthcoming book, Ormonde Plater uses a method of theologizing about ministry common in Nevada during Frensdorff's episcopacy. Plater turns to the liturgy for instruction about the ministry we all share through baptism, and for clues to the focal role of the office of deacon in the context of that ministry. Along the way he offers interesting comments and provocative opinions about the liturgy and the service after the service which we all share.

- Eds.

I n the late twentieth century, baptism and holy orders have changed places in importance. For many members of the church, ordination and clerical status formerly represented the fullness of membership in the church, while baptism was only the first stage in the journey to orders. Now, in the writings of theologians, in the teachings of bishops, in revised liturgies, and even (if slowly) in popular opinion, a shift is beginning to take place. We have returned to the traditions and belief of scripture and the early church, perceiving clearly that what it means to be a Christian transcends what it means to be a deacon or a presbyter or a bishop.

This change of positions has wonderful but frightening implications. The shift will take decades to implement in the practice of the church, and there is always the danger of a reaction to the earlier clerical model. I intend to examine some of the implications of this shift by analyzing the liturgies of baptism and ordination.

Baptized to service

The great discovery of our age has been the meaning and practice of baptism. Despite the ancient and still-revered practice of baptizing the infants of believers, baptism is primarily for adults. It draws its meaning, and its most appropriate occasion, from the Easter experience, as expressed in the Great Vigil of Easter. After the people have entered the church, the deacon begins the Exsultet by calling on angels, earth, and church to rejoice in the victory of Christ. The imperative *exsultet* means not only to rejoice, to feel a blissful emotion, but to leap up, repeatedly and even violently as in a wild dance. Although the action of the vigil tends to be sedentary, as Anglicans and other western Christians usually render it, I prefer to imagine the Exsultet as the deacon calling a boisterous square dance. The dancers — swarms of angels, the earth and all its inhabitants (the whole Noah's Ark entourage), and mother church (all the people of God, living and dead) — circle round and swing their partners. In cosmic steps the dancers recall the paschal Lamb and give thanks for the light of Christ. A square dance is energetic but not chaotic; the dancers rarely bump into each other or step on toes. It is orderly. The figures that all perform require precise execution, and the dancers listen carefully to the caller. The dance represents the order of creation brought to perfection through Christ. Exodus and crucifixion take place according to God's orderly plan. In one of the great prayers of the paschal vigil, a priest prays:

> *O God of unchangeable power and eternal light: Look favorably on your whole Church, that wonderful and sacred mystery; by the effectual working of your providence, carry out in tranquillity the plan of salvation; let the whole world see and know that things which were cast down are being made new, and that all things are being brought to their perfection by him through whom all things were made, your Son Jesus Christ our Lord.* [BCP, p. 291]

This prayer of the paschal vigil is used also as the collect at ordinations of all three orders. It reminds us that the perfect order of God's church — which to our dim sight seldom appears perfect or orderly — is grounded in God's creation of all things.

Into this perfect order people are baptized. The baptismal process involves shedding the old life of satanic disorder and taking on the new life of God's orderly plan. This plan is outlined early in the liturgy. After the candidates have been presented and examined, and have renounced Satan and turned to Christ, they swear the baptismal covenant. The covenant contains several elements essential to Christian life: *orthodoxy* (right praise of the triune God, expressed in the Apostles' Creed), *koinonia* (fellowship or shared communion), *metanoia* (change of mind or turning from evil), *kerygma* (proclamation of the gospel), *diakonia* (serving and loving Christ in others), and *righteousness* (seeking justice and peace).

The first three of these — *orthodoxy, koinonia* and *metanoia* — refer to the internal life of the church and its members. They are the location of priestly or presbyteral ministry, which teaches and encourages belief, forms and builds up community, and guides the spiritual life of the people.

The fourth — *kerygma* — is both internal and external, both priestly and diaconal. The church proclaims the gospel both to its members and to the world outside. In the evangelical question the celebrant asks: "Will you proclaim by word and example the Good News of God in Christ?"

The last two — *diakonia* and *righteousness* — refer mainly (but not entirely) to the external life of the church and its members. They are the focus of diaconal ministry, which serves the helpless and tries to cure the causes of poverty and oppression. The diaconal question is central to the teaching and practice of Christ. The celebrant asks: "Will you seek and serve Christ in all persons, loving your neighbor as yourself?" Out of this service of mercy flows a concern for justice, expressed in the last question: "Will you strive for justice and peace among all people, and respect the dignity of every human being?" The six questions will be repeated, in slightly different form, in the ordination of a deacon. In baptism, though, they refer to the service of all Christian people in church and world.

References to priestly and diaconal ministries appear in several other places in the baptismal liturgy. To consecrate oil of chrism (either within the baptismal liturgy or on some other occasion) the bishop prays "that those who are sealed with it may share in the royal priesthood of Jesus Christ." After the baptism and chrismation the people welcome the neophytes with these words:

> *We receive you into the household of God. Confess the faith of Christ crucified, proclaim his resurrection, and share with us in his eternal priesthood.*

The key word in both texts about priesthood is *share*. Royal or eternal priesthood is a function of the assembly. It is exercised chiefly through a shared society in which the members join in offering gifts to God: praise, intercession, confession, thanksgiving, bread and wine, incense, uplifted hands and hearts, money, food for the hungry, their own lives. All are priestly. But the emphasis is on priesthood rather than priests, on a group rather than individual persons.

The diaconal element is repeated and reinforced in the prayers for the candidates: "Teach *them* to love others in the power of the Spirit," and "Send *them* into the world in witness to your love." The element appears also in the blessing of chrism, when the bishop refers to Christ as "servant of all," and in the prayer after baptism, when the celebrant refers to these new "servants" of the Father. Like Christ at his baptism in the Jordan, each neophyte is sealed as a servant by the Holy Spirit.

In 1987, Richard F. Grein, then bishop of Kansas and now of New York, preached eloquently about the diaconal element in the blessing of the baptismal water. The blessing contains three images: creation, exodus, and the Lord's own baptism. When the deacon gathers up the gifts of all the people to be offered in the eucharist, Grein says, this act signifies "the great cosmic liturgy of all creation, for the gifts represent the people who are to be consecrated, a sign of our becoming in Christ — the new creation won by his cross and resurrection." When the deacon proclaims the gospel and gathers up the intercessions of the church for the world, these acts recall the Exodus, helping us to "go on a journey through the wilderness." When the deacon distributes the gifts of the altar, this act represents gifts "in the process of becoming through consecration, which the Spirit has blessed," and which the deacon takes into the world. The gift of water, Grein says, is thus related to "the gift of deacons in the life of the church."[1] Indeed, the water blessing (like the eucharistic blessing of bread and wine) is similar in structure and theme to the blessing or consecration of a new deacon. It begins with remembrance and thanksgiving, centers on epiclesis or invocation of the Spirit, and ends with a prayer for the fruits of blessing on God's people.

There is a difference between the priesthood and diaconate we receive in baptism and the gifts of God we receive in natural birth. Our lives show abundant evidence of natural gifts, revealed in the diversity of our personalities and skills and professions. We are given in birth a natural priesthood. Made in the image of God, whether we accept our likeness or not, we tend to praise God for creation. We are also given in birth a natural servanthood. Responding to the love of God who made us in his image, we tend to love and serve both God and others. The imprint of God on persons causes them to recognize the image of God in themselves and to adore the God they image. Although in society today God is not always recognized as the creator, a tendency to praise an external being and to serve others continues as a powerful force. The world is full of good, loving, caring persons who are not consciously Christian — indeed, who have nothing to do with a supreme being beyond a fuzzy-minded but stubborn refusal to believe and praise.

The gifts of baptism differ from natural gifts in their focus and particularity. As royal priests we praise God not only for creation but for the ultimate creation, the death and resurrection of Christ. The Spirit who hovered over the waters of primal creation now hovers over the waters of baptism and over the bread and wine, filling Christian lives with salvation and sanctification. Made in the image of God — as patristic fathers were fond of saying — we share in the divinity of Christ who humbled himself to share in our humanity.

As servants in Christ, we bring Christ to those we serve, we find Christ in those we serve, and at the heart of *diakonia* we identify the encounter of Christ with Christ. This is where communion meets service. The main difference between the two kinds of ministry, natural and baptismal, lies in the centrality of Christ in baptismal priesthood and service. Through acts of *agape* and *diakonia* to the poor, hungry, thirsty, homeless, sick, imprisoned, oppressed, and all those in need, we discover the presence of Christ who reveals his Father.

Ordination and service

What is the meaning of ordination, a "sacramental rite" (as the catechism calls it) that stands in the shadow of the great sacrament of baptism? In the modern church, in some circles, it is fashionable to speak of the three holy orders in base and disrespectful terms, as outdated and even useless. We are right to emphasize baptism. We are wrong to treat bishops, presbyters, and deacons as mere appendages who sometimes benefit the church but who are dispensable in an ecclesial priesthood and servanthood of all believers.

The preface to the ordination rites says that the three orders are "a gift from God for the nurture of his people and the proclamation of his Gospel everywhere" (*BCP*, p. 510). If nurture is shorthand for priesthood, and proclamation for service, the definition may be considered sufficient. But it needs expansion.

Christ shares his *diakonia* with his church. The service of Christ thus embraces and includes the whole Christian people of God. Their membership in the eucharistic body confers on them an indelible character of *diakonia*. They are one with Christ on the cross, a cross marked forever on their forehead. They follow Christ, they love and serve the Lord, they witness to the death and resurrection of Christ. They are the *laos*, the people, the essential ministers of the church.

But the *laos* are not one ministry, but many. The catechism misleads some readers when it refers to the "laity" (which, in the regrettable modern sense of the word, means unordained Christians) as one "ministry" and even implies that the "laity" are a fourth order. The whole *laos* are thousands of ministries. Some ministries are symbolic, and some are functional. Some are the ordinary share of the Christian life. They occur when Christians believe in God, share with each other, turn from evil, proclaim the gospel, serve the needy, and seek justice and peace — any or all of these and more. Some ministries take place in families, and some at work. Some are specialized, and some are recognized. Most simply happen in a quiet way. A few are ordained.

The preface to the ordination rites states, in a phrase dating from the sixteenth century, that different ministries, including but not limited to the three orders, have existed in the church "from the apostles' time." Christ did not establish holy orders, but the three orders came into being within the first generation of Christians, certainly within the first century, and they were "within the Church." Because they occur within the body of Christ, as a conscious and communal act of blessing, they are sacred. They convey meaning and have significance which other ministries of great value do not impart.

In modern writings about holy orders it is common to hear the terms *sacrament, sign, symbol, mystery* and *icon*. All mean basically the same, and despite subtle differences I feel free to use them interchangeably. Talk about ordained persons as sign, symbol, or mystery has a long history, going back to Ignatius of Antioch. Today the catechism says that each order "represents" a particular mode of Christ and his church, a term which emphasizes the *anamnesis* or Christ-recalling aspect of orders.[2] We may also say that each order is a "sacrament" or "sign," meaning that the order, in the language of sacramental theology, is "an outward and visible sign of an inward and spiritual grace," which is Christ in his church. Or that the order is a "symbol" which points to and contains a particular mode of Christ. Or that the order is a "mystery," a profundity beyond human understanding which somehow reveals the death and resurrection of Christ (the paschal mystery). Or that the order is an "icon" or image-window through which we commune with a particular face of Christ in heaven. In all these terms Christ is the point of reference.

These terms refer to orders as state of being. To take a far more common "mystery" (as the Prayer Book puts it, page 423), marriage is not a sacramental event in the past, the "wedding," but a living sign of the union between Christ and his church. Similarly, order is not the "ordination" but a living sign of a manner or mode of Christian life.

The terms contain two elements. A sign (or symbol or mystery or icon) contains the element *signifier* (which points to the meaning) and the element *signified* (the meaning). In a true sacramental sign the two elements must be unified. They must correspond in message. If a deacon helps AIDS patients (whose blood carries death), then deacon = servant, and those who receive the blood of Christ (which carries life) from the deacon perceive the sign deacon as unified. But if the bishop puts a deacon in charge of a mission, where the deacon serves bread and wine confected elsewhere (or on an occasion when a priest could be present), then deacon = quasi-priest (who cannot function as priest), and the people are confused. Either they fail to see the sign deacon or they perceive it as dysfunctional and disunified. In these and all other possible examples there is a third element, those who see and enter into the sign. Their perception of the sign depends largely on the strength of the unity, the correspondence between *signifier* and *signified*. The sign, thus augmented, exists for their benefit and fills them with the grace of its meaning.[3]

What distinguishes those in holy orders from other members of the *laos* is the authorized faculty to embody sign language, and the grace to embody it with God's help. They symbolize and incorporate in particular ways the numerous ministries belonging in a general way to all the people of God. This happens by a gift of the Spirit. The gift in ordination differs from the gift in baptism. In baptism the Spirit seals a neophyte as a member of the body of Christ. In ordination the Spirit bestows symbolism. The gift of orders does not bestow a personal or inner change of character; it extends and adorns the speech of the community. It is song for the speechless, dance for the lame. The Spirit helps the ordained person to act out for the assembly the sign language the church has authorized. But the sign, both *signifier* and *signified*, works differently for bishops, presbyters, and deacons.

If I were to pick a geometric figure (another type of sign) for bishops, it would be the circle. Bishops encircle the church. A circle protects and preserves what is within. It keeps the shape and the body. It is hands encircling the diocese and the whole church. Some bishops regard their main activity as adventure, risk, and challenge — hands pushing away and out into the world — but the sign language of episcopacy points mainly to catholicity and orthodoxy. The liturgy of ordination talks about the bishop as primarily "called to guard the faith, unity, and discipline of the Church." The role of the bishop is not static but dynamic, for the gospel requires constant reinterpretation in the world at hand. The role covers three areas, each emphasized by a patristic writer: presider in baptism and eucharist and leader of a diocese (Ignatius of Antioch), teacher of the truth revealed by Christ (Irenaeus of Lyons), and member of a college of bishops (Cyprian of Carthage).[4]

Presbyters or priests (even to give both titles reveals the ancient confusion surrounding the order) resemble bishops on a local scale. What bishops are in the diocese, presbyters are in the local church. (The term *local church* as currently used can refer to both diocese and parish.) They lead the baptismal and eucharistic life in parishes, join with other presbyters in a college of elders, and share in the bishop's oversight of the diocese. Can we give them a geometric figure? It could be another circle, or circles within the bishop circle, but let's try the vertical line. As priests they symbolize hands uplifted in prayer. Especially in this post-Constantinian church in which our high priestly bishops must usually be someplace else, priests express the royal priesthood of Christ which all enter at baptism.[5]

It is easy to speak of the meaning of deacons. In a tradition dating from Ignatius of Antioch, deacons are images of Christ the Servant. Although the practice of the diaconate has changed drastically through the centuries, the image has remained firm and constant. Deacons reveal the *diakonia* of Christ and his church. They bring into focus the great number and variety of Christian service. To this ancient tradition in modern times we have added a communal dimension. Deacons bring their sign of service into the *koinonia* of the church. They encourage, enable, enlist, engage, entice, model, lead, animate, stimulate, inspire, permit, organize, equip, empower, and support Christian people in service in the world, and they point to the presence of Christ in the needy. *They are signs of service who uncover and explain signs of service.* The human dimension of diaconal symbolism suggests that their geometric figure is the horizontal line, hands reaching hands.[6]

Ordination of deacons

The place to begin to study the diaconate is the liturgy of ordination. The liturgy begins with the presentation of an ordinand who has been legally "selected." The ordinand must declare the scriptures "to be the Word of God, and to contain all things necessary to salvation," and must swear loyalty and conformity "to the doctrine, discipline, and worship of the Episcopal Church." The people consent to the ordination and promise to uphold the person "in this ministry." After the singing of the ordination or other litany (all kneeling, although in some places the ordinand lies prostrate) and the collect, all sit for the readings.

The readings present some of the scriptural themes meaningful to the diaconate, especially those of proclamation and service. For the first reading, either Jeremiah 1:4-9 (the call of Jeremiah) or Ecclesiasticus 39:1-8 (the scribe who studies the scriptures) may be used. Of these, Jeremiah is especially appropriate. It refers to the prophetic call, the putting of words in the prophet's mouth, which we now see as part of the diaconal office through the deacon's proclamation of the gospel. The deacon serves as primary evangelist of the congregation. The Prayer Book gives three choices for the second reading: 2 Corinthians 4:1-6 (which refers to "seeing the light of the gospel of the glory of Jesus Christ" and to "ourselves as your servants [slaves] for Jesus' sake"), 1 Timothy 3:8-13 (which lists the qualifications of deacons and "the women"), and Acts 6:2-7 (choice of the seven to wait on tables). There are two choices for the gospel: Luke 12:35-38 (men with "lamps burning" wait for their master to return from the marriage feast) and Luke 22:24-27 ("I am among you as one who serves").

The preacher delivers a homily based on the readings which covers the meaning and duties of the diaconate. Since the bishop will cover the same territory, in the formal examination that follows, the preacher needs to be careful not to contradict the scriptures or the Prayer Book. There is a custom, whose origin and age I am unable to determine (the Prayer Book does not mention it), that the preacher close with a "charge," a personal address to the ordinand; some preachers omit the "charge" on the grounds that the homily should be addressed to all the people.

Talking to the ordinand is really the bishop's job. The bishop's address occurs principally in the formal examination (*BCP*, pp. 543-544), which every candidate preparing for ordination should study carefully. This is an important document for our understanding of deacons and service in the church. It contains two main parts, an address on the work of a deacon and a series of questions and answers. After a trinitarian prologue on baptismal discipleship and service — "every Christian is called to follow Jesus Christ, serving God the Father, through the power of the Holy Spirit" — the address proper consists of eight statements. The first and last statements form a bracket which opens and closes the other six. The six internal statements, each of which begins with the phrase "you are to," expand the meaning of the first, introductory statement.[7]

1. **God now calls you to a special ministry of servanthood directly under your bishop.**

A multitude of ministerial relationships makes up service in the church. What makes this one "special" is its bond between deacon and bishop. The ancient and primary bond of deacons, deriving from ordination, is with the bishop of the diocese — first the bishop who ordained the deacon, then that bishop's successors. If a deacon moves to another diocese, and the move is canonically approved through letters dimissory (a certificate from the bishop which sends the deacon to the new diocese), the bond transfers to the bishop of the new diocese.

The bond of deacons with the bishop differs from that of priests, since priests work "together" with the bishop in a college of presbyters and take a "share in the councils of the Church."[8] Other Christians gather around and work with the bishop, but they are free to come and go and serve in all sorts of ways, which are accountable not directly to the bishop (with the exception of a few licensed ministries), but to the entire community of the baptized, and they also take part in the governance of the church. No statement, in the catechism or in the ordination liturgy, gives deacons a formal conciliar role or grants deacons a vote in church governmental bodies. The role of deacons above all involves obedience to the bishop.

Deacons are subject to the bishop because the bishop oversees *diakonia* in the church. In the early church deacons served as the bishop's eyes and ears and as members of the bishop's household or staff. According to Hippolytus in *Apostolic Tradition*, a deacon is ordained "to the bishop's service, to carry out commands" and "makes known to the bishop what is necessary." The ancient bond between deacons and bishop does not translate easily into the late twentieth century. Today priests function much as bishops did in the third century, and much of the bonding involves deacons and priests instead. Deacons and bishops, however, are seeking new expressions of the ancient bond which combine collegiality with discipline. Deacons help bishops to carry out their own ordination vow to "be merciful to all, show compassion to the poor and strangers, and defend those who have no helper" (*BCP*, p. 518).

2. **In the name of Jesus Christ, you are to serve all people, particularly the poor, the weak, the sick, and the lonely.**

The main function of deacons is to serve those in need. Deacons share this service with all other members of the church, who serve the needy in many different ways. The difference is one of focus. Deacons are to be lights of service at the center of the church. The distinctive role of deacons is to hold up *diakonia*, just as they hold the paschal candle in the midst of all the smaller, hand-held candles of the Easter Vigil, so that the people, led and encouraged by an example of radiance, will go into a world of darkness with candles of service.

Earlier deacons found the needy mainly within the church: the poor, old, sick, and shut-in of the parishes, whom deacons visited and brought the sacrament. There is ancient precedent for this form of service — the deacon of the early church who took the sacrament directly from the eucharist to Christians who could not be present, especially those in prison. But the early deacon, such as Laurence, also found the poor in the world outside the church. In our age we regard ministry to those within the church as primarily pastoral, the work of the parish priest and certain other baptized persons.

Deacons now find the *anawim*, the poor of Yahweh, mainly in the world outside. Poverty, weakness, sickness, and loneliness are global conditions, too broad to be limited to the membership of the church. The experience of Israel teaches us that recognition of poverty within leads to recognition of poverty without. Servant of the needy has thus become a synonym for servant of the world. The bishop's instruction "to serve all people," while including the poor, weak, sick, and lonely of the church, points through the church door to vast numbers outside.

3. **As a deacon in the Church, you are to study the Holy Scriptures, to seek nourishment from them, and to model your life upon them.**

Do we not require this study of all the baptized? Such study, nourishment, and modeling are implied in the baptismal covenant question about proclaiming the gospel "by word and example." Two questions following the bishop's address to the ordinand indicate the special importance of scripture in the study and life of a deacon: "Will you be faithful in prayer, and in the reading and study of the Holy Scriptures?" and "Will you do your best to pattern your life (and that of your family, *or* household, *or* community] in accordance with the teachings of Christ, so that you may be a wholesome example to all people?" The bishop's address requires deacons to study the scriptures but also to live as imitators of Christ.

The personal life of deacons should include the spiritual disciplines common to all Christians (but not as widespread as one would wish): daily prayer (especially the daily office), family prayer (which includes all small groups), confession of sin, and the eucharist. The bishop's address also suggests that deacons adopt a program of regular, even daily, reading of the scriptures and commentaries. Deacons may expand on the requirement by forming and leading groups to study the Bible.

The reason for this emphasis on the scriptures lies in the special role of the deacon as chief evangelist, the reader whose formal proclamation of the gospel encourages others to bear the word into the world. The essence of scripture is the *logos* or Word who is Christ. To study the word is to feed on Christ. To model oneself on Christ is to adopt a life that is modest, simple, and humble. This is probably what the writer of 1 Timothy meant when he said that deacons "must hold fast to the mystery of the faith with a clear conscience" (1 Tim. 3:9). The mystery of the faith is the paschal mystery of Christ crucified and risen.

4. You are to make Christ and his redemptive love known, by your word and example, to those among whom you live, and work, and worship.

This statement bears on the symbolic nature of the diaconate. All Christians must relieve distress and seek out the causes of injustice. Deacons are also symbols of the *diakonia* of Christ and his church. As we have seen, diaconal function gives life to diaconal symbol. As servants of the church, deacons hold before it the whole ministry of the church as service. As symbols of Christ, deacons reveal to the people of God that they all have been baptized as servants.

As symbols of Christ, deacons occupy a special place in the *laos* as a living challenge to symbols of status and hierarchy. Although members of the clergy in canon law, they are also, in the ancient tradition of the church, members of the laity. Hippolytus said that the deacon "does not take part in the council of the clergy." The existence of deacons in the church raises profound questions about the historical development of the clergy (bishops and presbyters) into a professional estate above and separate from the vast majority of Christians. Deacons demonstrate that leadership does not have to be hierarchical.

The making known of Christ has a practical aspect, which is also controversial. As clerics, deacons have inherited special dress, titles, perquisites, and other symbols of clerical status, yet deacons should be distinguished as servants to those among whom they also live and work. There is some evidence that men deacons (and priests) find clerical titles and collars unnecessary, because in theological and other church circles men are assumed to be ordained, but that women deacons find them helpful as visible signs of ordination.[9] In places that deny the value of women in the church's leadership, women clerics sometimes feel compelled to adopt the signs of rank that men clerics use.

The decision about clerical dress and titles belongs to the bishop. Some bishops require street clothing as the norm for deacons, even on Sunday morning. Some bishops allow the clerical collar when a particular form of diaconal ministry requires it; some bishops require it on certain occasions, such as "when functioning as a deacon of the church." Some bishops specify "the Rev." as a formal title for deacons and "Deacon" for less formal address. In most American culture a clerical collar and "the Rev." signify someone professionally reverend, especially a hired pastor. Although clerical collars and titles are not an issue over which any Christian should make a last stand, the bishop needs to ask whether they accurately signify a servant of the church.

5. You are to interpret to the Church the needs, hopes, and concerns of the world.

Having served the needy in the world, as scripture directs all of us to do, deacons then return to the church in the role of *signifier*, or interpreter. This role has great value for the church. But I must first make a qualification. The bishop's direction to interpret the world to the church is not a license to preach. Preaching is interpretation of the good news (in the gospels) as it should be lived out in the world. It is a prescription for health. Deacons interpret the world in all its messiness to the church. They interpret the world because, as servants of the needy, they have continual access to needs, concerns, and hopes. Other servants of the needy also have access, but only deacons are directed to interpret.

If deacons are to interpret, they must be able to see and hear and speak. Part of the training of deacons should be to teach them the many languages of the needy. This involves skills in observation, listening, diagnosis, and speaking (including musical and artistic expression). It involves knowledge about how social and political systems, institutions, and organizations work. In her speech at the Kanuga conference in 1989, the Canadian deacon Maylanne Whittall told about a social worker, preoccupied with Jungian psychology, who began her first interview with a client with, "How do you feel?" The street person answered, "I feel *hungry*."

Whittall suggests three guidelines for listening and diagnosis: First, we must listen where others don't — "to children, to old people, to women, to street people, to natives, to people of color, to the voice of emerging nations." Second, we must voluntarily displace ourselves into situations not normal for us. Third, we must develop "the ability, the strength, and the willingness to make ourselves inconspicuous." These guidelines help us to be attentive to the needs, concerns, and hopes of the world in which we serve.

Deacons interpret the world to the church in several settings. They interpret when they "make known to the bishop what is necessary" (as Hippolytus puts it). They interpret the world when they speak out in the forums of the church (which is not the same as voting). They are expected to use their voice in conventions and on church bodies such as commissions and committees and vestries. In many parishes, deacons work with outreach committees. They interpret the world when they tell the stories and sing the songs and draw the pictures of the poor. In the liturgy, to "interpret" means to put the language of needs, concerns, and hopes into the language of bidding to prayer. This occurs in the prayers of the people. In the ancient language of the church at prayer, deacons are to list names and concerns of great need, so that the people can intercede through Christ to our Father in heaven.

6.   **You are to assist the bishop and priests in public worship and in the ministration of God's Word and Sacraments.**

I prefer to render this instruction in these words: "In the liturgy you are to serve the assembly as proclaimer of the gospel, interpreter of the world, and waiter on the table." The point of the diaconal role in liturgy is not that a subordinate assists the presider — who can just as well do without, and all too often does. The point is that a deacon, as a major performer in the assembly, plays a vital role in the complete action of the assembly by acting out major messages.

In the Christian liturgy, the people of God put on the masks of ancient Greek drama and bring about catharsis, sing the arias and duets and choruses of grand opera, kick up heels in a country dance, set fire and drown in water and rub oil and feed the hungry, perform for the pleasure of God. Liturgy is the closest experience of human beings to heaven on earth, and maybe it is heaven. But I speak idealistically, with a sigh for the often grim reality.

Aidan Kavanagh, in a witty little book about liturgical style, says that the deacon is "the assembly's prime minister" who must be able to perform the other ministries as well as anyone else: "singer of singers, cantor of cantors, reader of readers . . . butler in God's house, *major domo* of its banquet, master of its ceremonies."[10] There are three activities in the liturgy in which the deacon performs as angel or table waiter: proclaimer of the gospel (angel), bidder of intercessions (both angel and table waiter, delivering messages and reading lists), and table waiter at the messianic banquet (setting the table, preparing the dishes, serving the food, making sure the banqueters don't make a mess, cleaning up, telling everyone to go home). How this is done is a matter of combining ancient tradition with local custom, too complicated to describe in detail here.

One complaint about deacons, especially from bishops and priests, concerns their bumbling and bungling in the liturgy. Cooking a pot of beans for the hungry does not always translate into spreading table linens and setting bread and wine on the altar. Deacons need more help in the liturgy than we have been giving them. Training should cover two areas: reading (including singing, a form of discourse which pleases God) and serving tables. Deacons need to learn to function in the choreographed, stylized liturgy of a cathedral as well as in an informal small setting. They need to learn to observe when help is needed — the bishop has lost his glasses! — and to spring into action at a crisis. I would put prospective deacons into a restaurant for a month or two and let them learn to reconcile the uproar in the kitchen with smooth service in the dining room. Another idea is to conduct a school for butlers. In the old days of high-priced oil, an English butler ran such a school in Houston, Texas. Polite manners are equally proper in a hospital ward and a soup kitchen and a prison dining hall and the Christian liturgy. I would have the trainees spend an hour a day singing the Exsultet, gospel, prayers of the people, and dismissal (especially the Easter dismissal with alleluias). Even the tone deaf and others disabled in speech or hearing can be taught to make a joyful noise. Aidan Kavanagh writes: "A deacon who cannot sing is like a reader who cannot read, a presbyter (which means elder) without age or wisdom, a bishop (which means overseer) who cannot see, a presider who cannot preside."[11] It's a harsh judgment but all too often a true picture of what goes on.

If we train deacons to serve in liturgy, we must also train bishops and priests to live and work with servants. The main problem is to teach the presider to preside and not to serve. Presider, stay away from the altar until your time arrives, and be a model of quiet prayer.

7. And you are to carry out other duties assigned to you from time to time.

This requirement concludes the sentence above, about liturgical duties. Other duties (unspecified and hence unlimited) may be assigned by the bishop and such priests who have legitimate authority over the deacon, and the deacon must carry them out. What a threat of despotic control! Any sane ordinand who takes the bishop's address seriously must be tempted to turn around and run out of church. The bishop may tell you to quit your job and get another, move to another town, move to another parish in the diocese, leave the hospital and enter prison, stop preparing babies for baptism and start collecting the dead for burial, leave the old folks' home and open a shelter for street addicts. Does this sound unreasonable? Potentially cruel? Most bishops will exercise common sense and pastoral good judgment. But if the instruction has any meaning, any force, it constitutes a binding agreement that the deacon is now at the service of the bishop and of the church — a delicate act of balancing — to use for *diakonia*, wherever the bishop sees the need.

The instruction has another ominous meaning. Conventional wisdom, reflected in a doctrine such as the indelibility of orders, tends to place the isolated being of an ordained minister, what ordination does to the minister's character, ahead of the minister's being and function in the community. But an order exists for the good of the community, not of the ordained minister. Here the bishop is warning the ordinand against using the order for self: a deacon is ordained for service of others.

This statement is a variation of the vow of obedience, which the ordinand makes during the presentation. It is given its theological content by the last question following the bishop's address: "Will you in all things seek not your glory but the glory of the Lord Christ?" The deacon seeks God's glory by carrying out other duties assigned from time to time.

8. At all times, your life and teaching are to show Christ's people that in serving the helpless they are serving Christ himself.

The theological basis for the statement is Matthew 25:31-46. We are to feed the hungry, give something to drink to the thirsty, welcome the stranger, clothe the naked, care for the sick and visit those in prison — and serve all the rest who need. Alongside the tabernacle in the sanctuary are temples of the Holy Spirit, the poor clamoring at the door for food, shelter, and a listening ear. Christ is present in all the needy and helpless, and he can be found especially in those at the bottom of society. The distinct role of deacons in the church is to reveal the real presence of Christ in the needy and helpless, and to carry the message of that presence to the people of God.

This is what the modern church means by deacons enabling, helping, and encouraging Christian people to serve. Deacons are to give Christian people the Christian reason to serve. Without the presence of Christ, service becomes institutional and impersonal, while the role of servant reverts to its secular meaning of low and mediocre status. In the liturgy the revelation of Christ in humanity occurs vividly when the deacon comes among the people and proclaims the good news of Christ to the poor in whom Christ dwells.

The liturgy continues after the examination. The ordinand kneels facing the bishop, and all others stand while a hymn invoking the Holy Spirit is sung. This is almost always Veni Creator Spiritus in either the old plainchant version (Hymn 502 or 504) or the waltz-like responsive version sung by bishop and people (Hymn 503). The Pentecost sequence Veni Sancte Spiritus (Hymn 226) is also permitted, although at none of the ordinations I have attended in the last twenty years have I heard it sung. Both hymns are baptismal but point to the epiclesis or invocation of the Spirit in the ordination prayer.[12]

After a period of silence, the bishop begins the ordination prayer. It commences with a remembrance of Christ "who took on himself the form of servant, and humbled himself, becoming obedient even to death on the cross" (from Phil. 2:7-8). Through Christ "we know that whoever would be great must be servant of all." The bishop praises God for the diversity of ministries "and for calling this your servant to the order of deacons."

Then the bishop lays on hands and prays:

> *Therefore, Father, through Jesus Christ your Son, give your Holy Spirit to* N.; *fill* him *with grace and power, and make* him *a deacon in your Church.*

The bishop removes hands and concludes with prayer that the deacon be "modest and humble, strong and constant" (rough translations of similar phrases in *Apostolic Tradition* and *Apostolic Constitutions*) and "share in Christ's service."

The prayer of the Canadian church uses similar scriptural and patristic sources but arranges them differently. I find the Canadian version more coherent and graceful in style. There is one subtle but major theological difference. In the American version the bishop prays that the Father "make" the ordinand "a deacon in your Church." *God* consecrates. But in the Canadian service the bishop prays:

> *Send down your Holy Spirit upon your servant* N, *whom we now consecrate in your name to the office and work of a deacon in the Church.*

The Canadian prayer expresses the reality of the Spirit acting in and through the body of Christ. Filled with God, *we* consecrate. In both the American and the Canadian prayers, only the Father is asked to give the fruits of consecration.

The people shout "Amen" (the rubric says "in a loud voice") and the deacon is vested "according to the order of deacons" (*BCP*, p. 545) —

that is, with "stole worn over the left shoulder, or other insignia of the office of deacon" (*BCP*, p. 554). The rubric would be clearer if it specified "and/or dalmatic and other insignia" instead of "or other insignia." The stole or *orarion* originated in the east and the dalmatic in the west. The earliest custom (still followed in the Russian Orthodox and some other eastern churches) was to wear the stole hanging straight down from the left shoulder. The dalmatic in its primitive form was a full-sleeved white or off-white tunic, sometimes with colored stripes called *clavi* sewn from each shoulder to the hem and around each sleeve. In the early Roman church deacons wore the dalmatic without a stole. In the early Gallican church deacons borrowed the *orarion* and wore it on top of the dalmatic, still hanging straight down. Eventually the style spread to Rome. After about the eleventh century western deacons started to wear the stole beneath the dalmatic and for convenience tied the ends under the right arm. Meanwhile, in Greece and other Hellenic areas deacons sewed two stoles end to end and wore this double *orarion* wrapped about the body (the Byzantine style) as a mark of honor.

The distinctive vestments of the deacon are the dalmatic and left-shouldered stole. Both may be worn (in several ways), or only one may be worn. Vestments have nothing to do with personal adornment or status; they are the formal dress of the assembly, and the assembly should have a hand in their design. They are beautiful costumes (which attract the eye and capture the imagination), and they are emblems of dramatic parts (which convey action). In "solemn" celebrations one sometimes still sees dress which suggests a performance of *The Mikado*. Modern vesture conveys beauty through simplicity and honesty in fabric and shape. Does your dalmatic suggest and permit the active yet graceful movement of one who delivers messages and waits on tables? Is your stole visible? What should the messengers and waiters wear at *this* wedding?

The bishop then gives the new deacon a Bible — a remnant of the medieval *porrectio instrumentorum* (delivery of the instruments) — and says: "Receive this Bible as the sign of your authority to proclaim God's Word and to assist in the ministration of his holy Sacraments." All too often the ceremony suggests a private gift — another study Bible added to the one the new deacon already owns. It would be more meaningful to give a lectern Bible or book of the gospels (or lectionary), which signifies proclamation in the assembly. For the next revision of the Prayer Book, the bishop might say: "*N.*, receive the gospels of Christ, whose herald you are, and proclaim the living Word." Then I would like to see the bishop or someone else give a large white hand towel to the deacon as a symbol of table waiting and footwashing. (May the towel be considered "other insignia" and given under the present rubrics?)

The giving of Bible (or book of the gospels) conveys the meaning of proclamation — deacon as angel herald. For the rest of the liturgy, the deacon enacts the role of table waiter; if several have been ordained, they share table service. The bishop stays away from the altar until the new deacon finishes setting the table and preparing the food. Then the bishop comes to the table (and censes the altar, if that is the custom, whereupon the deacon takes the censer and swings it among the people — an angel task) and begins the eucharistic prayer.

During the prayer the new deacon hovers nearby, helps the bishop follow the text, protects the wine from spillage and insects, and during the doxological ending lifts the cup of wine in a gesture of offering, while the bishop lifts the bread. (Some bishops and priests prefer to elevate both bread and cup, some to elevate neither. The deacon needs to adjust to their custom.)

The new deacon serves communion, in one or both kinds. Usually the bishop takes the bread and the deacon the wine, but if there are several new deacons they may serve both. After communion the bishop leaves the remaining sacrament on the altar and the deacon performs the ablutions. The rubrics suggest that the deacon remove the vessels, consume the remaining bread and wine, and clean the vessels "in some convenient place" (either credence table or sacristy). The deacon gives the dismissal, which should actually send people out of church. (No post-dismissal hymns, concerts, or prayer services, please.)

After the liturgy, an ancient service may take place. The deacon may carry the sacrament, preferably both bread and wine, "to those communicants who, because of sickness or other grave cause, could not be present at the ordination." This obviously refers not to *nominal* Christians but to *faithful* communicants who would have been there if they could. I suggest that the new deacon publicly enlist lay eucharistic ministers to help in this extension of the body of Christ.

I have gone into detail about the ordination and eucharist in which the deacon first serves because they inaugurate the meaning of service. In every Sunday eucharist, in baptisms, and in the great liturgies of Holy Week and the paschal feast, the people learn through the drama of the liturgy that to be a Christian means to be a servant of the Lord and a servant of the poor. Their vow to uphold the deacon in ministry includes upholding the deacon in liturgical performance. The people are not passive listeners at a lecture on ethics, but part of the great drama of Christ the Servant on the cross. What they enact, they are. The old axiom *lex orandi, lex credendi* means: the law of prayer [is] the law of belief. The original version, by Prosper of Aquitaine in the early fifth century, clearly subordinates belief to prayer: *lex supplicandi legem statuat credendi*, the law of prayer establishes the law of belief.[13] Worship constitutes and forms belief. Liturgy forms the people of God in the life of Father, Son, and Holy Spirit.

Here is another axiom. Those who serve in liturgy (especially those whom the church officially appoints) must also serve in the work of service in the world. When one who serves the poor also proclaims the good news, calls on the people for prayers of compassion, and waits on the table, and the people recognize the connection between deacon's service without and deacon's service within, liturgy forms the people of God in life of Christian service.[14]

Notes

1. Richard F. Grein, "Homily of Richard of Kansas" (6 July 1987 in Kansas City, Mo., at the North American Association for the Diaconate conference) *Diakoneo* 9:3 (Nov. 1987), 3-4.
2. The catechism also speaks of "the ministry of the laity" as "to represent Christ and his Church," but this representation differs from that of orders. It is general, diffused, and various and does not contain the focus of authorized particularity. It is baptismal, the property of all the baptized, including the ordained.
3. For a linguistic explanation of semiotics, or the science of signs, see Walker Percy, *Lost in the Cosmos: The Last Self-Help Book* (New York: Farrar, Straus & Giroux, 1983), pp. 85-126. Other disciplines which contribute to our understanding of signs are anthropology (Victor Turner on tribal rites of passage) and psychology (Carl Jung on the symbols of dreams).
4. For a summary of Anglican thought on bishops, see Richard A. Norris, "Episcopacy," in *The Study of Anglicanism*, ed. Stephen Sykes and John Booty (London: SPCK; Philadelphia: Fortress Press, 1988), pp. 296-309.
5. For a summary of Anglican thought on priests, see John B. Webster, "Ministry and Priesthood," in ibid., pp. 285-290.
6. For extended definitions of the diaconate, see [Timothy Blavin], *Deacons in the Ministry of the Church: A Report to the House of Bishops of the General Synod of the Church of England,* GS 802 (London: Church House Publishing, 1988), pp. 77-99; Anglican Church of Canada, Committee on Ministry, *A Plan to Restore the Diaconate in the Anglican Church of Canada* (Toronto:Anglican Church of Canada, 1989), pp. 4-8; and Sr. Teresa, CSA, "An Anglican Perspective on the Diaconate," Distinctive Diaconate Study 29 (1988).

7. Although I speak here mainly of the ordination of a deacon in the Episcopal Church, the 1985 rite in the Anglican Church of Canada is almost identical, with minor differences in order and text (*The Book of Alternative Services*, pp. 652-658). The rites of other Anglican churches also agree in theology and practice.

8. One problem with regarding a priest as also a deacon (if the diaconate is indelible) is that the bishop's instruction to a priest to work "together" logically contradicts and repeals the prior instruction to a deacon to work "under."

9. As observed by Sr. Teresa, CSA, in a discussion group at the 1989 NAAD conference at Kanuga, *Distinctive Diaconate News* 24 (Sept. 1989), 6.

10. Aidan Kavanagh, *Elements of Rite: A Handbook of Liturgical Style* (New York: Pueblo Publishing Co., 1982), p. 76.

11. Ibid., p. 32.

12. The same cannot be said of two other ordination favorites, "God of the prophets" (Hymn 359) and "I bind unto myself today" (Hymn 370). Both belong instead at baptism.

13. W. Taylor Stevenson, "Lex Orandi - Lex Credendi," in *The Study of Anglicanism*, p. 187 n. 1. See also Aidan Kavanagh, *On Liturgical Theology* (New York: Pueblo Publishing Co., 1984), pp. 3, 46.

14. Gail Ramshaw describes how this happens: "Simply said, here is the liturgical logic: that the weekly ritual of assembling around Christ in prayer for the world will form in Christian people the mind of praise and the habit of service." (Speech at the National Liturgical Conference "The Baptismal Mystery and the Catechumenate" 8-11 Feb. 1988, at Grace Cathedral, San Francisco.)

Chapter 12

PRIVATE FAITH and PUBLIC RESPONSIBILITY

Jean Haldane

Wes always gave me the feeling I was on his team, and that what I was doing was important. His friendly smile, usually accompanied by another terrible pun, made me feel that ministry was a most joyful thing. I learned from him, I admired him, I had great affection for him.-JH

I n the videotape "Faith on a Tightrope"[1] Robert Bellah says it is vital that people (of the Episcopal Church) "find ways to connect private faith with public responsibility."[2] If we don't, he warns, the church will become more and more remote... "a small enclave repeating formulas we no longer believe and enacting rituals that no longer have meaning for us."

Are laity concerned about connecting private faith with their public responsibility? I believe so. But in our churches relatively little happens to help laity do this. We need to listen to laity's experience, invite them to share their insights about being a Christian in their work, their family, their community.

The promise of this sharing is first, that lay people will get a lot clearer about the connection between faith and daily life. Second, they will become teachers of one another. Third, as laity perceive the crucial nature of their work of ministry in the world, their theological and faith questions will become clearer, and this will impact the church's agenda.

At St. Stephen's Church, Seattle, a number of lay people were interviewed about how they act on their faith on a daily basis, and how the church empowers them for it. One of the questions asked them to describe an "experience beyond the walls of the church, when you felt compelled to speak or act, simply because you felt it was right." At first many could not think of such an experience. But the idea provoked serious thought; eventually almost all described experiences that came to mind. One man on the faculty of a local university said, "I learned about a proposed policy related to faculty that I felt would be unjust and divisive. I spoke up, and said it was wrong." Weeks later both his colleagues and the dean's office agreed that it was wrong. The whistle blower said, "It is hard to stand alone. Yet I knew my action was right, so it wasn't hard."

He seemed pleased to have identified that experience beyond the gathered church community; it seemed satisfying to have connected his Christian commitment with his responsibilty in academe. "One doesn't always reflect; . . . this has helped me," he said later.

Scores of examples outside this study suggest that lay women and men are concerned about how their faith relates to their responsibilities in daily life. They do think about it, but it usually remains a private concern until they are asked about it.

Ministry on a daily basis is a very individual process for laity. Much of it is costly in time and effort and uncertain in terms of outcome. But there is enormous promise — not only for the specific situation and people in it, but for the world which God so loves.

The results of the St. Stephen's interviews were written up as a report to the congregation.[3] People were excited and moved by this chronicle of ordinary lay people acting in society with courage and sensitivity, motivated by their Christian commitment, for the good of others. This was heartening to other lay people and to the clergy. The group researching how laity acted on their Christian commitment in daily life was known as the Ministry of the Laity Development Group (MLDG). They were broadly charged by the vestry to find ways of supporting and enabling laity for ministry. The MLDG decided first to find out what ministry meant to lay people, and if and how they were ministering. We shall return to St.

Stephen's later in this chapter.

A new book that raises the whole question of connecting private faith with public responsibility is *The Political Meaning of Christianity*,[4] by Glenn Tinder, professor of political science at the University of Massachusetts at Boston. He is a Christian and a Protestant. I was struck by what his Roman Catholic reviewer, Michael Novak said: "He takes up one of the central traditions of American life — that of prophetic Protestant Christianity — and shows how an intelligent participant in such a tradition interprets several basic concepts of American politics."[5] Tinder's book shows us a way to bring Christianity's contribution to the world's deliberations about the future of this planet and its peoples. Novak is excited, admiring, and he wonders why so few in the sciences who have Christian backgrounds have not done likewise.

One reason that occcurs to me is that it's a risky thing to do. Any professional, especially in academe, can lose credibility if he or she introduces religious considerations. A more subtle obstacle to those who would follow in Glen Tinder's footsteps is that the churches do not, generally speaking, expect that much of their laity.

The call of lay persons in any of the professions carries with it enormous challenges in today's world. Laity in these arenas of power and influence have been neglected by the church.

One layman in a church expressed a desire for greater intellectual stimulation. This was interpreted as a need for better sermons. (Then he became senior warden and too busy to pursue his desire.) Theological and historical grounding is not sought for those who could become the Tinders of the future. More likely they will be pointed in the direction of seminary or theological school to follow their "interest," where the possibility of a new vocation — ordination — may remove them from the lay ranks.

In Bill Moyers' television program, "A World of Ideas,"[6] he interviews men and women from many fields, from sociology and medicine to history and the arts. Bill Moyers listens and questions in such a way as to bring out, not only the expertise of each person in his/her field, but the wisdom of a thoughtful mind and the spiritual values implicit in the ideas. They are truly theological discussions. Moyers, himself an ordained minister as well as a nationally known television journalist, says that in these conversations he found "a kingdom of thought, rich in insights into our times." But most of all, he adds, "I found a love of sharing, a passion for connectedness. . . ." And he sees all of these women and men as teachers. For those of us who heard them publically "thinking aloud," it was indeed a thrilling learning experience.

Not quite a "Bill Moyers" event, a scientist was asked by his church to speak about his work from the perspective of his Christian faith.

He said he gave it much thought and found it very satisfying to share his viewpoint with other lay people. He said he considered this invitation to speak a ministry to him; he felt ministered to. Perhaps there was a desire, a hunger even, to pursue the meaning of his faith in relation to his life's work — and a need to articulate that within the faith community.

A research project that holds promise for insight into the ministry of professionals in academe is "Leaven" directed by Dr. Alda Morgan.[7] Christian faculty come together to explore what their Christian commitment calls for in that setting. They explore what ministry may be possible, how personal faith can be connected to their public responsibility of teaching, thinking and writing. No one can tell these lay men and women what and how to do it; they must do the hard thinking for themselves.

Ministry in a world of strangers

The laity of the Episcopal Church include all sorts and conditions of women and men and they all have gifts to share. They are not all scholars. Yet all are challenged to act out of their deepest held values and beliefs in the unique circumstances of their lives. A woman, known at St. Stephen's, Seattle, for caring and responsible ministry, could not think of an example "beyond the walls" of the church. The interview was coming to a close, when she said "I've just remembered something. . . ." She had parked her car at a shopping mall when she noticed a woman get out of the next car and disappear into the mall leaving behind a small child. Feeling concerned for the safety of the child, she stayed in her car for thirty minutes or so until the woman returned. She then said something to her about the danger of leaving a child alone in a locked car, to which the woman reacted defensively, got in her car and drove off. Asked by the interviewer, "Would you do it again?" she replied, "Oh yes, you'd have to, wouldn't you?"!

Beyond the gathered community is a world of strangers. Circumstances are unexpected; often the challenge is to act now on behalf of others. There may be no one else around to do it, no overt support, no witness. Is the ministry of the laity, in part at least, the capacity to act with courage in the world God so loves? To care for the helpless, to act rightly — is this not loving one's neighbor as oneself? The laywoman's action, small and unobserved, helps build the community of all God's people. And it sounds very much like connecting one's faith with public responsibility.

There are dozens, hundreds, thousands of experiences that could be cited of lay people acting on their faith in daily life. They do not always experience hostility; often the strangers are friends, and church people are the ones ministered to. Nor do they always act alone; rather, they link with others in society to address issues of justice and need. And there are many who have thought deeply about the relationship of private faith to public responsibility. These laity do not need to have their awareness raised about "ministry in the world;" they are becoming almost bored with the talk. . . . A recent example of this comes to mind.

A diocese asked me to help them put together a year-long lay training process. The start-up would be a conference on the ministry of the laity. Some time later, I received a phone call, "No one is interested! There's no interest in lay ministry." Bored about the ministry of the laity?! The focus changed. It is now on how a congregation might help people to live as Christians, in other words, to make a better connection between Sunday and Monday. The projected conference has become a consultation, with clergy-laity teams, open-ended outcome, and projected next steps. Pre-involvement is planned, both to communicate diocesan thinking, and to get responses to it.

It is time to move, to act on the words in a total way.

Accountability for baptismal vows

Baptism is, of course, the bedrock of our entry into communion with one another in Christ's church. When we speak of the minstry of the baptized, we are speaking of our lifelong task of fulfilling our vows to love God and our neighbor as ourselves. We're speaking of constant search and discovery, "with God's help," for ways we can carry out our vows at each stage of our life and in our unique circumstances. We're speaking of the diligence we must employ "with God's help" to know our gifts, to develop and use them to carry out our vows. And we're speaking of a vocation which embraces every part of life — family, work, friends, strangers, recreation — learning and serving in the institutions and structures of society.

Seeing the baptism of a baby is always a wondrous occasion, warm and tender, as well as astonishing as we hear parents and godparents promise on behalf of the baby to "renounce Satan and all spiritual forces of wickedness." It reminds us of our creaturely stance before the Creator and the need for God's help; the fortitude we will need for the journey, and also the support and strength of the faith community, past as well as present. Baptism is a hopeful ritual, giving us all another chance to vow "with God's help" to follow our calling, to claim our freedom, to walk by faith, and to work for the spread of the kingdom.

More frequently these days, we renew our baptismal vows as part of eucharist, Lenten programs, and on other occasions. Valuable as this is, it can become a "vain repetition," unless there is accountability for our vows, a way to give an account of ourselves before God and one another in the body of Christ. People need to share their experience of daily ministry, for they are, in many ways and in many places, being accountable to their baptismal vows. Sharing and reflecting on this with one another gives meaning to the vows and authenticates the ministry.

Integrating faith with life

One pastor writes about identifying the central issue in her congregation. Attendance showed there was a lack of interest in Bible study; unwillingness to talk about one's personal faith; absence of leadership in the church. The central issue appeared to be the inability of laity to integrate their faith with their lives: and failure of the church to develop a program which might help them with that central task. They decided to concentrate for a couple of years on learning about the daily lives of their members.

Laity came together in occupational groups. A listening team led members to talk about their work lives. Ongoing support groups were formed for laity who wanted to connect faith and life, and specifically in the workplace. The Rev. Davida Foy Crabtree, pastor of the Colchester Federated Church in Colchester, Connecticut, says, "We discovered an important principle. By beginning with their lives we were validating the authority of the laity and empowering them to reflect on the faith."[8] Eventually day-long conferences on "Discover Your Gifts," "Beyond a Sunday Christianity" and other topics took place. Tools of laity's work were offered on the altar during eucharist, with laity in that job or profession standing while the congregation gave thanks and prayed for them.

Crabtree notes that when laity were provided an opportunity to talk about their work and reflect on the impact of it on the rest of their lives, they developed confidence and trust, began to ask theological questions and started to wrestle with the scriptures! As their workday lives were brought into worship, the process "began to bridge public and private worlds."

The key to what the leadership at Colchester Federated Church did was in reading the behavior of the congregation. They did not resign themselves to 'uninterested laity,' nor did they rush to provide more attractive programs. They said in effect, "how is it that lay people are not interested in these life-giving traditions, the means of grace?" In other words, they allowed that a different problem could be behind the inertia. Davida Crabtree finds satisfaction in seeing an alive and growing laity, for whom her pastoral gifts and teaching skills are abundantly needed.

A variety of gifts

"Gifts are so central," Crabtree said. Why is that? The discovery that God has given "me" a unique configuration of gifts and talents is empowering! Nothing has to to be added. Lay people are already prepared for ministry, for their gifts actually shape their ministry. They are assured by this knowledge that they are needed; for no one can replace their unique contribution. When laity have this understanding, confidence grows, and along with it a new sense of responsibility. Not only do they have gifts to use, but they have gifts to develop, to educate, to train.

There are a numer of processes of gift identification.[9] My own bias is for a process that leads a person to see a pattern of strengths, talents, and abilities demonstrated in their own life experience. All are gifts from God and all have the potential for use in ministry. Our gifts can lead us to a ministry made out of whole cloth, that is, without the false duality of *church* ministry and *world* ministry, so that it becomes simply a matter of living the Christian life.

Finding ways to use our gifts appropriately in a given situation is a deep and delicate task. Both laity and clergy need to explore this with one another. On occasion we must use our gifts boldly and to the full; at other times we must exercise restraint in using them. Justice and right action will be one guide; another will be the love of brothers and sisters within and without the church. Gifts can be used and misused, but until we know our gifts we cannot choose how to use them.

St. Stephen's Church followed its interviews of laity with an "Exploration of Personal Resources for Ministry" to help laity name and claim their gifts, and be clearer about their life's work.

Developing and growing our gifts gives continuing education, training and the like a different focus, for it can mean growing our talents "ten-fold" or "a thousand-fold." Some growing will take the form of skill training; some will mean going back to the classroom; some will involve retreat and waiting on God. Some growing will mean finding a job or a career that will use a person's gifts; some will mean occasional review of all activity in church and society to bring into view how one may use one's gifts better. Knowing one's gifts gives laity another criterion for making choices in their ministry, both in the church and in the public domain.

There is an underside to gifts, precisely and well described by Elizabeth O'Connor in *Eighth Day of Creation*.[10] She refers to the envy and jealousy we are all prone to. We envy "her" ability, we are jealous of "his" skill . . . . These are the silent sins considered so unattractive in our culture and our church that few of us dare admit to them. These feelings are at the root of many difficulties between clergy and laity, between laity with other laity and clergy with other clergy. It is a kind of mental and emotional seething that grips us, which, carried to its ultimate conclusion, destroys relationships we'd like to have, despises gifts in others we want to appreciate, and buries our own gifts instead of enhancing them. Fear of another's gifts often lies below the envy and jealousy, especially when the other's gifts are in "my" area. It is the fear that another will be thought more valuable than I am. It is the fear that others will replace me.

One antidote to this sad and difficult bias is, first of all, to help laity and clergy identify their gifts in each other's presence, so that mutual appreciation becomes possible and probable. Second, the development of a collaborative climate. For example, every task group in the church could go through a shortened form of gift awareness, a team building process. This would help each to value the others, and enable assignments according to people's gifts. It would relieve the strain of competition and replace it with collaboration among mutually gifted people.

In one Christian denomination, the pastor's doctor of ministry project was about gifts. His research focused on laity identifying their gifts and the impact of that on the congregation and the pastor. He wrote in his dissertation, "I am aware of a greater interest I now have in what people do for a living, how they view their work, what their struggles and joys are. . . . I am feeling less of a sense of burden in the parish, and less loneliness and isolation than I once did. I don't have to do it all. I believe I have much more sense of "we" and mutual ministry. I know this work with gifts has contributed to my growth here. . . . I've always respected the laity. . . . This respect has been deepened through our work with gifts for ministry. The lay people of our churches have much to teach us pastors about God, about faithfulness, about ministry, and about the spiritual journey."[11]

At a laity conference on employment, the keynote speaker, Kevin Starr, said "Each of us has a work to do. . . "[12] not a job, mind you, but a work. A work to do would encompass a number of jobs or even careers: certainly our family work, our community work, our church work. . . . Perceiving our life's work is one of the most important things we can do. If a person misses this, misses developing and offering his gifts and talents, his life will often be without meaning. There will be a sense of loss.

Connecting inward and outward

There is another way of looking at the connection between private faith and public responsibilty. Our Christian tradition of spirituality has always emphasized the connection between inner life and outer action, and the importance of growing that connection so that each informs and fuels the other. Retiring or retreating into our private inner life, whether we label it faith or spirituality, can result in a compassionless and self-serving outer life. The reverse is true; we can throw ourselves into all kinds of good works, but this can become lifeless unless tied to our motivational source. The inner and outer connection is the stuff of the spiritual journey. And Christian ministry is the public expression of our inner sense of meaning and our relationship with God. Evelyn Underhill, one of our Anglican mystics, says, "it is this constant correlation between inward and outward that really matters."[13] In other words it is a movement, back and forth from a centered reflection to a giving action in the world.

Recently, I was asked to speak to a network of men and women commited to career development. They work in a variety of organizations and institutions, and for all I know, may belong to a variety of churches. The person who invited me asked if I could speak about spirituality and career: "No one has ever done that!" I felt challenged to find ways to communicate about spirituality in an environment where faith language is not the norm. I also wondered how to take the church with me.

I found that the notion of life as a spiritual journey was unanimously accepted. As we pursued the connection between our inner and outer worlds it became obvious that it only required someone to give permission for people to move and speak with relative ease within this frame of reference. I drew examples from my work and my "organization" (the church) as and where it would be helpful for the purpose of communicating something about spirituality and career.

After the presentation and participant sharing, several people came to speak to me. One spoke of hunger for inner spiritual exploration, another spoke of her sense of connection between inner and outer; and another said he used to belong to the church; "I was an acolyte. At some point it just didn't seem to relate to the rest of my life." Inside and outside the church there is need to connect inner and outer worlds. This could be a great opportunity for the church to serve many in the community.

Privatism and diversity

Inner and outer — both are adventures involving risk, growth, expansion of the individual's ways of perceiving, thinking and acting. It sounds a wondrous journey, and it is.

Being human, however, we are not always courageous; in fact we are often beset by fear of the unknown, both in the inner world and the outer. Struggling to control the degree of contradiction and ambiguity, we meet constant diversity and change; and we can begin to shrink our lives to a narrower world of known ideas, known people, known things to do. If this is carried too far, we begin to live in a private world which becomes the context for "my life." This state is called privatism, and as Parker Palmer says, "If Americans didn't invent it (privatism), we have elevated it to unsurpassed status."[14] He suggests that privatism "caps" both the inner spiritual life and the outer ministry by closing off our openness to growth.

How does privatism impact the laity of the church? We are as susceptible as other human beings to the anxieties of living. We can make our God too small, and we can make God too comfortable a support for our lives. Also we can ignore other laity who seem to have a different concept of God, or we can try to impose our way as *the* way to worship God. The root fear is of a diversity of spiritual experience. If we were to be open, we would have to live with the ambiguity and contradiction that we dread. If we stay with a narrow spirituality, our inner spring of new life will be "capped." Similarly, if the world is becoming too diverse, too complex, too uncertain, we can remain silent about public issues, we can solidify our opinions until they become uninformed prejudices, we can live within our circle of family, friends and certain other groups — like church. Sometimes the gathered church community can be a major part of privatism. The reality for some laity is that the gathered church never really "scatters." This contributes to the idea that ministry of the laity is synonymous with service within the congregation. Ministry beyond the walls of the church stays unappreciated, unknown — in other words, capped.

A dreary picture? Overplayed? Perhaps.

Parker Palmer says the church can do one of two things: push the people further into privatism, or call us out and encourage us for the spiritual journey — both inner and outer. If laity are to come of age and be the church, it must be the latter.

Leadership and morality

Another follow-up to the interviews at St. Stephen's was an Exploration of Effective Leadership. This was not a skill training event as such, but rather an orchestrated discussion by lay people.

Two lay people set the tone — one describing her leadership of the board of a local hospital and the other telling of his leadership in the community around the issues of desegregation and abortion. The layman had brought community organizations with opposing views together, and helped them to find some common ground. As each lay person described what they had done, two stories of courageous and effective leadership emerged. The scope of their influence, their ability to live with ambiguity and conflict, and their constant effort to act rightly was inspiring. Each had gone way beyond his or her "job description" to contribute to society and to work for the common good.

On the evaluation form, participants were asked what relationship they saw between leadership and ministry. One wrote, "In order to minister, a certain degree of leadership is involved." Another wrote, "(our talk about leadership suggests) a more responsible and aware ministry" and "Ministry is leading a Christian life in its communal context." Many asked for support groups, mentors, life inventory/ministry counselors, whatever would encourage and equip them for effective ministry. They also asked for volunteer opportunities in parish and community.

Great excitement about leadership! Why?

Barbara Tuchman, the historian, in an interview with Bill Moyers said, "We (Americans) have a lapse in initiative and the exercise of activity toward a goal."[15] She attributed this lapse and lack of a common goal to "a loss of a moral sense." When asked what she meant by moral sense, she responded, "the sense of what is inherently right and wrong and of following your belief in what is right."

The leadership exploration discussion defined leadership as taking responsibility and acting rightly in our day-to-day life. This meant that leadership can and must be exercised by everyone — whether in the large arenas of the world we live in, or in the more immediate arenas of family and work, church and community. Taking responsibility for recycling the family trash and international strategizing in response to deforestation are both about protecting the environment. The issue is the same; the scope is different.

Could it be that these laity saw that they had been exercising leadership in many ways, and that now they wanted to take more initiative and work toward renewal of a moral sense in society? Such leadership has to begin with a vision and a goal. When the vision and goal are held in common with others, powerful action can follow.

Two lay people in Tucson, Arizona, Nancy Bissell and Gordon Packard, put it this way, "If we call ourselves Christians, then our lives should reflect that commitment in everything we do."[16] They began a soup kitchen for homeless men in 1982. Nancy Bissell writes, "In my innocence I was only able to picture the simple act of passing out a bowl of soup and a sandwich to a needy person. . . ."[17]

She and Gordon soon found that they had begun a journey that would involve them not only in relationships with the poor, but in confrontations with city hall and conflict with other church people. They would also have a volunteer force of 500, and lives would change. . . not only those of the poor but those of the helpers, mostly middle-class Episcopalians. A suit was filed against them by a neighborhood organization, citing "the transients are frightening people. . . ."

Nancy and Gordon report, "One of our goals was to serve the poor energetically, paying special attention to their humanity and their individual needs. But another goal, far more provocative, was to reach out to churchmen and churchwomen with a challenge: how does your experience of the teachings of Our Lord translate into direct action? Are you taking risks? Are you speaking out against injustice? Will you allow yourself to be a little less comfortable so that others can be more so?"

Leadership means we will be tested. There will be victories, there will be defeats; moral dilemmas will continually face us. And there will undoubtedly be a shift in the way laity see things. A lay woman put it this way: "we might have to clarify and tighten up the connection of theology-spirituality and our service in the world." We need to make sense of a worldly ministry. Our faith and our service must be connected.

A theology for everyday life?

A paper written by an Anglican from Australia is titled, "What is the Theology of Everyday Life?"[18] In it, David Milliken, Director of Religious Programming for the Australian Broadcasting Corporation, differentiates between two kinds of theology. The first answers the question, "What is the irreducible content of Christianity?" The second addresses the question "How does the Christian faith make sense of life?" The first is the work of professionals and required by the demands of life in the church. The second is a process required by the life of Christians in the world. The primary focus of the first is ecclesiastical; the primary focus of the second is the mundane. It is the second theology that Milliken calls Theology of Everyday Life.

Milliken points to the parables of Jesus as examples of a theology of everyday life. They provide insight into the meaning of faith in the midst of the details of work, the family, and so on. The experience of lay people in the world is fundamental to this process of theological understanding. Consideration of the mundane, life's everyday experiences, "makes re-assessment of our faith a necessity." This exercise, this reflection will strenthen lay people's faith and enlarge their understanding of the biblical and theological tradition. As Davida Crabtree said, we must *start* with laity's experience, for that is where they have authority. Then they will begin to look to the scriptures and theology for meaning, for empowerment of their lives.

A lot of adult learning is re-learning, which means re-assessing old meanings, affirming those that hold up, and re-framing those that need change in light of new experience. This process raises questions which can form the basis of teaching and preaching.

Haven't we always done this? NO! NO! NO! We almost always start with scripture and theology, the authority of tradition, and HOPE people will apply it in daily life.

Fredrica Harris Thompsett has written a wonderful book called *We Are Theologians*[19] in which she returns the focus of the church to its members. She points out that Anglicanism, from its beginnings in Reformation England, had "a generous inclusive definition of membership (which) grew out of the optimistic expectation that most church members would want to know basic biblical principles of the faith and would in time become theologically informed, whatever their particular occupation. The goal of these early reformers was an educated church in which all might be theologians."

There was a time when clergy were the best educated, and often the only educated people in the church. Later, seminaries were founded to make sure the clergy were equipped to teach largely ignorant (lay) people the faith, the Bible, and the application of same in daily life. Today we have a different situation. Many laity are well-educated in many fields of study, from medicine to electronics. They are not "lay" any more in the sense of being ignorant, though many are uneducated in the area of theology and biblical study. Almost all laity could bring their theological education up to a level that would be more useful to them; some could go beyond, way beyond. The point is that laity today — for the most part — have the educational background to pursue these subjects. They can become theologically astute.

A friend of mine is both a physican and a lawyer. He is more than well-read. He has an incisive mind. He is a man of deep faith and a thoughtful layman in the Episcopal Church. He's sought after for terms on the vestry, for search committees, as a speaker. I do not believe the church has communciated to him this vision of a theologically astute laity.

Are we clergy and professional lay people anxious about or even afraid of persons like this? Certainly the prospect of laity being the equivalent of Ph.D.s in theology and Bible as well as law and medicine, gives me a lot to be humble about. But this is not a contest! The world needs competent people in every field who in addition to their professional expertise, can draw on the Christian tradition to address issues in their work. The church needs clergy and lay professionals who will listen to such lay people, encourage their questions, put in their way opportunitites to meet the scholarship of the church through books and in person, and arrange discussions for "above average" intellects to come to grips with how the tradition relates to public life. Somehow the church first has to embrace a literate laity. Then, perhaps, my friend will hear the invitation to become a theologian.

Of course, there are a growing number of lay people who have pursued theological education (four years of Education for Ministry, some diocesan schools of theology programs, and the Lay Academy in California, for example). Many have a thirst for it, a desire to get hold of the books and study their Christian heritage and so become theologically informed. My worry about these programs is that, good as they are, many people are somewhat at a loss to know what to do after such a program is finished. A rather high percentage of graduates go on to be ordained. Talk in one diocese was around "how to use the EFM people more." What theological education is for is not clear, not if one is a lay person and feels called to continue as a lay person. The connection between theological education and ministry is crucial. Laity are invited to pursue theological education in order that they may be more effective in daily and worldly ministry.

Implications for the church

Some say — clergy among them — that clericalism cripples the ministry of the laity. I think it is something else. At root, it is our ecclesiology that is defective.

Henrik Kraemer, the Dutch theologian, asked if a theology of the laity is possible, "not as an appendix to our existing ecclesiologies, but as an organic part of a total ecclesiology."[20] He then goes on to enumerate three essentials for a total ecclesiology. First is the "dimension of the world," second, "the perennial call for renewal," third, "the church's life and expression are taken from the church's being and calling." He adds the need to have a full awareness of the risk of faith. If this whole doctrine of the church were to be identified and embraced, a genuine theology of the laity would be possible as an indispensable part.

Kraemer wrote this in 1958. His vision has not been realized, though some important steps toward it have been taken. The notion of total ministry and a totally ministering church is a big step toward a whole doctrine of the church. All called, all sent, all gifted, all baptized into Christ's death and resurrection, is another way of affirming one church, one ministry, one mission. This, we say, is the nature of the church's being and calling. The church's life and expression is not yet fully tied in to this re-definition of its being and calling. There is slippage between who we say we are and the way we act that out. The need for theological clarity around the relationship of church and world is urgently felt; creation theology, liberation theology and feminist theology are responses to that.

Renewal and the risk of faith challenge me greatly. A total ecclesiology that includes the laity and charges the laity to be the prime ministers in the world would be renewal indeed. I feel hopeful (always) that this will come to be. But clergy who were interviewed in a national survey about the source of changing expectations of their role in the church today rarely referred to the laity, and the world beyond the church; that makes me wonder if professionals are up too close to see the total transformation that is needed!

Loren Mead said recently that we must "re-invent" the congregation.[21] He was referring to the new centrality of the laity in the church, and their primary focus of ministry beyond the institutional church.

There are two distinct images I have of a re-invented congregation. One is of the laity, now come of age, fully integrated into the ministry and mission of the church, fully expected to act on their faith in their public responsibilities, and with the help of clergy and lay professionals acquiring the biblical and theological acumen necessary for that. The other image is of the clergy now finding freedom in their traditional role of preaching, teaching, liturgy, pastoral care, and with the help of laity, developing a mission strategy centered on enabling laity to connect their faith with their everyday life.

In order for those images to become goals, a number of shifts in mindset need to take place. Here are some that I can see.

1. *Clergy's sense of their role: From* being "the leader" for both tradition and mission, *to* a recognition that clergy are ordered to minister primarily in the church, to the church. And I believe deacons as well as priests are so ordered. (Their charge to seek out and respond to the needs of the world makes their ministry a significant outreach of the church. They are still not in the world in the same way that a lay person is in the world.) Lay professionals are in this category too. All are to support lay mission and "mind the store." And if this sounds limited, I must be wrong about the significance of congregational life and worship.

2. *Laity's sense of their role: From* seeing themselves as primarily ministering in the church, *to* seeing themselves as primarily called to minister in the world. They are central to the church's mission. They are to take responsibility, with the clergy, to see that they are educated for this ministry. They are also to contribute to the ongoing life and agenda of the congregation.

3. *Who listens to whom: From* laity listening to the professionals, *to* professionals listening to laity . . . to better understand their daily

experience so that the church's program will centrally equip laity for ministry.

4. *Teaching and learning: From* the lecture format as primary teaching model, *to* a variety of methods in response to the multiple ways of learning. Lecturing by itself encourages privatism by discouraging community conversation and peer learning.

5. *Privatism or connectedness: From* pre-occupation with in-church concerns, *to* community issues that affect people's lives. A congregation could seek other congregations unlike their own and invite public discussion. Multi-cultural and inter-racial, intergenerational and ecumenical groupings could gather around appropriate issues.

6. *Clergy and laity expectations of one another: From* expectations arising from an old role model, *to* expectations geared to the new definition of role. Persistence in modeling clear role definitions, using every forum the church has (meetings, committees, etc.).

7. *Confirmation: From* a rite-of-passage for youth, *to* a sacramental rite for confirming adults in their call and ministry. This could be a significant liturgical experience for laity, comparable to ordination. It might evolve that on any one evening the vestry could be commissioned, several laity could be confirmed and one or two persons could be ordained to diaconate or priesthood.

In conclusion

To return to St. Stephen's interview process, another question that was asked was, "How does your church experience support, nurture and nourish your ministry?" Most responded positively and pointed to worship, a caring community, and appreciation for the example and nurture by clergy and other laity. No terrible lack was uncovered. The leadership as well as the rest of the congregation felt affirmed. But there were four recommendations: 1) Get to know one another in terms of call, ministry and gifts. 2) Develop curriculum for lay education. 3) Use the best leadership — lay and ordained, indigenous and beyond St. Stephen's — to enable ministry of the laity. 4) Connect people's gifts with needs in parish and community. The congregational leadership never took up these items though they approved them. Nothing has changed in a systemic way, except the vestry moved to make the Ministry of the Laity Development Group a committee of the vestry and charged them to continue to find ways to affirm and build up the ministry of the laity. The research changed a lot of individual's thinking about themselves as "ministers" on a daily basis. It did not, after a year, appear to impact the way in which the leadership set goals and prioritized them.

Why? First, it is very difficult to see how to take immediate advantage of research such as this. Second, a management group such as a vestry has an enormous weight of in-house agenda to take care of, as well as grappling with larger issues that are pressed upon them from outside, to say nothing of the personal concerns of members themselves around matters like stewardship and pastoral care. There is turnover of leadership too. An agenda item like "What would it take to bring center stage equipping the laity for ministry in the world?" does not lend itself to a fast briefing on the problem and a programmatic response to it. In fact, a whole retreat on the subject does not necessarily mean that the leadership, both clergy and laity, will be convinced that this is, or should be, center stage.

So how can a local church grapple with its own "being and calling," via research such as this? The key first step is to stop and look at the evidence. The second step is to ask, "What does it mean?" And this takes time. The third step is to be open to the impact this might have on "our" way of being a congregation. St. Stephen's tried, but we are left wondering why we were so strangely uplifted by the evidence of lay people who, in going about their ordinary lives, appeared to be ministering with courage and imagination. Utilizing this kind of research is rather like the story of Moses who saw a bush burning in the desert and turned aside to look at it. And we read that "when God saw that Moses turned aside to look, he called to him out of the bush. . . ." If we can look at the evidence, ponder what it means, stay open to possibilities, we may hear God's call. Davida Crabtree and her lay leaders in Connecticut did that, and bold action and newness of life followed.

Notes

1. Office for Ministry Development, "Faith on a Tightrope". (New York: The Episcopal Church Center, 1989).
2. Robert Bellah, ed. *Habits of the Heart* (Berkeley: University of California Press, 1985).
3. Lee Porter, Chair and Jean Haldane, Consultant, "Report on the Ministry of the Laity at St. Stephen's Parish." (Seattle: The Diocese of Olympia, 1989).
4. Glenn Tinder, *The Political Meaning of Christianity* (Baton Rouge: Louisiana State University Press, 1990).
5. Michael Novak, George F. Jewett scholar in religion, philosophy and

public policy at American Enterprise Institute, Washington, D.C.

6. Bill Moyers, *A World of Ideas* (New York: Doubleday, 1989).

7. Alda Morgan, Leaven Project, based at the University of California, Berkeley.

8. Davida Foy Crabtree, "They Bring Their Work to Church." *Action/ Information*, Vol. XVI, No. 1. (Washington D.C.: Alban Institute, 1990). See also: Crabtree, *The Empowering Church: How One Congregation Supports Lay People's Ministries in the World.* (Washington D.C.: Alban Institute, 1989).

9. Jean M. Haldane, *Ministry Explorations with Gifts for Ministry* (Seattle: Wellness Behavior (N.W.), 1981).

10. Elizabeth O'Connor, *Eighth Day of Creation*. (Waco, Texas: Word Books, 1971).

11. Erick Johnson, Unpublished Doctoral Dissertation (Detroit: Ecumenical Theological Center, 1989).

12. Kevin Starr, Address at the Employment Symposium. San Francisco, California: The Lay Academy, (1983).

13. Evelyn Underhill, *The Spiritual Life* (Wilton, Connecticut: Morehouse Barlow, 1955).

14. Parker J. Palmer, "All the Way Down. A Spirituality of Everyday Life." *Action/Information*, Vol. XVI, No. 1. (Washington D.C.: Alban Institute, 1990). See also: Parker J. Palmer, Barbara G. Wheeler, and James W. Fowler, eds. *Caring for the Commonweal: Education for Religious and Public Life* (Macon, Georgia: Mercer University Press, 1990).

15. Barbara Tuchman, historian, in Bill Moyers, *A World of Ideas*, Pg 5.

16. Nancy Bissell and Gordon Packard, co-founders, "The Primavera Foundation: Trickling Up and Breaking Through." (Tuscon, Arizona: The Primavera Foundation, 1987).

17. Nancy Bissell, "Choosing to Act: Reflections on Running a Soup Kitchen." *Smith Alumnae Quarterly*. (North Hampton, Massachusetts: Smith College, 1984).

18. David Milliken, "What is The Theology of Everyday Life?" *Laity Exchange*, No. 33. (San Leandro, California: Laity Information Service of Vesper Society Group, 1987).

19. Fredrica Harris Thompsett, *We Are Theologians* (Cambridge: Cowley Publications, 1989).

20. Henrik Kraemer, *A Theology of the Laity* (Philadelphia: The Westminster Press, 1958).

21. Loren Mead, President of the Alban Institute, Washington D.C.

CHAPTER 13

EMERGING ISSUES:
A Dialogue

Josephine Borgeson & James A. Kelsey

Introduction

    When Wes Frensdorff came to Nevada as bishop-elect, he brought with him a vision of the church in mission, a church which could truly make a difference in the wider community of which it was a part. But he faced a struggling institution with low income and minuscule endowments, with great geographical distances, with a mental image of what Episcopal congregations should be: an image not achievable with the resources, or even the potential resources, at hand. He reflected, he listened to the experience of other dioceses throughout the Anglican Communion, and he came up with <u>a plan for systemic change</u> so that the church in Nevada could be a church in mission.

    The outline of that plan, now known as the Nevada Total Ministry Program, was laid out <u>in four principles.</u> These four principles were foundational in Nevada, and have also been embraced by other dioceses and *regions who have subsequently moved toward total ministry.*

(1) Each congregation is to be a "ministering community" rather than a community gathered around a minister, sufficient in ministry from within its own membership, including local deacons and priests wherever possible.

(2) Each member of the church will have the opportunity to serve our Lord in church and world, through ministries which will vary greatly according to gifts, available time and opportunity.

(3) Seminary-trained clergy and laity will increasingly be trainers, enablers, supervisors and pastors of trainees. Congregations will become less dependent on seminary-trained people as the doers of ministry.

(4) The diocese, as the primary unit of interdependence in the life of the church, is the support system. The diocese will provide training and support for the various forms that ministry can take, including local priests and deacons.

There are probably few leaders in the Episcopal Church today who would not give nodding assent to these four principles and accept them as valid, at the very least in someone else's context! Yet those who begin to own these principles and practice them realize that they have embarked on a course of sweeping systemic change. Each of the original total ministry principles gives rise to a host of questions, issues and imperatives for further change.

What follows is a dialogue between Phina Borgeson, Los Angeles, and Jim Kelsey, Northern Michigan, around these four principles. It's the kind of dialogue one is apt to get caught up in at a Sindicators meeting.

-Eds.

I. Each congregation, a ministering community

Phina: I think it's easy to talk about being a ministering community if we're preoccupied with institutional maintenance. Wes used to use the image of "unpacking the one man band," which he borrowed from Bishop Michael Marshall. Well, unpacking the one man or woman band is easy if we only hand out the instruments. "Here, you take the cymbals, and you look like you've got a gift for the triangle, and I'll hang on to the harmonica, and we'll probably make better music than we did when I played everything and you only listened." We know from experience that small rural and urban congregations can do at least as good a job of carrying on parochial pastoral ministry by sharing the tasks as they do when depending on one paid presbyter. But is that really a ministering community?

Jim: I think it's very important that we stress from the start that total ministry development does not simply attempt to spread out the task assignments of "doing church" in the old, familiar model, but that we are breaking new ground and reshaping not only *how we* will organize ourselves as the church, but also *what* we plan to do as we act out our faith.

At the 1987 national forum on congregational development, Arlin Rothauge drew a distinction between three different kinds of change which he called *developmental change, transitional change,* and *transformational change.* Those of us who were there to present a workshop on regional ministry development found it to be a helpful distinction.

Most church leaders, in our effort to help shepherd congregations through constructive growth and a deepening of commitment, begin by initiating *developmental change.* Perhaps because of the basically moderate (if not conservative) bent of our tradition, we first seek to improve the existing structures, to improve the skills of our present personnel — to straighten up our act, as it were.

But when it becomes apparent that something more drastic is called for, we move boldly ahead into another level of change: *transitional change.* We reorganize our committees and commissions. We rewrite job descriptions. We hire new people for new positions. We restructure and we let everyone know that we mean business.

As dramatic a process as we might feel this sort of change management to be, the truth is that it is still pretty tame when it stands next to the third type of change, that which Arlin calls *transformational change.* Let me illustrate by using a favorite analogy of retired Bishop William Gordon, of Alaska.

If developmental change would involve special training events for the crew on board a cruise liner, and transitional change would involve hiring a new captain who in turn would rearrange the work schedule and bring on board a new cadre of senior officers to oversee a whole new way of serving the passengers during their two-week vacation cruise, transformational change would involve gutting the whole craft and turning it into a cargo ship, transforming its whole identity; making it into a whole new vessel with a dramatically different mission. So much so, that you might even want to change the ship's name, for indeed, it will have become something quite different from what it was initially.

Phina: Exactly! A ministering community must take a look at the wider community or communities in which its members move, and be responsive to the struggles and hopes found there. At the same time, a ministering community must take a realistic look at the gifts and needs of its members. A ministering community that is to be self-propagating, to borrow Roland Allen's term, must look to the places where the gifts and opportunities of its members meet the mission context in which it exists, rather than squeezing its members into a platonic ideal of "The Episcopal Parish." The first principle, then — the ministering community — does not exist independently of the second, the giftedness of all the members. Taken together they suggest an entirely different way of being the local church.

"Sufficient in ministry," a phrase Nevadans struggled with, does not mean that every parish will have every thing we have believed the ideal parish ought to have. It *does* mean that every parish will be making the most of its gifts to meet the challenges in mission in its context. Anyone with a track record in working with small congregations can tell you that gifts are not distributed equally! At one time I worked with one congregation of under fifty communicants which had no keyboard musician, while another of comparable size had four. "Sufficient" implies that we work with the gifts we have been given, and that we develop and build on our strengths. Congregations are thus freed from the sin of envy, and from working out of a scarcity model. But there's the rub. When they move into wider circles of the church's life they discover that most of the church does work from a scarcity model and assumes a closed system, fighting over turf and limited dollars. So the ministering community can become a misfit in the community of communities we know as diocese, national church, household of the faithful.

Jim: What we are trying to do is really quite counter-cultural. So often, these are congregations which have felt like misfits for many years, mostly out of a sense of inadequacy. Now, the very offer God makes to them for a new future makes them nonconformists of a different breed. For some, it might seem to be too much to ask. For others, it might be just the challenge to kick-start a new beginning.

Phina: In Nevada we had people move, or simply attend a church meeting, and experience deep frustration in trying to share the new vision they had caught. Fortunately, there have also been some very successful encounters which have brought new pride to the congregations who felt most inadequate. Jean Orr uses the analogy of produce deliveries. The small grocery store in Pioche (see their story in Chapter 10) is at the end of the line for the produce truck. They get what no one else along the route wants. Once in a while it's something surprising like fresh raspberries, but usually it's lettuce beginning to brown. The people of Christ Church used to feel that way about their church life; now they can feel they have something to offer instead of receiving what no one else wants. Still there are difficulties when they come up against unreformed structures in the wider church.

Jim: And the truth is that most of our structures are anything but reformed. And it is also true that all of us who live within the institutional church are ourselves products of the structures we are seeking to reform, and in that sense, we are, all of us, part of the problem. My bishop, Tom Ray, has a powerful way of talking about how we ministry developers still carry within us the virus we are trying to eradicate. We preach and teach against clericalism and top-down management styles, but then we repeatedly catch ourselves using old vocabulary or taking actions which discourage shared decision-making and which perpetuate old models of a priest-centered ecclesiology. We talk all the time about the ministry of all the baptized, but we never fail to find new ways to elevate the clergy, to encourage patterns of dependency and co-dependency, and to nurture parent/child relationships between the ordained and the rest of the community. As I heard Wes Frensdorff say more than once, our model and our message don't match. I see this inconsistency in myself and my own actions as clearly as I see it in my colleagues.

Phina: Another thing we have discovered with great implications for the future of ministry development: a ministering community is not just a series of ministers, but an organic unity. Actually we need go no further than Paul's Corinthian correspondence to see this notion set forth. You, collectively, are the body of Christ, he said.

You are not a bunch of individuals doing his or her own thing, each running off in the direction of his or her particular enthusiasm, but an organic whole, where mutuality, not equality, is the governing principle. Mutual discernment, mutual accountability, mutual support, mutual discipline, mutual celebration, are the ways in which the local Christian community is ordered. In the typical total ministry congregation we have done a good job of holding up the principle of the giftedness of every member. We have done a reasonable job of identifying those gifts and beginning, through new forms of theological education, to develop them. But we have only begun to scratch the surface, to identify the areas where change needs to happen in the structures of our common life, if we are to be ministering communities governed by mutuality.

What would Sunday worship look like in a ministering community ordered by mutuality? Clearly it would not be lining up a list of personnel alongside the service order, but would be an exchange among a variety of personnel, a dance of mutual ministry with referents in the community's ministry throughout the week. But what does that look like?

Jim: I wonder how many of us stop and reflect upon our standard liturgical practices in light of those questions. Think for a moment how we reinforce hierarchy and unhealthy dependencies in our worship, the way we dress up the clergy and selected others and prance them out in a procession which pinpoints each person along the pecking order. The cathedra-type chair for the presider. The way we infantalize one another by printing hymn numbers in the bulletin, posting them on the wall, and then *still* announcing them, and so on. We are inadvertently undermining our own efforts to discover new expressions for Christian community. Tom Ray tells a story about a time he visited a congregation and as he stood outside in his cope and mitre waiting to take his place at the end of the long procession, a little boy pulled at his mother's dress and said with awesome wonder: "Look, Mommy, a King!". And Tom suggests we might well consider what has happened to a church which dresses up her servant leaders as if they were royalty. All of this is a part of our problem of incongruence. Again, our message and our model don't match.

Phina: There's a lot to tackle there. I've always felt that if we have processions, they should be arranged functionally, suggesting the roles people play in the liturgical dance, not a pecking order parade.

Jim: Look at some of the ways we put forward a pretense of shared leadership while still maintaining all sorts of controls and mechanisms by which we assure ourselves of the last say. What can we learn from the Native Americans and the Quakers and other cultures and traditions about alternatives to the hierarchical leadership style and top-down management approach so prevalent in our society and so deeply interwoven into the fabric of the historical church? As we seek to dismantle those old hierarchical models, we are still left with the challenge of discovering new models for decision-making.

Phina: We need to remember, I think, that hierarchy was a gift from the medieval church to the world as a way of doing business. As rigid hierarchy breaks down as the only way of doing business in most institutions, perhaps we need to search our tradition and the work of people in other disciplines today to find the sources of new models.

Jim: I find myself challenged by Edwin Friedman's thinking in *Generation to Generation*.[1] He quite skillfully dismantles the hierarchical model, but then goes on to raise questions about what we have sometimes called the "collegial" approach. Does our new understanding of the church as the body of Christ demand leadership by consensus? If so, how do we avoid such pitfalls as the corporate loss of imagination, the tendency to panic and to develop high anxiety, strength given to extremists who can hold the group hostage, the danger of developing cultic tendencies, and so on. Friedman offers an alternative which he calls "self-differentiated leadership". I'm not sure I fully understand what he means — or if I do, I'm not all that comfortable with it — but in any case, my experience has been that his warnings about the potential dangers of decision-making by consensus are not without some foundation. Could it be that these sorts of dangers are simply the cost of investing in a community life which is based on unconditional love rather than self-interest? Or are there more creative and effective ways we have not yet discovered to deal with these challenges?

Phina: The real struggle, of course, is to get rid of the worst of hierarchical leadership without getting rid of leadership altogether. I think we need a repertoire of decision-making styles that we can draw from. The style we select in any instance will depend on our cultural context and on the matter at hand calling for a decision. And mutuality, which is our governing principle, does not imply an absolutely flat democracy; it leaves room for those who exercise leadership based on their gifts and the authority they've earned in community.

Go back, for a minute, to our ministering community ordered by mutuality. Areas such as parish communications, administration, education and prayer would all be affected. Newsletters, bulletins, telephone trees and reports would, ideally, reflect the life of many ministering in a variety of contexts, not just in the church building, and as one body. Vestry meetings might be radically different — or even non-existent. (Family-size parishes in Nevada have the option of four congregational meetings per year.) How would various programmatic ministries be coordinated? What would the budget categories look like? How would stewardship of wealth and income be understood and practiced?

What would education look like, and who would set the educational agenda? What would prayer look like in our community? How would the community's prayer life be related to the tasks of discerning and supporting gifts and vocations? How would praying the scriptures be related to active, outward-facing ministry? How would a mutual spirituality, a communal spirituality rooted in the church's lore and the congregation's mission context, take shape and be nurtured?

At a recent meeting of the Council for the Development of Ministry, I was pleased to see that a sense of the importance of community discernment is being incorporated in discussions, particularly of recruitment and selection of people for ordination. Could it be that some of our fringe efforts are influencing national thought and decision-making?

Jim: I think so. This basic principle of mutuality is not the invention of modern day small-church management theorists. It is fundamental to the gospel, and sooner or later any faithful Christian leader is going to feel drawn back to this scriptural understanding of Christian community. People like Wes Frensdorff have offered the whole church a way to get back to our roots, as it were, with regard to restructuring our corporate life as the body of Christ.

But it is easier said than done! So many times we find ourselves heading in the wrong direction. Since we are doing something different from the recent past, we want to be careful about keeping things from getting out of hand. Yet, as long as our agenda is that of creating controls, rather than unleashing the freedom of life in the Spirit, we will be forever creating and reinforcing distinctions and gradations. I have watched some diocesan leaders initiate quite radical total ministry models only to end up spinning their wheels over such questions as who gets to vote at convention, who should and who shouldn't wear clericals, and who is allowed to attend clergy conferences. We have a sad and destructive tendency to drift back into issues of ordination and leadership status. We need instead to keep focused upon matters related to baptism and church *membership*. We keep forgetting that the main arena for ministry is not within the walls of the church but in the midst of daily life, and that the main players are not the clergy (whether imported from the seminaries or ordained indigenously) but all of the baptized. And the sum of this points towards a total reshaping of the life and mission of the church as we have come to know it.

Phina: Clearly "each congregation is to be a ministering community" is a simple statement, easy to assent to, but church-shaking, and if we do it right perhaps world-shaking, in its implications!

II. Each member, a gifted minister

Phina: It's impossible to have talked about the ministering community without also having considered the second principle, the giftedness of every member. How we discern, develop and support each member's giftedness is ministry development in its most universal form. The process of enhancing existing skills, refining them for an ecclesial context, or for use from an ecclesial base, and reflecting on their use in the light of all Christian experience, is what we have usually called theological education.

Jim: As we consider theological education and the development of gifts, it might help to state again that the main arena for ministry is the world. Yet so often in ministry development circles, we become preoccupied with questions of in-house ministry. When you talk with any group of Christians about baptismal ministry, it is not uncommon for them to assume you are discussing who will preach, who will visit Aunt Bessie in the nursing home, and who will counsel Fred and Gladys when their marriage is falling apart. This should hardly be surprising to us, since we have for so long equated "ministry" with the paid priest who has concentrated much time, skill and energy on this sort of agenda. Even in a diocese such as Northern Michigan which has been *very* careful to focus on adult Christian responsibility in the midst of life, as our covenant groups complete their preparations to be commissioned as ministry support teams, we are still finding people who consider the team to be for *delivery* rather than *support* of the ministry of all the baptized, and to be engaged primarily in in-house responsibilities.

Phina: This makes me wonder — have we really caught on to the fact that talking about gifts in ministry is not just this year's Lenten program? Too many people have been frustrated by attending a church program to identify their gifts, then attending another program where they learn a bit about scripture and church history and how to reflect theologically, and then never having their gifts, knowledge, or ministry recognized by their congregations again. We've got to get serious about the fact that respecting the gifts of all our members is an ongoing process. We put far too much emphasis on education as a way of getting permission to use one's gifts, and almost no emphasis on deploying gifts in response to opportunities, giving an account of how we're using our gifts, and continuing to challenge and enhance our gifts throughout our lifetimes. Could this just possibly be a hangover from preparation for church careers or residential presbyteral formation where there's been front end loading of pre-ordination education, and far too little emphasis on lifelong vocational development and continuing education? If so, then we still don't have a theology of ministry rooted in the intersection of gifts and opportunity, but one that sees all ministry as derivative of the traditional parochial, pastoral, presbyteral role.

Jim: I couldn't agree more that we have not yet effectively connected "gift" with action for most adult Christians. I have led and participated in numerous gift discernment workshops, yet I always seem to go away frustrated. There's a good deal of affirming and supportive talk, but I'm never convinced that participants have had something click for them in such a way that they are led to a renewed sense of their own involvement in God's work of redemption. "Gosh, I guess I'm not such a loser after all" is an important insight, but we haven't quite gotten to the place where people understand themselves to be engaged in the ministry of reconciliation, servanthood, stewardship, and evangelism.

Phina: We could go on forever talking about the principle of giftedness of all the baptized, but I do want to raise one practical question for ministry developers. I hear, increasingly, comments like these: "When we began our ministry development strategy in the diocese we put too much emphasis on having the right educational materials." or, "If you want a good diaconate program, put the emphasis on the selection of candidates and on their ongoing support and education."

In the congregation, what's the balance between formal educational programs, and informal education, that is, taking advantage of educable moments for small bits of hands-on learning, or topical conversations which are theologically reflective? Have we overvalued having the right program and the right materials, and undervalued creating a climate in which eagerness in learning is a given, and theological reflection a daily habit?

Jim: I think you've really hit on something there. The most effective regional ministry developers are those who almost never work alone. They are always inviting people to go with them to visit the sick, to co-teach some session, or to share in responsibility for this project or that. Walk with me, watch and experience what it's like to be involved in this aspect of our community's life and mission, and then, next time, you'll be ready to try it on your own, and in the meantime as we drive together to the next county, let's reflect on the theological implications of what's happening. A simple technique, yet so often our method has been to talk and talk about Christian ministry in the abstract, never getting out of the workshop setting.

I have always looked to that moment in Jesus' ministry when he turned to the seventy and sent them out, two by two, to visit the towns and villages before him. He was prepared to treat his followers as mature and responsible adults who could be entrusted with responsibility for carrying on his work. He knew that they would learn the necessary skills as they went, and he was prepared to risk everything by putting into the hands of the uneducated and inexperienced even the most important of missional tasks. But you notice that he sent them out two by two. By working together, mistakes were minimized, and the opportunities for balance and corrective measures were greatly enhanced.

This illustrates how central to the life and ministry of Jesus was the creation of a ministering community. His intent was not to credential a collection of individual ministers, but to give birth to an organic corporate body, which would regenerate and grow by drawing into itself new members who would themselves participate in the missional task entrusted to the whole. And the only way it could work would be for each member to discover his or her unique set of gifts and to use them generously for the welfare of the entire community.

III. Seminary-trained personnel as support and resource people

Phina: As I've worked with these principles, I've come to see that the third one is less a principle than a strategy for transitional change. When we started out, it looked like a principle, but with almost a generation behind us, it now looks like a stage in total ministry development. It assumes that what's right for the transitional generation, i.e., those who embrace total ministry as a concept and take the first steps toward making it a reality, will also be right for subsequent generations. We have learned that there are those among that first generation who themselves have the potential to be ministry developers. They've caught the vision and they have the gifts to strengthen others in ministry. Will they be relegated to the position of volunteer ministry developers, of helpers of the "real" ministry developers who have seminary degrees; or will we have the courage to re-think our categories and recognize that we may have stumbled onto that which was our Roland Allen-esque goal —a truly self-propagating church which can raise up, not para-leaders and para-professionals, but true leadership for the future?

Jim: For me, that's the most exciting challenge of the adventure. Our task is not to redesign an organizational structure, but to help midwife the birth of a whole new organism. The hardest part for the ministry developer might be the task of stepping aside to allow new leadership to emerge from the midst of the community which until now had been so dependent upon outside support. I suspect most ministry developers would protest: "Are you kidding? That's what we've been working for all along! I live for the day when I can exit from center stage and allow the local community to stand on its own feet." That's what we say, but when it comes down to the day-by-day decision-making process, it's a lot harder than first imagined to allow other people to make different choices than you would have made.

Of course, our model and inspiration is Jesus' own ministry. He did exactly what we are trying to do: hand over to the local community responsibility for its own life and mission. "I no longer call you servants, but friends," he said at the Last Supper, and he was true to his claim. We ministry developers are called to do the same. We are called to invite newcomers into our midst as colleagues. And at times, that will involve not so much a "promotion" of certain individuals to our "status" as an emptying of ourselves and the status with which the institutional church has saddled us.

This points to a distinction which I think is most important for ministry developers to keep in mind. Certainly, most church leaders today would seek to move beyond clericalism, which I would define as an ecclesiology which views the priest as "*the* minister," and all others as passive consumers of ministry. Our first alternative to clericalism is what I would call "team ministry," by which the priest is seen as the *primary* minister, but s/he receives assistance from a select few, hand-picked lay persons who serve together as a ministering team; all others in the community are still passive consumers of ministry. Certainly, this is a positive step, moving away from the one-person show, but it still perpetuates a sense of elitism. The cadre in control will now assume the role once held by the autocratic cleric, and old dependencies will continue to be nurtured.

In contrast to these approaches is what we have come to call total or mutual ministry, which might be defined as an ecclesiology which understands all ministry to be Christ's, with every baptized person as a participant therein, each according to gifts. This is an important shift because it moves the ministry development task away from simply "training" local clergy or even a collection of ministry team members toward an effort to educate entire congregations for adult Christian responsibility.

Phina: My point is that in some ministry development situations we may be running the risk of simply changing the competencies desirable in our paid leadership. Instead of being the doers of all ministry, they will now be the trainers of all ministry, in perpetuity. Dependence is still dependence, no matter its criteria.

Jim: That is so true. I have watched too many clusters and other regional arrangements simply create new patterns of dependence. At the same time, I think that it *can* be legitimate to maintain the role of the regional ministry developer indefinitely as an extension of the episcopate (or, as we would say in Northern Michigan, as a part of the apostolic ministry of oversight and support). In this, I have always turned to the missionary methods of St. Paul for my basic imagery (especially as informed by Schillebeeckx's *The Church With a Human Face*[2]). Leadership on the local level is to be shared and indigenous. Leadership on the more-than-local level is to be shared and itinerant. I don't find a problem with establishing an ongoing relationship between congregations and persons identified as ministry developers. Of course, we will need to continue to work as hard as we can to keep from developing unhealthy dependencies, just as we always will in any setting and in the midst of any series of relationships. And the real key, as you say, is to welcome indigenous leadership into the ranks of the ministry developers, learning to embrace one another's gifts and to grow together into our future.

One thing is certain. There's no way around the increasing demand for regional ministry developers. As more and more dioceses initiate total ministry and regional ministry development efforts, the shortage of experienced, competent persons to serve in leadership roles in these settings is becoming a growing problem.

Phina: Let's talk about some of the things we learned when we surveyed regional ministry developers a few years ago. We can't say that our sample of those who responded was particularly scientific, nor can we say that they were effective ministry developers. We can only say that these were people committed to being ministry developers, since they were comfortable identifying themselves as such, and generally happy with their work despite many stresses and problems. We can, from that group of respondents, say two things about ministry developers. They are, by nature and acquired habit, collegial persons. They like working *with* others, and they tend to make colleagues of those who in a hierarchical scheme would be identified as superiors or inferiors. The second thing is that ministry developers are ongoing learners and reflecters; they have a working theology of church and ministry, and value and foster the ecclesiological enterprise.

It seems to take just the right combination of aggression and serendipity to be educated as a ministry developer. A course here, a book there, and a mentor over there — all in the context of learning from those among whom one ministers. There were, at the time of our survey, a few curacies and internships in ministry development sponsored by dioceses, but these were the only intentional efforts to develop the skills for ministry development which our church increasingly seeks in its professionals.

Jim: Our track record in trying to work with seminaries to revise curriculum, initiate internships, and create helpful continuing education opportunities for this purpose has left us frustrated beyond words.

Phina: Isn't it too easy to look to the seminaries for help? This is a ministry development concern, and that means it's a challenge to the whole system, the church, not just the seminaries.

Jim: You bet. Internships and curacies need to be initiated by dioceses themselves. Of course one of the challenges we face is that it may be the smaller dioceses with the least number of resources who most need these sorts of programs and who, in some cases at least, may have the most to offer potential interns and curates. It will be important to identify and tap potential sources for outside funding as needed.

We also need to recognize that there are internal struggles for those who would be ministry developers. Again, the virus is within us.

Phina: I think the growing literature on addiction and related behaviors in organizations may hold further clues to what a ministry developer is and is not. Clearly a person who works with others so that they can claim their own gifts and authority and begin to work in adult, mutual and interdependent ways has the opposite traits to the co-dependent we find so often among the clergy, other church workers and other helping professionals. To help in such a way as to perpetuate dependency is what most clergy have been asked to do. To smooth things over so that the outward appearance is One Big Happy Family is an expectation we have of most bishops and presbyters. To put personal approval ahead of risking the changes that could bring about a church in mission which truly practices what it preaches is an easy sin to commit. This is not just somebody's fault; it's everybody's fault. We face a systemic problem which is reinforced on the one hand by the behaviors that we learn early on in most of our families, and on the other hand by societal norms which scream loudly of the behaviors which support addiction.

Jim: The desire to be successful at those institutional tasks of membership recruitment, group motivation, and conflict avoidance is a driving force in the hearts of those of us who have been socialized by generations of role models and countless numbers of subtle (and sometimes not so subtle) rewards and punishments doled out to the career cleric by the establishment. I find the metaphor of the addictive system to be really helpful. The first of the twelve steps, of course, is a personal surrender; an acknowledgement of one's powerlessness. This is a deeply personal and spiritual step, and I really do believe that if one is to serve as a ministry developer, there has to be a level of spiritual depth and maturity which allows for self-examination and self-transformation. We have to be willing to confront ourselves and to challenge ourselves to change. I don't know how you talk about this without sounding preachy or moralistic.

Phina: I suspect one way to avoid preachiness is not to get stuck pushing recovery programs as the solution to every problem, but to remember this is one model which helps understanding and healing. We need to remember that ministry development starts with God-given strengths. This holds for developing professionals in ministry just as it does for our work in congregations.

Another item I would like to flag is the warring over scarce resources that inhibits the collegiality necessary to effective ministry development.

Jim: Warring over scarce resources not only inhibits collegiality; it also badly distorts the agenda for any ministry development effort. Ministry development is not a cost-cutting gimmick.

Phina: Then there's the fact that the press of conflicting demands arising from many notions of what the church (read *the clergy*) should be leaves precious little time in the lives of our leaders for intentional reflection and planning where we really ought to focus our energies. This is especially true for those ministry developers who work in a transitional situation. They must juggle two sets of expectations. One we might call the traditional pastoral expectations of parochial clergy; the other, the emerging expectations of ministry developers. The juggling act can collapse, and the ministry developer is stuck as the supposedly omni-competent person around whom the church's life revolves.

Jim: I think things begin to move when ministry developers themselves live and work out of a collegial model. There is such strength in mutual support; it establishes a solid foundation for everything that happens. Ministry developers learn from one another when they teach and consult in teams, and when they gather for regular collegial review and feedback. They learn even more when they open themselves up to receive input from the members of congregations as well. It is only by working together that new images can be forged for the church of the coming century.

Phina: I guess the last thing I want to say about this, at least now, is that those of us who have made the transition from self-selected providers of ministry to developers of ministry under the discipline of Christian community need to share our stories of transition.

When I began my work in ministry development, I took to heart the words of Bill Gordon, retired bishop of Alaska, who said the first thing you must train people to do is that thing you love most, never the thing you didn't want to do anyway. So, I set about trying to encourage teaching, trying to empower those without formal residential theological education to teach other adults, trying to grow a second generation of teachers. Then comes that moment when someone you have trained handles a teaching situation better than you could have; when someone you've trained is more sensitive to the needs and questions of learners than you were; when a learning community begins to set its own agenda without a prod or a process from you. It takes all the grace God can give to become a participant in a learning community rather than the expert. Yet this was the transition I was called to make to help fulfill the vision of an interdependent ministering community. If congregations are to become less dependent on seminary-trained folk as doers of ministry, then seminary-trained folk must learn how to receive ministry and grow in interdependence, even as far as recognizing that those with whom they minister may have gifts in teaching, enabling and supervising.

IV. *The diocese as the primary unit of interdependence and as the support system.*

Jim: The first time I learned in any detail about what was going on in Nevada was as late as 1984, when I read the CRW Management report, *Living Out the Vision*.[3] At the time, I was serving in a small New England diocese which was struggling with many of the same challenges of increasing fiscal demands in the face of rapidly declining resources, as was Nevada. One day at a mission planning meeting, when I brought up ideas from the report I had read, the bishop leaned over the table and stated firmly, "We're not Nevada, Jim!" and that was the end of the discussion.

I suspect that my experience was not unique. For many years, diocesan leaders watched the creative efforts of Wes Frensdorff and others in Nevada with detached curiosity if not downright suspicion. It's not hard to find reasons why such bold and innovative experimentation might be justified in those far off places such as Alaska and Nevada and Utah without allowing the insights gained there to raise questions about the *modus operandi* of mission work back on the homefront.

But over the past half decade or so, things have changed rather dramatically. Those basic concepts of the mutual responsibility of all the baptized to support the life and mission of the church have been taken more seriously every year in an increasing number of dioceses across the country. Bishops and mission commissions in virtually every diocese of the church are now confronted with many of the symptoms which stimulated innovative thinking in Alaska and Nevada two or three decades ago, and in many places diocesan leaders are now beginning to say, "We may not be Nevada, but we're not what we used to be either." And for the first time, many more mission planners are ready to look at the Nevada experience as one of the more helpful reservoirs for learning.

Phina: I've worked with a lot of different dioceses who have begun to be receptive to new directions in ministry. I've concluded that most diocesan structures and staffs resemble fire companies. Some are highly professional; others are like rural volunteer fire companies. Some diocesan structures and staffs may be so progressive as to be in the fire insurance business; while others seem to be centered on providing relief and first aid to survivors of serious fires. Very few could be likened to fire prevention programs.

Yet it may be that the implication of the fourth principle is that dioceses aren't in the fire business at all, but are themselves ministering communities, practicing interdependence and mutuality between congregations, and between each congregation and diocesan staffs and structures. Such a transformed view of a diocese's identity and purpose would lead to overwhelming changes. First, the diocese would need to begin with the assumption that each congregation is uniquely gifted in mission and for ministry. Instead of putting the emphasis on congregations in trouble or in transition for diocesan staff attention, dioceses would need to pay attention to all congregations and how their unique opportunities and strengths could be developed.

Jim: Again, it's a question of learning how to build on our strengths instead of harping on our weaknesses; to respond to and to support people's competence instead of simply trying to "fix" their incompetence.

This touches on another important issue. Those of us who have been engaged in total ministry development over the past few decades have taken as our starting point the existing "mission field" as it has been handed down to us by those who first gathered Episcopalians in our part of the world. If some eager archdeacon started visiting a small lumbering town or a farming community a century or so ago, thereby initiating a worshipping community, and some remnant of that group still remains, we feel a moral imperative to keep it going at any cost. And that, so often, is the starting point for our mission strategy. "How are we going to keep those poor little places out there from going under?" I do not intend to be cynical, but I do want to raise this question.

So far, our total ministry development efforts have been directed toward the goal of transforming existing congregations from communities gathered around a minister into ministering communities. Should we at some point be getting more serious about initiating new worshipping communities which embrace total ministry as their normative ecclesiology, not of economic necessity, but out of choice? I realize that this has been attempted in certain isolated settings, but what would it mean for a diocese to shift its agenda from that of sustaining and/or resuscitating dying congregations to that of sowing the seeds for whole new expressions of Christian community? We have much to learn from the base Christian communities of the Third World. Of course, new forms of worshipping communities and traditional congregations do not have to be mutually exclusive.

We can indeed continue to be faithful in our efforts to invite the existing congregations of our dioceses to explore and discover for themselves new and more appropriate ways to be the church in their place at this time in human history, and at the same time become more creative in our efforts to initiate new communities. The problem is that most dioceses are failing to do this. We are using total ministry development as a way of "dealing with" small struggling congregations, while still clinging fast to the familiar priest-centered ecclesiology in those new work efforts in the suburbs and urban settings which offer promise of institutional growth and stability. What would happen to a diocese that might direct its focus not upon church growth (in the categories of the three Bs: bodies, bucks, and bricks), but rather invest its resources in the broader agenda of total ministry development: that of extending and strengthening ministering communities?

Phina: One of the congregations where I served in Nevada was a new one, founded on total ministry principles. I wouldn't have traded the opportunity to be a part of a congregation where people can challenge one another toward growth in ministry. But we kept coming up against your evaluating criteria of the three Bs, which frustrate our work as a ministering community.

Before we get carried away on issues of what diocesan staffs could initiate, though, let's step back a moment. Truly transformational change will need to be initiated by both the bishop and other diocesan leadership and by leadership in the congregations. Diocesan programs and projects, I believe, need to arise in response to the goals and needs of each parish for education in ministry, consultation, support, and linkage. It can't just be the diocese wreaking transformational change on the parishes. The diocese has to be transformed into a ministering community, articulating its vision of ministry and allowing its structures and ways of doing business to be transformed in fulfillment of that vision.

We have some clues to what's involved in diocesan change from the experience of a handful of dioceses that have embraced total ministry; changes may mean such things as developing truly collegial working teams, rather than the more customary structure of committees setting policy and staff carrying it out (or sabotaging it). This requires a considerable investment of time.

Jim: I couldn't agree more. The development of truly collegial working teams needs to take place at all levels. If the bishop and other diocesan leaders are not working hard at this, how can we expect anyone else in the diocese to take it seriously? It's a lot easier to spot control mechanisms, manipulation, and authoritarian tendencies in others than it is within yourself, and yet we all manifest these behaviors. The question is not whether or not you manifest them, but how honest and self-reflective you can be about identifying them and making yourself change your own behavior.

Phina: Some other changes which may need to happen are:
- having a commission on ministry which takes seriously its canonical charge to plan for the future ministry needs of the diocese, rather than simply reacting and screening.

- having a bishop who spends time articulating a plan and a strategy, and, in the meantime, lets some fires burn themselves out and resists pouring water on grease fires.

- having a bishop and other leaders who are willing to stick with a strategy for the generation of change that 's required, rather than having renewal in ministry be this year's diocesan theme.

Jim: That last point is vital. I think this is the incredible gift of Wes Frensdorff, because he really gave his life to ministry development; for him, it *wasn't* just a short-lived tactic to accomplish institutional equilibrium.

Phina: We've talked about redeploying professional clergy who work with aided congregations. But we also need to note that just as total ministry congregations will need to question business as usual, so will total ministry dioceses. If the budget and reporting and communication systems of the diocese haven't been re-thought, probably not much change in the congregations will be sustained and supported.

And since I dared to mention budget. . . When all of this is set in the context of the financial situation of most dioceses — that they have increasingly fewer real dollars to work with — it begins to seem like dreaming the impossible dream. The good news is that while many feared that strengthening congregations as ministering communities would weaken interdependence and the diocese as a unit, quite the reverse has happened in dioceses that have tried it with deliberateness and consistency. Developing a diocese as ministering community does require an intensive input of time on the part of many people, staff and volunteers, and it requires a systemic, thoughtful, strategic approach; but it does not necessarily mean a greatly increased bottom line.

Jim: That's important for diocesan leaders to understand from the outset. If the motivation for total ministry development is to enhance the fiscal stature of the institution, there will no doubt be disappointment somewhere down the road. But if the intent is to provide a whole new framework for building up the body to pursue its mission, there could be no more promising approach. This, of course, implies something far more than a passing commitment to a so-called "experimental" program.

I have recently been exposed for the first time to the world of computers and word processing, and as I have learned about it, an analogy has come to mind. I believe that too many times people think of total ministry development as if it were one more software program for the computer. In fact, it's the Disk Operating System (DOS) that makes the other programs work and communicate with the rest of the system.

Phina: When total ministry began to take shape as a diocesan-wide strategy in the Diocese of Nevada, one rector of a large parish was heard to comment, after listening to several of Wes' sermons, "Last year all we heard was world hunger; this year it's ministry,

ministry, ministry. . . ." How wrong he was to think that "ministry" would go away (or world hunger, for that matter, which continued to be a concern for Wes and many others in the diocese)! Total ministry is not just a way of renewing or retooling one department of the church's life; it has implications for every department and facet, and leaves no business as usual unchallenged. The structures and patterns of each congregation, the life of every gifted baptized person, including those with leadership responsibilities, and the meaning and role of the diocese — all are called to radical transformation, to be the church in mission.

Notes

1. Edwin Friedman, *Generation to Generation.* (New York: Guilford Press, 1985), Chapter 9.

2. Edward Schillebeeckx, *The Church with a Human Face* (New York: The Crossroad Publishing Company, 1985).

3. CRW Management Services, *Living Out the Vision; an evaluation of Nevada's total ministry program.* (Arvada, CO: Jethro Publications, 1983).

Chapter 14

AUTHORITY AND
THE THEOLOGICAL ENTERPRISE:
An Invitation to Dialogue

Frensdorff and Colleagues

In October 1987, Wesley Frensdorff circulated a paper — four pages of notes actually — titled Exploring the Theological Enterprise *to a few close associates. The paper consisted of a series of questions concerning a future desirable state of the 'enterprise' under four headings: 1) the ongoing study of scripture, its meaning (theology) and action(mission); 2) theological education (education for all Christians); 3) leadership development; and 4) the seminaries as theological resource centers. As the paper was circulated shortly after the publication of* Challenge for Change, *it seemed that he might be beginning to stir the pot for a new challenge — this time in the area of theologizing and education. Given the time and perhaps the stimulation of dialogue with others — Wes' usual method of conceptualizing — he might have come up with a new section to the*

Frensdorff dream. But time was not to be given.

However, it did not seem right to simply let it go. In February 1990, we took the paper to the Sindicators meeting and asked members — all reasonably familiar with Wes Frensdorff's thinking — to respond to it. We came out of that meeting with a substantial stack of notes from small group sessions. From there we decided to keep the dialogue going via a continuing circulation of notes among interested people, not because we felt competent to answer the questions, but because we thought the questions too important to ignore. So it is that the contributors to this chapter are many: members of Sindicators, members of the editorial board and others. This synthesis was prepared by Phina Borgeson, Steve Kelsey and Chuck Wilson. The chapter is not, in any sense, a final product. It is a moment in a conversation that continues. The pot still needs stirring.

-Eds.

I n the Pioche story (Chapter 10), it was noted that one of the concerns before the church in Nevada in 1983 was the suspicion that theologizing or theological reflection was the domain of the professionals. Somehow it must be set free. Ministry isn't *total* ministry if 1% of the ministers hold priesthood and diaconate captive — nor if they control theologizing. It may be that the 1987 Frensdorff paper had its roots in those 1983 evaluation sessions. If so, and even if not so, the underlying theme in the questions put forth by Wes in 1987 would appear to be power and authority. With this as a premise, let us begin with a little background before picking up the Frensdorff challenge.

In 1976 a committee report, *Changing Patterns of the Church's Ministry in the 1970s* (subsequently referred to as the Krumm Report, after the committee chair, Bishop John Krumm, Southern Ohio), was reviewed by the General Convention of the Episcopal Church. The concern of the report was the rising number of aspirants for ordination then being processed through diocesan schools instead of through accredited seminaries. It sounded the alarm; perhaps as many as one-third of our new ordinands would soon be products of non-traditional academic preparation.

The Krumm Report set forth the committee's conviction that for the foreseeable future the principal mode of ordained ministry in the Episcopal Church would continue to be the ministries of those in full-time parish positions and that the standard preparation would be the full three-year program of an accredited seminary. The main concern before convention at this point was with education for ordained ministry and the perceived threat to the seminaries as standard setters for excellence in academic preparation and formation. The convention called for further study. And the seminaries rallied in an attempt to tighten the canonical standards.

Three years later the Rev. Richard Kirk, on behalf of the Board for Theological Education, prepared a new report, *Paths to Ministry: Some Alternatives in Theological Education.* It was largely based on a survey of diocesan schools and other non-seminary programs, and was presented to the 1979 convention. In the meantime David Cochran, then bishop of Alaska, Wes Frensdorff and others had gathered their forces to defend Title III Canon 8 (the canon, sometimes broadly interpreted, under which most local training programs for ordination operated — and the target of the seminaries).

The Kirk Report, however, dispelled a lot of the fear. The agenda of the local training programs was found to be BIG; training for local ordained personnel was only part of it. The vision of total ministry was driving it. And the need for professionally trained, paid personnel had not diminished. However, the changing role of the full-time professionals was not noticed. The job was growing in scope and changing in substance. Full-time parochial jobs were beginning to give way to various kinds of regional or diocesan positions in support of parochial ministries. And an increasingly larger percentage of ordinations consisted of people taking on *volunteer* ordained ministries. There were signs that the Krumm Report norm of full-time professionally trained people in parochial positions was beginning to erode, but they were largely ignored.

The Kirk Report went on to discuss issues of quality control, accountability, sharing of resources and spiritual formation. Accountability in the seminaries tends to be a matter of mutual accountability within the teaching profession, as distinct from accountability to the client dioceses. Seminaries are independent. Accountability in the diocesan schools is clearly to the diocese. Thus, while seminaries may be relatively insulated from diocesan influence, local schools may be insulated from each other and subject to local bias and fad — a situation that could result in very different kinds of ministry from diocese to diocese.

In any case, Title III Canon 8 survived, and Title III would subsequently be revised, clarified and strengthened, much better to reflect a vision of total ministry and the normalcy of the ordination of local presbyters and deacons. Today there are all kinds of local education and training programs in the field, but questions of role, authority and relationships remain.

During the years of the Krumm and Kirk reports and right up to the present, another deployment question has dogged us: the question of clergy surplus or shortage which has been used (depending on one's view) to justify aggressive recruitment programs or moratoriums on accepting new aspirants. In fact, the number of full-time clergy jobs in the domestic dioceses of the Episcopal Church has been running in the range of 6,200-6,400 over the past 10 years with hardly any discernable trend. There are, additionally, some 2,000 non-parochial/diocesan jobs — so around 8,300 jobs receiving a full year's credit with the Church Pension Fund in an average year. However, when we include local clergy, retired personnel, those in non-church jobs and everybody else, there are over 15,000 ordained people. Some move in and out of church employment depending on opportunities or sense of vocation. In any case, the total pool of ordained personnel is large and growing. Bishop Alexander Stewart, vice-president of the Church Pension Fund, concludes in his study of these data, that there is no shortage except, perhaps, of people willing to accept a call to "undesirable" locations or in situations with insufficient resources to cover a salary.[1]

It takes around 230 ordinations a year to cover deaths and retirements — a figure we greatly exceed. Thus it might be argued that there is a surplus, but this is no problem unless we assume that the purpose of the church is to guarantee jobs for ordained people.

What *has* changed significantly over this period is (as noted above) the scope of the average job. In 1974 the average full-time job was associated with a parochial base of:

> 126 people in church on Sunday;
> $39,000 in general purposes income;
> $12,800 salary (stipend and housing).

Today the figures are (estimated):

> 180 people in church on Sunday (+43%);
> $139,000 general purposes income (+49% after inflation);
> $38,800 salary (+26% after inflation).

For the able rector who has, over these 16 years, gone from a $39,000 parish to a $139,000 parish, it is clear that the job today is much larger, better paid, and it is a different kind of job — a program church, not a pastoral church. But the total picture is much more complex. Back in '74, a large percentage of employed clergy were actually serving as rector of an (on average) $39,000 congregation. *Today at least 75% of our congregations are no longer able to employ a full-time presbyter.* So every year an increasing proportion of those 6,200-6,400 professionally trained people are finding their way into various positions of support services for local clergy and lay leaders. And we may see the day when *most* seminary-trained people end up as professors in diocesan programs, consultants, regional archdeacons, etc. — as we say, a trend not picked up in the Kirk Report, apparently not noticed by seminaries today, but quite obvious to Wes and others years ago.

Out of something like this background, Wes Frensdorff, in 1987 set forth a list of questions then on his mind. We turn now to those questions.

I.   Ongoing study of the scriptures, its meaning (theology) and action (mission)

Frensdorff: Who does the theologizing and where does it happen? How do theology and tradition develop? What is the ecumenical dimension? What part do theological and historical research and scholarship have in it? (What are the ingredients — research? writing? for whom? How is scholarship disseminated: publication? lectures? to whom?) How is it all funded?

The fundamental concern here is trying to make sense out of life — trying to understand our beliefs concerning meaning, purpose, life, eternity, God. If we have a sense of direction, a place to go, a ministry to perform, we have purpose. Pursuing that direction within a framework of recognized values beyond ourselves contributes a sense of morality and meaning. Working out such matters in our own minds and in dialogue with others is theologizing, or theological reflection. So considered, we have to assume that everyone, by virtue of human self-consciousness, engages in the theological enterprise. You, me, St. Paul, Shirley McLaine, old folk, kids, philosophers and peasants. For some of us the dialogue called theological reflection consciously (and maybe even scholarly) engages voices out of scripture and church tradition. The process seems to be at least partly a function of community or group life: a base Christian community, an EFM group, a seminary or a parish — again, settings in which the voices of scripture and tradition are brought into dialogue to help inform thinking on contemporary life issues.

One of the questions directed to diocesan and other grassroots programs in ministry education has been, "What will happen if we don't have learned clergy?" Part of the Episcopal Church's self-concept is a belief that we value great learning in our leaders and open wrestling with difficult questions. This may indeed be a mark of the Anglican Communion, but so is indigeneity. At critical points in the history of the church in England we see a commitment to developing local leadership and respecting indigenous culture. In the sweep of the Reformation we see worship in the people's language valued, and a commitment to accessibility and familiarity with scripture for all the faithful.

Total ministry has stressed the ministering community as fundamental. The handmaiden of a ministering community is a theologically reflective community, knowledgeable in its basic traditions. To put it simply: instead of a community gathered around a minister, a ministering community; instead of a community gathered around a learned person (parson), a learned and reflecting community.

The calling of local persons, primarily volunteer, to leadership positions is not an anti-intellectual movement, because that calling is set in the context of a community whose biblical literacy and capacity for theological reflection are improved and enhanced. Thus the Anglican value placed on reason, knowledge and inquiry is upheld, at the same time that the Anglican value of indigeneity is recovered.

If theologizing is everybody's business, inclination, need or right, the question can't be "Who does it?" or "Where does it happen?" but rather, "Who authenticates, censures, codifies, approves?" It is a question of leadership or authority. The Frensdorff questions could be interpreted to imply a sequence in the theological enterprise something like this. 1) Scholarly innovation: The professors study the sources and come up with new insights. 2) Testing: Papers are published in journals for other professionals to read and critique. 3) Permission (or canonical provision): New ideas gaining credibility among the scholars are translated into books, new canons, liturgies or courses for popular consumption or experimentation. 4) Delivery: Something goes into the field. It is an ongoing process of interpretation, translation and application of gospel truths once received.

However, the questions could imply a different sequence, something like this. 1) Historic event: Something happens because of a crisis, new possibilities, or combination of factors, and action is precipitated (the Exodus). 2) Interpretation: People try to make sense of it in retrospect; they theologize about it, they tell their children about it and, in time, a standard interpretation — a story — emerges (the book: Exodus). 3) Celebration: Liturgies are created to re-enact the event, and remember. 4) It is a tradition, part of a new community consciousness contributing to new interpretations of events and responses in action. It is a process of discovering gospel truths in contemporary experience.

Actually, of course, both processes are in use. Scholars, delving ever more deeply into scripture and tradition, are providing us with tremendous new insights about the formative period of our faith. And action in the field, in confronting new realities, is generating new reflection, theory, story and tradition.

Both are needed, legitimate, and they are interdependent. But who is "authorized" — has a right — to do which? Is one sequence superior (more basic or legitimate) than the other? If so, does that mean that the "superior" one is, therefore, "authorized" to pass judgment on the product of the other, but not vice versa? At first glance it might seem that the scholar engages in the former process and the minister in the field in the latter. But we can't leave it at that, each isolated from the other, not informing each other, at loggerheads and not interdependent.

Edward Schillebeeckx,[2] considering the relationship between practice (of ministry) and theological reflection, says that "practice must never wait for the permission of the theologians." Practice, whether right or wrong, proceeds from faith. Then comes critical theological review, to test in light of scripture, tradition and practical need whether the practice be justified. The process presupposes Christian community which is, "in fact the sphere in which theology is born." . . . "However, we would have an ideology if theology were put *directly*, i.e., without the mediation of hermeneutics and in accordance with its own laws, laws in this sense independent of all practice — at the service of practice . . . ." But who is the theologian? Schillebeeckx seems to assume that the scholar or professional is the theologian. Even at that "the theologian does not have the last word here," but has a special contribution to make in the formation of what might be called the "consensus of believers" which is eventually expressed in such ways as canonical revision.

So the scholar can't be effective when isolated from the community in action, and other "believers seeking consensus" must also be theologians. In fact, that we are all theologians is an Anglican heritage — a central theme of Fredrica Harris Thompsett's book, *We Are Theologians*.[3]

Questions of stewardship also are related to questions of authority and leadership. If we believe that theology is the work of the community of believers, how are our dollars, time and energies being used to act on that belief?

We look back wistfully to a church where the catechumenate involved three years of study, and a person with needed gifts of leadership might be called from among the catechumens and ordained deacon (or even bishop) immediately following baptism. The catechumenate is being recovered, but is at most a six-month or one year part-time process, while the majority of those ordained do three years of full-time study. The total cost to the system of one year of full-time seminary study is pushing $20,000. What average sized Episcopal parish has $20,000 a year to spend on the part-time education of 100-200 ministers, even taking into account a portion of the salaried leaders' time?

In defense of the status quo, we assume that there is a trickle down effect, and that some of that expensive seminary education is being shared with the local theologians. Yet it seems a rare presbyter or bishop who gives serious time to her/his role as teacher. And if they do, many stop at imparting facts, concepts and opinions, rather than modeling theological reflection as integral to all of Christian life. That stopping short may be due, in part, because few seminary-trained professionals do theological reflection well. When a conference design includes provision for a "professional theologian" who will "help us reflect theologically on what we are about," odds are that what comes out in the theologian's meditations was prepared beforehand, not drawn out of the conference.

Another authority/leadership question concerns how we measure progress — or, as industry would put it — maintain quality control. The Frensdorff questions cry out for some kind of opened, expanded or revised evaluation base. We have seen a big shift in VISION of ministry and education — obvious in this very volume. In some places the vision has been formed into goals, objectives and strategies. These action plans surely must contain, or at least imply or point to, the evaluation criteria. If what we seek is the support and authentication of all baptized people in their ministries, the evaluation of the strategy must be against the end product: the confidence and behavior of Christian people in their ability to think and act theologically. But we haven't done that. Instead we seem to have a compulsion to evaluate the *educational component* of the total strategy with seminary criteria: grades, degrees, accreditation processes, etc., presupposing departmentalized curricula and "justifying" the local schools.

And why this almost exclusive attention to education? Are we neglecting other matters of ministry support such as structuring, deployment, innate gifts, performance review and other means of authenticating or empowering ministry so that, finally, it is the test passed, degree earned or license granted — not baptism — that authorizes one for ministry in the Lord's name? Are we unwittingly sending the message that education is the basis for authority in ministry, rather than the means of enhancement for particular functions in ministry? If so, educators become the power brokers in ministry, and education, with its standards, hoops, licenses and all the rest, may, in the final analysis, be a block to ministry.

Can we, then, stand up to the challenges:
* To quit thinking of the seminary as the norm for Christian education (instead of one of the resources) and get basic education for all the baptized back to the center of the church's agenda (as with the catechumenate in the early church)?
* To develop program evaluation criteria and procedures — not copied from academia, nor based on doubts about the legitimacy of

local programs, but truly related to program goals that insure effective, confident, theologically sophisticated Christians in ministry in the world?

* To encourage bishops who take seriously the teaching and theologizing aspects of their office, presbyters who work to build up learning and reflecting communities, and deacons who support the laity in engaging theological and ethical issues in the wider community?

* To learn to collaborate among many centers of influence with diverse strengths and approaches, in addressing the theological enterprise, in an environment in which the power to determine the nature and scope of theological education is more dispersed?

II. Theological Education

Frensdorff: What is included in theological education for the whole church? How is the whole church enabled in its theologizing? (Who does it: the theologizing, the enabling? Where does it happen? How is it resourced? How is it supported?) How does education take place? (What are the prevalent educational theories? How are these applied to the church? local communities? congregations/dioceses? special communities? Who are the teachers and how are they taught what and how to teach?) How is the "product" of the theologizing enterprise, including theological scholarship and research, "delivered" to the church's theological education process? How can "theological centers" be effective resources to the church in this process? Are theological scholars the best teachers?

There is a desperation about theological education in today's church that is most disturbing. Despite the rhetoric about empowering all the members, and the benefits of a theologically astute laity, most of our attention focuses on the preparation of candidates for ordination. Thus real authority is limited to those who make it through three years of a traditional seminary program.

Theological education is seen, essentially, as preparing candidates for priesthood, with the understanding that some of them, some day, will be our bishops. This presents some significant political concerns. It colors decisions about who is educated, by whom, and in what manner — in short, about who has power and how that power is wielded. It influences maintenance of the institutional church we know, including staying within the familiar boxes of *educating* aspirants for ordination and *training* members for "church work." We seem afraid to explore new ways of living, ministering and witnessing as a faith community in a rapidly changing world.

As long as "theological education" is concerned primarily with the making of priests and bishops, it will continue to be turned inward toward institutional concerns. Deacons, who are largely ignored in this preoccupation, direct the mission focus of the church beyond the walls — the places where 99% of the members live and move and have their being. If ministry is really being done at the supermarket, YMCA, corporate headquarters and the dentist's office, what happens to the power and authority of the ordained leader whose work is centered in the institutional church?

The great fear on the part of many priests is that their clout, as well as their jobs, will diminish; no one will listen to them and they will have little to do. They will not be esteemed. The truth is that empowering others does *not* reduce one's own power. It also means, however, that the traditional ways of being the parochial leader don't work well anymore. "Father" or "Mother" isn't the only preacher, teacher, pastor or counselor. Rather, Jim or Sarah is pretty busy supporting a whole host of people engaged in these ministries. They do their priestly ministries, of course, but in a new atmosphere of collegiality rather than hierarchy. And *everyone* teaches and learns.

What if "theological education" in our church were geared toward nurturing lifelong learners rather than focusing on qualified candidates? What if we were primarily concerned, not with formation of candidates for ordination, but with the formation of the baptized to live out their vows? We could take the current practice of

call > education and discernment > ordination > ministry

and turn it into

ministry and education > call and discernment > ordination >
education and ministry.

Perhaps then we would find theological education in pursuit of a broader agenda, while still concerned with preserving and proclaiming the memory of who we have been as church. We might also be concerned with who we and the world for which Christ died are becoming.

Consider the questions asked of baptismal candidates, and then renewed by the whole community, baptism after baptism (*BCP* p. 304f):

Will you continue in the apostles' teaching and fellowship, in the breaking of bread, and in the prayers?

Will you persevere in resisting evil, and, whenever you fall into sin, repent and return to the Lord?

Will you proclaim by word and example the good news of God in Christ?

These are the areas in which most priests are well trained, and thus are the themes taught to children in most conventional church education programs. (Most religious education in our church is directed at children, culminating in a confirmation ritual which establishes an adolescent level of theologizing as the norm for adults.) But what of the next two questions?

Will you seek and serve Christ in all persons, loving your neighbor as yourself?

Will you strive for justice and peace among all people, and respect the dignity of every human being?

These are the areas where deacons' leadership is focused. The vows call for baptismal candidates to be more than contributing members of the church. We are being invited as well to grow into our calling to be contributing members of God's mission in Christ: *"to restore all people to unity with God and each other in Christ"* (BCP, p. 855).

Now, when we begin to talk seriously about who we are as "the church sent out" ("Let us go forth into the world . . ."), the institutionally preoccupied get nervous. Most conventional "theological" study programs steer away from these concerns because they are not in the areas of expertise of those "trained" conventionally by the church. Thus, laity seldom encounter in the church an opportunity to reflect eagerly upon their lives and general human experience in light of stories and passages from scripture, history and personal encounter with God.

We *can* dream of a church, as Wes Frensdorff did (Chapter 1) "in which every congregation is free to call forth from its midst priests and deacons, sure in the knowledge that training and support services are available to back them up; in which members, not dependent on professionals, know what's what and who's who in the Bible. . . a church *without all the answers, but asking the right questions."*

What would a church in pursuit of this sort of theological education look like?

Perhaps we would be a church in which it is understood that all of us are lifelong learners, that no one small group possesses all the answers which they impart to others, but together we seek answers to a wide variety of questions and concerns — and even ask new questions. In this church all the baptized are educated for ministry in their own life situations, within the life of the church, and through the life of the church. Together with other Christians, we share the gospel, help persons in need, shape and change society through public service and citizen involvement, all the while reflecting upon this adventure with others similarly engaged in their local praying community.

Young women and men, awakening to a sense of vocation with all the abundant energy and zeal which so often accompanies this discovery, would not automatically be whisked away to seminary to be "formed and trained." Instead they would exercise their baptismal ministry in the community of the faithful in which the vocation was heard, where elders share their religious experience with younger brothers and sisters, and the story is interpreted not merely as informing who we are as church gathered, but also how the story forms our day-to-day lives.

A renewed diaconate would hold up the church's theological agenda regularly to the "needs, concerns and hopes of the world." Deacons, rejoicing in their charge: "At all times, your life and teaching are to show Christ's people that in serving the helpless they are serving Christ himself" (*BCP* p. 543), are living reminders of the church's servanthood. This in itself would broaden the theological agenda of the church. Deacons would be trained not as "para-priests," but with skills which would heighten their capacity to bring and interpret this agenda to the church, and empower all the baptized to proclaim the gospel to the world.

We might see regular, small gatherings of the baptized (lay and or- dained, professional and not, employed and not) meeting regularly in each congregation or cluster of congregations for mutual support, story-telling, scheming and dreaming about local mission and ministry, Bible study and eucharist. Here the more experienced and those awakening to their ministry teach, inspire and challenge one another. Seminary graduates continue their education in the context of the local faith community. Seminary professors visit such gatherings from time to time to learn and enter into a dialogue with those who are actually applying what the seminaries seek to impart. "Ministering communities," rather than individual ministers are engaged in theologizing, and there is opportunity for exchange between these local, theologizing faith communities, so that the theology emerging from the grassroots is in dialogue with and informing the seminary agenda.

Theological education would focus on education *in* ministry rather than education *for* ministry (in which the primary objective seems to be to screen out those deemed "undesirable" for ordination). All the baptized are recalled to ministry — those who will one day be ordained with those who will not — so that as the community does ministry and continually reflects theologically upon it, it becomes apparent who the leaders are, some of whom are called forth by the community for ordination. And as the community calls forth gifted people into various leadership positions, it is understood that distinctions in role are not distinctions in rank, but in function. Thus those who are in ordained ministries are less concerned with preserving their "theologizing turf" and more concerned to develop the gifts of all members and the community's opportunities for mission.

The local faith community might be like a theological/ministry "playground," a safe place in which to try new ideas and behaviors, exercising the imagination, reaching beyond what we can control and contain, to new, sometimes risky, but potentially exciting and effective avenues for ministry, where every member has opportunity to tell her or his story as it continues to unfold.

Our faith community would have opportunities to be revolutionary, engaging in a "subversive" activity beginning with the reformation of our own hearts, souls and minds. Instead of theological education preparing us to manage the *status quo* and believe the myth of the establishment (that the way things are is the way they will always be), education will strengthen us to embrace the changing order of the world in which we live in such a way that rather than being paralyzed by fear or overcome by anxiety, we will embrace even that part of life which cannot be controlled, even by a "well educated" church.

In such a church we might at last discover how to call the broader communities in which we live to reflect upon the serious theological issues related to ecology, population explosion/control, environmental pollution, resource depletion, economic injustice, political systems, war and peace, medical and sexual ethics. Empowered Christians, equipped to engage in theological inquiry consciously and confidently, could effect significant changes in the social order. The strength and courage to tackle the issues comes from our participation in local faith communities, where the mustard seeds we all carry around can be planted and nourished.

III. Leadership Development

Frensdorff: How is leadership exercised in the church? (Is this changing? How are the medium and the message more consistent?) What varieties of leaders (taking into account varieties of situations, cultures, locations, sizes, etc.) does the church have? need? How does the church identify/call/select/choose persons for leadership and how does this vary from one type of situation to another? What are the expectations for each position or office? What is the relationship of lay and clergy leadership? What are the qualifications for different leadership offices and positions — ordained or lay? How is leadership — volunteer/employed, lay/ ordained — educated and trained? How are dioceses and congregations responsible in the initial call or identification of the person? in supporting the person so called? What are prerequisites for each position or office and how are the qualifications assessed — and by whom? How does this differ for varieties of leaders and situations? Where and how does the training take place? What is best done locally? as contextual education? through other institutions/programs?

That is quite a list of questions. We will begin with a summary of the contemporary leadership issues in which these questions might be rooted, examine the nature of community in need of leadership, then come back to a more thorough analysis of the issues.

Issues

* The church seems shy about leadership: about exercising it, accepting it, admitting that it is needed or desirable. Leadership seems akin to power and a stranger to love. The church approaches it . . . tentatively.

* There is confusion over how leaders are chosen. Are they "raised up" by the community or "called by God" (which might mean "self-appointed")?

* Many cultural models and ideas about leadership equate it with heavy-handed, autocratic styles, inappropriate for the church (or any system). The images are still predominately adult, male, white and left-brain — images of reason, preservation and continuity, with little appreciation for the feminine, childlike and playful — images of fun and creativity.

* We persist in confusing leadership with orders. Yet one frequently hears the complaint these days that the community no longer holds the local pastor in the same high esteem as was the case in an earlier era. The pastor "is no longer considered a professional," they say (which may be as true of doctors and lawyers). Involuntary terminations are commonplace. Far too often we seem unable to get authority and accountability working smoothly, creatively, effectively. The pressure of discontent builds until an explosion wrecks havoc on all.

* Leadership training is traditionally much more decentralized than theological education. Seminaries largely skip it. Our national church, since World War II, has played a big role. Many independent agencies, church and non-church related, help. It is almost exclusively on-the-job training rather than preliminary education.

* Leadership in the church tends to be equated with pastoral services (not supervision, delegation, organization, etc.) which, of course, follows for a system that deems it routine to subject a theolog to a quarter of clinical-pastoral training, but would have grave questions about asking a student to spend a summer as a foreman intern in a factory. So it is that a bishop and diocesan staff facing problems getting their act together will probably hire a clinical psychologist instead of a management consultant.

President Wilson defined leadership as the task of transforming grand visions into crude deeds; Harold Shapiro (Princeton) more recently, as "the act of bringing an institution to understand and accept a new set of changes and values, and to inspire a common will to bear allegiances to them."[4] Taken together we can see that leadership has to do with moving forward and it includes the messy job of compromising and getting agreement on specific strategies — i.e., "crude deeds." Perhaps, for the church at least, we could define leadership as a range of ministry functions which arouse the constituent elements of the church in a spirit-filled response to God's mission. Leadership is a gift, a charism, a ministry. And like all ministries, rooted in a life in God, in personal prayer and in the eucharistic community.

Prior to questions of leadership, however, are questions of community. What is the nature of the community for which leadership is presumably needed? It is a tricky question, since the kind of leadership presently in place is certainly influencing the nature of community as it evolves over time. Thus it is not enough to be simply analytical in responding to the question; we must also be idealistic. Our models of leadership must devolve from our ideals of community. Our *strategies* for leadership development must certainly deal with current realities. But they must also be guided by a vision of the kind of community we seek. The task of envisioning requires, in this case, that we look at community first.

Frank Kirkpatrick, in *Community*,[5] examines three basic models. The first one we might call *mechanical,* as descriptive of the way the parts relate to one another. This model is basically rooted in the fear that an elite group or individual will seize power and impose (their) will on the rest of us. Each individual is an autonomous unit and the model assumes that individual freedoms are of paramount interest. Thus each member of society, each unit or "atom," legitimately pursues his or her self interest: looks out for number one, to put it baldly. The model accepts this human condition as natural and understandable. With this understanding of the nature of things, the design objective is to provide for the maximum in individual freedoms consistent with being fair to everybody. Of course this means imposing *some* constraints; no unit can be unconditionally free. So we "contract" for arrangements that will alleviate fear and provide the best deal for ourselves and our interests under the circumstances. (Kirkpatrick calls the model "atomistic/contractarian" and observes that it is "really, an anti-community model.") The function of leadership in this case is that of helping us get the contract together and revised under evolving circumstances, and of making sure that everyone operates within the terms of the contract. It's a model we are familiar with.

The second we'll call *organic* (Kirkpatrick: "organic/functional").

In this model it is assumed that true freedom is not rooted in individualism, but in the individual functioning appropriately on behalf of the whole. Thus the individual is a cell or functionary of the organism: a body part: a mechanic or nurse or teacher or (even) leader, and therein lies the meaning of individual existence and "true freedom." Everybody is important — sort of — in terms of the function and the gifts and abilities each brings to the overall good of the enterprise. But, on the other hand, functionaries, like bees in a bee colony, can be replaced. The meaning of community in the organic model is the community itself, the organism; it is not in the parts. "Person" apart from function certainly has no meaning. If we raise the question of what *is* that meaning of community, that apparently is supposed to be self-evident. And what about the role (another "function," of course) of leadership? Well, every organism needs a head.

In critique of the first model, we as a society (says Kirkpatrick) struggle to reconcile our western liberal insistence on the freedom of the individual with our desire to enter into interpersonal relations with others. ". . . We accept our freedom and the primacy of self-interest as givens and then search desperately for some kind of bond with others that will transcend or mitigate the despair and loneliness which goalless freedom and self-interest have imposed upon us."[6] But the others, objects of our self-interest, must be treated with fear and distrust, for *their* self-interest could be in conflict with ours.

While organic models overcome some of the loneliness and autonomy of the mechanical model, ". . . they still seem curiously limited either by their emphasis on the functional subservience of the individual to the greater whole, . . . or the absence of an enduring individual capable of sustaining ongoing relations with others, and, most importantly, on the absence of any serious discussion of what the purpose or end of cooperative behavior should be."[7]

We now turn our attention to the third model, *relationship* (Kirkpatrick: "mutual/personal"). The starting place for this model (for Kirkpatrick) is the biblical view that life is meaningful only in a community of love. He draws on Martin Buber for his initial consideration of this. Buber writes of two primary words which are hyphenated words: 'I-thou' and 'I-it'. The 'I' of 'I-thou' is not an individual, but a total person in relationship. The 'I' of 'I-thou' has its meaning and fulfillment in the relationship, not in the shell of the individual. The 'I' of 'I-it' is an individual dealing in a world of things. Thus the 'I' of 'I-it' is itself a thing among things. Whether the other is 'thou' or 'it' (person or object) depends on my attitude (*I*-thou, or *I*-it), not on its innate qualities. Furthermore, the center of a community where a mutual I-thou stance is taken is the eternal *Thou.* So establishing community is a cooperative and interdependent effort of God and people in relationship. Kirkpatrick then turns to the writings of John MacMurray to further his case. MacMurray, contending with the popular "I think, therefore I am" atomistic philosophy of persons, suggests that it is better to understand persons primarily as agents rather than thinkers. Knowledge is not, first off, what one *thinks* correctly, but what one *does* correctly. Thinking is important — in community or in support of action — not in and of itself. Group thinking can, of course, be synergistic, creative and stimulating. MacMurray isn't denying that. He is trying to upend the individualistic "I think, therefore I am" premise of the mechanical model and lay the groundwork for a new model of community in which the person is not sacrificed for some larger organic entity (in reaction to the mechanical model), nor left as an atomistic thinker. Agent in relationship is his offering. Thus the philosophical starting point for understanding community is not me thinking about it, but me in the relationship. This brings us very close to a second premise in the relationship model, which has to do with the nature of ultimate reality. Ultimate reality *is* relationship. Or, to paraphrase, God is love. Persons (agents) in relationship are then in harmony with ultimate reality. This is where we are supposed to be; it is true to our nature. This is "where it's at." *Reality.*

The point is treated as a theological premise as well as a truth that is self-evident. Take, for example, a micro-community, a mother and infant. Picture the mother bending over the baby, cooing and tickling and gitchy-gooing; the baby, arms swinging, feet kicking, giggling and laughing. In that picture the mother, totally subjective, unselfconsciously *is* (lives and has her being) in the relationship. Each, oblivious to anything else, is present for the other and takes their joy and delight in the other. And there we have the meaning of community: to delight in the other. Even in *The* Other. "Humans exist for awe's sake — to be radically amazed and to draw radical amazement from one another."[8]

But from this glimpse of community can we envision it on a large scale and enduring over long periods? A good marriage might give us another view. Here each partner loves and delights in doing things for the other. Each desires the best for the other without attempting to remold the other in some image. Each, unselfishly and unselfconsciously seeks ways to serve and bring joy to the other. What happened to "self-interest?" No need for it, for the relationship is mutual. "The self always has worth, but this is the gift of another's love, not the product of self-concern."[9]

Can we envision such a community on, let's say, the parish or diocesan level? Or national or worldwide? Maybe not on such a grand scale. But surely the church should be about the business of modeling it for the world. After all, it is we who claim that the model is not merely ideal, but Ultimate Reality. It is in harmony with God's creation and the New

Creation. And it is ultimately God's love that sustains us, justifies us, gives us worth and reason to risk the model in faith.

One is called not only to love and take delight in the other, but also to care for the other's needs. In a sacramental world we need material things: food, clothes, shelter. And while we live essentially in Christ, we walk this world existentially with Adam — a world in which self-consciousness deteriorates to self-concern and "love" is another strategy at one's disposal — a world in which material needs are not met for everyone.

So when the church claims that our ideal community is a community of love, that claim is greeted with amusement or suspicion, for "love" in common usage has no clout. It is mere emotion alongside hate, anger, joy and sympathy. As a guiding principle for community, it is naive. It means "overlook every transgression, turn the other cheek, skip justice— — for love transcends all of that. It's like a sweet syrup exuding over all, but expecting nothing. We need, therefore, a more adequate understanding of love.

Paul Tillich, in his ontology of love, power and justice,[10] has shown that these three "categories of being" are ultimately one. In God, love, power and justice are united: one reality of being in Ultimate Reality. To say that "God is love" is to impute the categories of power and justice, as part of love, to Being Itself. In *essence*, love, power and justice are one. In *existence* they tend to separate. If we lose sight of their ontological unity in dealing with love, power and justice in "the real world," each tends toward distortion. Love, for example, is the drive toward reunion of everything estranged; it is not mere emotion. Power is not the ability of one to impose his or her will on another. That is destruction, and a reduction of power in both the other and the one who imposes. Power is the self-affirmation of being over non-being, "the possibility of self-affirmation in spite of internal and external negation."[11] In their distorted forms love and power may be seen to negate each other. Actually, "love is the foundation, not the negation, of power" and "the more reuniting love there is, the more conquered non-being there is, the more power of being there is."[12] The truth of this is readily observable in organizations. An insecure or jealous supervisor who hugs all authority to himself effectively reduces the ability of associates to function and diminishes his own power as well. While the supervisor who caringly and lovingly encourages and authenticates others generates power all over the enterprise, including her own.

And love is not the transcendence of justice; that would be chaos. "Love does not do more than justice demands. Love reunites; justice preserves what is to be united. It is the form in which and through which love performs its work."[13] Law (in the Hebraic-Christian sense) is not an imposition, but a revelation; law (as in "laws of nature") is not arbitrary, but revealing of the structure of love from which we are estranged. "(For this law) is not too hard for you, neither is it far off . . . but the word is very near you; it is in your mouth and in your heart, so that you can do it." (Deut. 30:11-14) Of course "laws" in this fallen world can be imposed, arbitrary and contrary to God's design for humanity. But righteous laws and creative justice are of grace, the gift of and form of love. What does all this imply for the adoption and administration of standards, regulations, rules and procedures in our organizations?

In our "relationship" model of community, then, our concept of love must include love as the foundation of power and the principle of justice. Love nurtures the power to be in the other as well as in the self. And it insists on justice for the other as well as for the self. Given the realities of a fallen world, our structures for community must include elements of the mechanical model and the organic model. (Kirkpatrick also speaks of the relationship model as an inclusive model, not a clearcut alternative.) Given our human limitations, no one can stand in an intimate relationship of love with everyone else. Yet even with these givens and limitations, our emphasis can be on the intentions; every human encounter can be approached with the understanding that there is a potential for love. And our community structures can reflect the intention that this is a community of love, not a collection of frightened self-seekers under contract or submissive functionaries in a more important organic blob.

Our relationship model of community would seem to imply that leaders are called to specific leadership functions in accordance with gifts and other qualifications, by the community under the guidance of the Spirit. Leaders are not imposed or self-appointed. They are identified and called into service. We shouldn't even say "raised up," implying that leadership is a superior ministry. If Paul is right, all ministries are of equal importance. Of course, how one is identified and called depends on the nature of the community (congregation, diocese, national church, etc). Elections are not ruled out. The principle that leaders are called forth by the community can hold in a political process. In the more enlightened episcopal or rector "searches" these days, the principle is adhered to. Potential nominees are not asked to "run" for office, or compete, or prove themselves. They are asked to join with the community for a while in a process of seeking God's will and matching qualifications with the job. In the end, if no one sabotages the process, no one is a "loser."

Within the Christian community, leaders are sheep called into service because they love Christ. (John 21:15-17) They are not shepherds; there is one Shepherd. Leaders are learners, always unfinished people, always challenged by the call to metanoia. Leaders hold to the basic premise that change is possible. We are capable of a turn around, a new awareness springing from our roots upward. Leaders are graced, thus led: leaders with a Leader. Leaders grow in Christ, becoming people filled with hope about possibilities, not stuck in the rut of "we've always done it this way." Thus leadership includes the capacity for intentional and deliberate interventions for the purpose of bringing about planned change (conversion) in communities and individuals.

Leaders are called to lead — not abdicate, not pussyfoot around, but to "arouse the constituent elements of the church in a spirit-filled response to God's mission;" to lead in love with power and justice. "Authority" is power at work in community. "Just authority" is power sanctioned by the community for the good of the community. There is no leadership without authority. Authority may be rooted in special gifts, abilities, knowledge or even in the position itself; in this respect all members of the community are not equal. But leaders are called to lead with just authority. "It is not unjust that in the struggle between power and power, one of the beings involved shows a superior power of being. The manifestation of this fact is not unjust but creative. But injustice occurs if in this struggle the superior power uses its power for the reduction or destruction of the inferior power."[14] Thus the proper exercise of authority in community will not be without its occasional confrontations. But the leader is challenged to make the confrontation creative, not destructive.

Still, the context is community; followers create leaders. Questions of leadership are questions of a community of leaders and followers. What kind of leaders does this community really want? How much "superior power of being" are we willing to tolerate? We probably get (in a given community) the kind of leadership we deserve or can tolerate. If we are fearful of the ministry of leadership — that we might be led too far, or see too much, or be challenged beyond what our courage can support — then followers can call forth wimps who, in their inner being are afraid of ambiguity and anxious about conflict. Do we live in a community in which (collectively and perhaps unconsciously) it is preferred that leaders abdicate responsibility and avoid tough decisions? Are we nervous about leaders who do not sniff around to see who might support the cause before proposing it, or salute the flag before running it up the pole, or who do not straddle the fence on tough issues? Thus, community and leadership are interdependent. And together, in their brokenness, they must attempt to figure out which ditch this community is willing to die in . . . for the living of the gospel.

We live and serve at a period in history when the church is beginning to recover a sense of the distinctive characteristics of the three orders. Instead of a linear progression,

baptized member > deacon > presbyter > bishop,

we are beginning to see each of the three offices reflecting some dimension of the church's general ministry and related to that general ministry in a leadership capacity. There are those who advocate direct ordination to priesthood or episcopate as a way of eliminating the sense of progression.

This is not to imply that only ordained people are leaders, but that everyone who is ordained is expected to be a leader in some way. It may be, as the distinctiveness of these offices is reinforced, that we discover a kind of core image of leadership for each office. That doesn't mean, for example, that every bishop has the same gifts or the same position description as all others, but that a core of behaviors or metaphors could be found that would sum up the essential meaning of that ministry. Or, to take another example, "eccentricity" has been suggested as one metaphor for the diaconate. Deacons tend to work the margins, fringes and undersides — in ministry and liturgy. It's a different kind of leadership from the center-stage presence of those who preside in community life.

The total picture is much broader. Add to the three offices the several canonical licensed lay ministries (catechist, preacher, eucharistic minister, etc.) and the various elected or appointed leadership roles (warden, treasurer, etc.) and we have a wide range of distinctive ministries. Then remember that an office or license is not a job or position description (a bishop isn't necessarily the *diocesan*; a presbyter isn't necessarily the *rector*).

In fact, it might be interesting to see in place somewhere a professionally trained, full-time lay rector of a parish or cluster working with a team of volunteers, including local presbyters and deacons. That might help us get at the distinctiveness of each ministry. And maybe we should print baptismal certificates on 17" x 24" high grade stock, suitable for framing, and make ordination and consecration certificates 5" x 7" for easy filing. Why, by virtue of ordination alone, does one have a seat in convention? (Yes, it's implied in the priest's ordination service, but why?) And why a vote by orders, or even a bicameral convention? These are some of the questions beginning to be scrutinized today. Continued study should lead us to new insights concerning leadership functions and the distinctions in each.

The variety of leader ministries even in a small relationship community is considerable, and questions of relationships among them, of authority and of structures of accountability necessarily arise. There is a lot of popular resistance in the church to "hierarchical models," usually based on observations of bad examples involving heavy-handed, dictatorial leadership styles. Yet some kind of structures of accountability are needed if we are to avoid chaos and aimlessness. The simple truth is, it's a lot more fun and meaningful to be part of a community where structural matters are effectively covered: position descriptions for individual ministries, task descriptions for groups, lines of authority clear, structures and standards of accountability known, etc. In such a community one has a sense of focus in the effort, purpose along the way and pride in accomplishment.

It is difficult to see how one might provide structure in community without some kind of chain of command. A relationship community is not an endless heavenly banquet with everyone looking out after the others. There is a mission to be defined and strategies to design and implement. There are opportunities for many to assume responsibilities of various kinds. Some kind of responsible structures of accountability are demanded. It may be that our problem is not with structures, but with the autocratic style of leadership we sometimes see in industry, government and, yes, in the church. But there are many good examples of leadership in those sectors too. Naive hang-ups about organization must not deter us from the task of providing creative structures and learning how to lead well.

Leadership can be thought of as the stewardship of the resources of the community. A steward is one who takes charge (of some area of responsibility) and who is accountable to a master. Another term for stewardship is management. But, alas, here we have another concept church members shy away from, again, probably because of the bad examples with which we are familiar. But here, too, there are many good examples. More to the point, there is a lot of good literature on the subject. It may be that the term "management" can't be resurrected in the church, but if we lose sight of the fact that the best authors on the subject, Peter Drucker, for example, are really dealing with what we would call organizational stewardship, we will have cut ourselves off from the best resources available. And the opportunity for continued growth will have diminished.

The tools of leadership development are experience/reflection, education and training (skill development). The starting place is the person and that means everyone in the community. More particularly, however, the starting place is the *strengths* of the *individual*. All good "job power" programs (those developed by Bernard Haldane, for example) are based on this key point. What are the person's "motivated gifts?" Motivated gifts are discerned in the activities the individual enjoys, does well and is proud of. And what kind of a person is the individual (for example, in terms of Myers-Briggs typology)? These gifts and personal characteristics one brings to the job, if they are known, are the strengths to build on. And if the community builds on the strengths of each of the members, the weaknesses become irrelevant. This is what good management does: builds on the strengths. This is good stewardship of community resources.

However, "the church" doesn't like the term "management." Even when management courses or consultations are offered, with some notable exceptions, the basic resources used are those from a field called "organizational development" (OD), rooted in psychology and sociology, and, for the church, in the sensitivity training of the '50s and '60s. "Management" then becomes a proposition of loving, understanding, respecting and trusting one another. Other management disciplines, such as thinking through the precise purpose of a job, providing for functional and healthy corporate and staff structure, planning, etc. — if dealt with at all — are subsumed under the basic premises of OD: incidentals, if you will. But accountability is not elicited via admonitions to love and trust. It is generated by having the job clearly defined, negotiating specifics, getting people into positions they are eager to be in, occasional performance review, authentication, and confronting and dealing with differences above board. Affection and trust are byproducts of competent management, not premises. On the face of it, OD seems appropriate for a "relationship community." And, indeed, sensitivity training and its spin-offs have made a contribution. But it does not represent the main missing ingredients. (Thus the oft heard complaint: "We've had enough of that touchy-feely stuff.") With a denial of power and authority and in the absence of the form or structure of love (justice), love has lost its clout and is reduced to some kind of an emotional state (trust/respect) we are supposed to sustain in spite of obvious confusion, injustice, ineffectiveness and aimlessness.

With all good intentions, then, the church inclines toward addressing the chaos of its own life with a clinical style of "management" and therapy becomes the point of entry. "Leadership development" focuses on the full-time, professionally trained personnel (instead of everybody) and looks for pathology (instead of strengths). There is no denying that the community must deal with illness when it crops up, but that's not the point. We are dealing here with a strategy for leadership development, and that means knowing, developing and taking advantage of strengths. One could even add that where this is done effectively, there will be less illness, since people will be involved in creative accomplishments and enjoying them. However, in our therapeutic model of leadership, performance review, for example, (a valued management discipline related to "experience/reflection" in leadership development) is reduced to looking for flaws and providing therapy. Top leaders are "chief pastors," middle managers, "pastors" and community members, "sheep," or dependents. So in the final analysis, what the church doesn't want (a hierarchical model of leadership) is precisely what she creates. Out of her fear of organization, power and authority, and her ignorance of leadership rooted in suspicions of "management," a paternal/dependent organization — not a relationship community — is the result.

How do we break out of that?

IV.   The Seminaries as Theological Resource Centers

Frensdorff: What place do seminaries have in all of this? Can they be "re-formed" from primarily being residential institutions to primarily being theological resource centers — for research/ scholarship? for more effective delivery to the church's total theological enterprise? Didn't seminaries develop out of both the university and the monastic model? (How much of this is effective today? What in it impedes?)

Marked changes in the thinking of Wes and others engaged in local theological education and ministry development underly this set of questions.   The seminal thinking in Nevada's total ministry strategy included two very distinct tracks of preparation for ordination. One was the calling and education of persons in the context of their congregation. Theological reflection and preparation were to be done with others engaged in ministry in the local setting.   The other was what Wes unabashedly called the "career track." Persons anticipating employment by the church, whether called to be deacons, presbyters or lay professionals, would be educated in the accredited seminaries of the Episcopal Church. There was no call for the residential seminaries to be anything other than what they were: schools which provided a basic academic and applied education for those seeking to be church professionals.

As total ministry strategies began to be lived out in Nevada and other dioceses, though, expectations of what seminaries should provide began to shift. Yes, we still needed seminary graduates as teachers, consultants and linkage persons between congregations, and between congregation and diocese. But were our seminaries providing at least an introduction to skills such as adult education and management needed by stipended people? Most of the dioceses developing total ministry were small and lacked the money and staff time to develop the full range of educational resources needed. They turned to the seminaries in search of visiting teachers, and of print, audio and video resources. With the exception of a few professors who enjoyed working with a general adult audience, the Education for Ministry Program from the University of the South, and a few helpful bookstores, little help and few resources were available. In Nevada and some other dioceses, people locally licensed or ordained are required to pursue continuing education. As their numbers increase, some seek specialized education and skill development which are impractical to provide at the local level. Again, as this need emerged the first logical place to look seemed to be the seminaries. Sometimes the programs needed were there or could be created; at other times the search for appropriate resources was an exercise in frustration.

What developers of local ministry, including Wes Frensdorff, learned was that you cannot make radical changes in one part of the system without affecting the other parts. Changes in how we conceive of and educate in local ministry meant changes would need to be made in how we conceive of and educate in the extra-local ministry of church professionals.

ISSUE #1: There is confusion about where the center(s) of theological education and ministerial formation is or should be. Definitions of the center follow views on what ministry is and where it is focused.

When you hear the word "ministry," what comes to mind? If you think of the work of the church, both gathered and dispersed, in which all baptized Christians are engaged, then you will probably envision education in ministry as taking place in the local worshiping community. It is there that values are formed, tradition is handed on, skills enhanced or adapted, and theological reflection engaged in.

If you think of the whole range of roles and offices that the church ordains or licenses or elects; i.e., if you come at ministry from the viewpoint of church order as reflected in constitution and canons, you will probably see education in ministry as taking place in diocesan programs, or in some way guided, shaped or contracted for by the diocese.

If you think of the paid parochial presbyter as the norm for ministry, you will think of the church's residential seminaries as the venue of education in ministry, and the norm for theological education that takes place elsewhere.

In other words, where you stand in understanding ministry will determine what you view as the center of ministry development and what you see as supplemental resources. Let's make two caricatures to explore this further.

Mary Jones is a middle manager in a medium size corporation in a small city. She often feels caught in the crunch between those she supervises and those to whom she reports. Mary wants to deal with her co-workers in a way that is consistent with her Christian faith. Mary also wants to use the small amount of influence she has in the corporation to bring about a sounder policy with respect to the environment. She sees this as ministry. Mary attends an average size Episcopal parish. She looks to this parish as the place where support and education for her ministry should take place; that is, she sees it as the center. And it is from this center that she will begin to explore resources: a study group led by the rector; a gathering of like-minded people from several parishes, perhaps ecumenical; reading; a spiritual director; a diocesan retreat or workshop; perhaps even a provincial or national event in support of total ministry.

Tom Smith teaches homeletics at your average Episcopal seminary. He sees his ministry as one of nurturing and challenging students, with all that implies, as well as reflecting on and being an advocate for the church's preaching ministry. For him the center of theological education is the seminaries. The resources he relies upon are libraries and his own scholarly pursuits, formal and informal dialogue with colleagues, feedback from students, the parishes where they do their fieldwork and the occasional opportunity to lead a clergy conference program in one of the neighboring dioceses. Sometimes the experience of committed lay people, such as Mary, can be a resource for Tom in his ongoing theological education.

Clearly, where the center of ministerial formation and theological education is depends on where one stands. There is a need for all people involved to take others' perspectives seriously if there is to be new agreement on where the center of theological education is and what the resources are. (See Issue #2, below.) Budgeting and legislation in the Episcopal Church suggest that currently the Episcopal seminaries are seen as center and norm. But rumblings among local ministry developers and those reclaiming the ministry of the baptized are beginning to organize themselves into a call for a shift in perspective church-wide. The centers for theological education will no longer be seminaries or national and diocesan buildings and staffs, but all the local places where Christian people gather for worship and for reflection for the living out of their lives in ministry.

ISSUE #2: A perceived conflict between seminary programs and diocesan and other local programs gets in the way of genuine dialogue about ecclesiology/missiology and of potential cooperation in ministry education.

Certainly conflict and competition between seminaries and diocesan ministry education programs is both felt and expressed. The word "perceived," however, is used in the statement of the issue to suggest that while there are signs of conflict, it need not necessarily be so, particularly if both seminaries and local programs would look beyond business as usual to how they might best use their particular gifts in a changing ecclesial environment.

One diocesan coordinator of ministry education who also served as a seminary board member was surprised to discover that seminary faculty were accepting of programs which did theological education in the local congregation or cluster and used the local clergy canon for ordinations, but more critical of diocesan programs which could be described as weekend seminaries. Why was this so?

Persons prepared locally for local ordination were usually seen as people who wouldn't be seminary material anyway. Distance and employment would make it next to impossible for them to attend. Many did not have college degrees, and for some English was a second language.

It was also seen by seminaries that the development of local clergy would continue to require seminary educated people for teaching and oversight. Even though there is no requirement in the canon that local clergy not be stipended, most are deployed as volunteers. Hence local clergy were not seen as a major threat to jobs for seminary graduates.

By way of contrast, larger diocesan programs of the weekend seminary variety sometimes produced graduates who found their way into part or full-time church employment. In crude marketing terms, a product produced more cheaply is always a threat to business as usual.

Beneath these questions of competition in producing persons for employed church leadership lay a deeper question. Clearly Christian education and ministerial formation are to be done in community. Residential seminaries offer a quasi-monastic community of study, prayer and shared daily life. Local programs which stress the calling of persons to ordination take advantage of an existing gathering as the locus for education, the local worshiping and ministering community. Centralized weekend diocesan programs bring together people whose neighborhoods, workplaces and week-to-week worship all happen in different places with different groups of people. Even with well designed deliberate attempts to build community, the natural advantages of a residential seminary or congregation are missing. (It probably should be noted that at the same time that diocesan programs grew and wrestled with questions of community, seminaries in highly populated areas were showing an increase in the numbers of commuter students, hence also raising questions about education and formation in community.)

So the conflict perceived between seminaries and local programs focused on two things: a threat to the seminaries' basic product, the M. Div. intent on a career in the church, usually as a presbyter, and a concern for the importance of integrated community life as the context for theological education.

There are at least two other areas of concern which also add to the perceived conflict. Both grow out of changing understandings of ministry fostered by local programs and the recovery of baptismal ministry.

Good local programs require that the seminary graduates they employ have skills in education and ministry development. It's quite easy to see how seminary faculties view this as yet another thing to be added to an already unwieldy curriculum, along with stewardship, evangelism, sexuality, spiritual direction, addiction counseling, racism and the other things in which every General Convention asks the seminaries to provide additional education. Instead, what may be required is a radical reform of seminary curricula seen against the church's total system of ministry education. (More on this below.) The goal might be graduates whom Fred Borsch, bishop of Los Angeles, has described as "practical pastoral theologians," capable of ongoing theological reflection and motivated to pursue continuing education and skill development in ministry, and capable of sharing what they had learned and were learning, and motivated to draw others into the process of theological reflection.

Recovering the importance of the ministry of the baptized and developing interdependent ministering communities have challenged the model of the omni-competent paid parochial presbyter. Encouraging people to identify their gifts and strengths and to use them in mutual ministry has revealed that the most effective and happy priests are not those who try to do everything well, but those who develop their strengths rather than belaboring their weaknesses, and appreciate and trust the strengths of others. A new understanding of priests who are not interchangeable parts challenges some of the underlying assumptions of both seminary and local curricula. No wonder that there is conflict in the air, given this jumble and flux of expectations and understandings of education in ministry.

What might provoke wonder, though, is to gather those concerned with theological education to ask some basic questions. What is the church? What is ministry? What sorts of ministries are we educating for? Once the sorts are sorted out, the practical and strategic questions could follow. Where is a particular ministerial role best prepared for? With what style or format of education? What resources are needed? From where? etc.

Whether or not such a major systemic review of theological education ever takes place, there are points where cooperation between seminaries and diocesan programs could begin, helping to capitalize on the strengths of each and minimalize the problems. For example:

* Seminaries can be a resource and venue for continuing education opportunities for diocesan-educated clergy and lay leaders. The Church Divinity School of the Pacific had modest success for three summers with a continuing education week for deacons. Most of the participants were diocesan-educated volunteers who took vacation time to attend. They welcomed the opportunity to get to know deacons from other dioceses, to meet and talk with seminary faculty, and to visit libraries and bookstores. Similar efforts could be tried elsewhere; they can pay for themselves and build good will for the seminaries.

* Diocesan programs can provide delivery systems for seminary extension programs. This is already true for Sewanee's Education for

Ministry Program in many dioceses. And some local programs will occasionally have a seminary faculty member as a guest speaker. Between these two extremes are a lot of other possibilities, such as shorter courses using print and electronic media, and continuing education institutes for seminary-educated folk and others. Diocesan programs are in touch with local needs and have structures for organizing events, publicizing opportunities and distributing materials, which means that seminary faculty and staff could concentrate on developing ideas and resources.

      *   Local programs and seminaries could share their experience with teaching formats and methodologies. All too often seminaries have been caricatured as using only pedagogical teaching styles and local programs as marvels of relevant adult education. Let it be said that there are innovative teachers and co-learners in both systems. A gathering of faculty members from all sorts of programs, including seminaries, to experience different teaching styles used to achieve different educational goals is a dream. A more modest suggestion would be a sabbatical exchange program, where seminary faculty could use part of their sabbatical time serving as co-teachers in diocesan or other local programs, and teachers in other programs could do the same in a seminary setting.

      *   Seminaries could do more to encourage their use for sabbaticals for church professionals. These need not be three to six months stays with elaborate projects and learning goals. One or two weeks of time to mull, sort, write and read would provide much needed sabbath time. Members of the seminary community might also be encouraged to learn from these practitioners, to hear about what is happening in the church beyond the seminary and its fieldwork parishes.

      *   Some of the burden on seminaries to offer training in 101 ways of applied theology (see above) might be lifted by developing internships for seminarians and recent graduates in relationship to diocesan ministry development programs. Adult education skills could be learned by practicing them. Stewardship theology and praxis could be learned by interns working alongside the best practitioners in a diocese, together with volunteers there. The mix would be enriched by the freshness of the interns' theological knowledge. *Dioceses would, thereby, assume more of their responsibility for training candidates for ordination and employment.*

The Episcopal Church's accredited seminaries could be a more effective source of resources for the total enterprise of theological education. But it will never happen if the seminaries continue to defend the *status quo* of their basic product, nor if dioceses and ministry developers continue to make seminaries their whipping posts. What seems called for is an acceptance of the fact that there are many centers of ministerial education in the church today, and that each has real gifts and strengths. Then we can get on with a genuine exploration in our time and in our many cultures, and substitute some concrete experiments in partnership and cooperation for a vague climate of competition and mistrust.

> *The pot still needs stirring!*
> *We have good ingredients. The recovery of the catechumenate as the process and norm for basic Christian education. Members of the baptized who have claimed their ministries and are asking for more support, information and opportunities for reflection. Local ministry development programs which hold up a vision of developing leadership in the context of the local ministering, learning and worshiping community. New emphases on leadership development and mission discernment at the Episcopal Church Center. Base communities which engage the gospel and struggles for justice, wholeness and inclusion in the human community. Seminaries whose financial future is not such a preoccupation thanks to a broader base of support through the 1% resolution of 1982. Diaconate programs which are exploring new ways of integrating knowledge, prayer and action in preparing for specific ministerial roles. But as any competent and creative cook knows, once we have assembled the good ingredients, exact proportions are not as critical as the method we use. And it seems that is where we must focus our efforts: on ways of bringing together representatives of the various efforts in, and centers of the theological enterprise.*
>
> *If a new consensus on the nature and authority of the theological enterprise is to be reached, we must have methods for continuing dialogue and mutual evaluation that are carefully chosen and intentionally applied to respect the diversity of persons and educational agendas in the church; and our methods must be consistent with our vision of a church where all the baptized share in ministry. Otherwise the pot we've stirred won't produce a tasty and nourishing dish — but the same old institutional food!*
>
> *- Eds.*

Notes

1. Alexander D. Stewart, *Episcopal Clergy*. Church Pension Fund: New York).
2. Edward Schillebeeckx, *The Church with a Human Face*. (Crossroads Publications: 1985), pp. 10-11.
3. Fredrica Harris Thompsett, *We Are Theologians*. Crowley Publishers: 1989).
4. *Harvard Magazine*. May-June, 1990, p. 68.

5. Frank G. Kirkpatrick, *Community, A Trinity of Models.* (Georgetown University Press: 1986).
6. Ibid, p. 137.
7. Ibid, p. 138
8. Matthew Fox, *The Coming of the Cosmic Christ.* (Harper and Rowe, 1988), p. 51
9. Kirkpatrick, p. 198.
10. Paul Tillich, *Love, Power and Justice.* (Oxford University Press: 1954).
11. Ibid, p. 40.
12. Ibid, p. 49.
13. Ibid, p. 71.
14. Ibid, p. 88.

Chapter 15

UMBRELLAS AND BIG SPOONS

Charles R. Wilson

It was during the 1960s, while John Hines was presiding bishop, the cities burned, college students took on the establishment, churches were presented with demands for reparations and the baby boom generation graduated from high school; it was then that a white, newly affluent middle class, finally able to afford a boat, camper, snowmobile or skis (or all of the above) took off for the recreation areas, and the mainline churches crashed. Many studies attempted to relate the decline to the "crazy social action programs" of the churches at the time, but the only clear correlation ever established was with the graduation of the baby boomers. Finished with diapers, measles, PTA and Sunday school, mom, pop and the kids went fishing. Since then other studies in the U.S.A. and Canada have shown that lapsed church members and the non-church public are not angry with the church, consider themselves believers and want the church around for occasional services and special needs — all of which tends to confirm the earlier findings. Apparently the church growth of the

'50s was more of a social than a religious phenomenon. Most of those seeds had not fallen on fertile ground.

In any case, the reckoning came in the '60s. The college chaplains were the first to go, and we lost contact with the young people. (Dick Bolles of *What Color Is Your Parachute* fame originally got into his job counseling career at this juncture. As head of the campus chaplaincy program in the western province, he boned up on job-finding skills in an attempt to help his unemployed chaplains find new jobs.) Next went the inner city church, then thousands of small churches across the land were closed. Parochial support of the diocese and diocesan support for the general church program crumbled. A rural and nominally Christian nation had become the secular city.

It must have been about 1967, while I was a member of our national church staff, that Ernie Southcott, an English evangelist, made one of his tours of the states that culminated in a visit to the Episcopal Church Center in New York City. I was among those invited to meet with him and hear him reflect on the state of the American church as he had come to see it. He pointed out, in his unhumble way, that we had five major blocks to church renewal: the altar, the *Book of Common Prayer*, the organ, the pews and the building. He went on to explain that one way to insight and discovery leading to renewal is to do a familiar thing in an unusual setting, or do something different in a familiar setting. Out of such experiences one might learn something about where we are stuck and get unstuck — sort of like surfacing unconscious assumptions or premises to see if they are valid or needed. However, (claimed Southcott) we couldn't do much of that. The altar was anchored to the east wall and the pews bolted to the floor. The organ was so good we couldn't try something else. The prayer book kept us in a straightjacket liturgically and the building was held in such reverence that we were unable to see that all of God's creation is holy.

I wouldn't claim that Ernie Southcott had much to do with it, but that whole set of blocks was about to get jarred loose. The altar was pulled away from the wall, guitars and other instruments began supplementing the organ, a more flexible prayer book was adopted, and in some places the pews went out and flexible space use came in. But that was only a start. Folk music was added to the standard repertoire of hymnody, balloons, banners and kites enhanced ceremonial, ministry exploded beyond the domain of the ordained, and the male stranglehold on church leadership was broken — in the ranks of the acolytes, in vestries, in the lay deputation to General Convention and, finally, in the ordained ministries.

During the '70s and '80s, trends in the Episcopal Church turned around, not dramatically, but significantly. Contrary to the reports of those who know only how to count baptized members, there were new and clear signs of growth: a couple of percentage points a year in Sunday church attendance, increases in general revenue outstripping inflation and substantial increases in giving for world relief and local outreach programming. Today we are a leaner, more committed church with some 40-45% of us at worship on Sunday instead of under 30% (as in the '60s). The ministry is immeasurably richer and our understanding of baptismal ministry much more in sync with patterns of the ancient church. And in a secular society where there is no particular social or business advantage in being an Episcopalian or Presbyterian, it really does mean something to claim one's Christian identity. Now we (Episcopalians) face the "decade of evangelism." Can we do anything with that challenge? Well, a substantial foundation has been laid.

That era we have just briefly reviewed approximates the period of the adult ministry of Wesley Frensdorff, one of its prime movers and shakers. That we can address the decade of evangelism with some degree of hope and confidence, in no small measure results from that ministry. Wes and the Diocese of Nevada were not the first to tackle reshaping ministry. In 1965, Bishop Norman Foote and the Diocese of Idaho, with a vision of total/ indigenous ministry, launched a serious and well-conceived program that anticipated most of the principles and issues that were to come up later. But that program was not sustained and eventually died without influencing much outside. There were, here and there, creative local attempts in reshaping ministry, but, as was soon to be seen, isolated local efforts couldn't carry the day. Ministry development would have to be big on the diocesan—eventually national — agenda for much to happen.

It was at a December, 1967 conference in Fort Yukon, Alaska, that Bishop William Gordon announced his commitment to indigenous ministry. It was at the same conference that Dr. Boone Porter, General Seminary, and for years a Roland Allen devoteé, introduced that voice into the dialogue in the field. Bishop David Cochran, Gordon's successor, reinforced the effort with intensive educational programming, and Bishop George Harris, his successor, followed through. All three bishops have been articulate advocates and interpreters of total ministry. But would a form of ministry created for the unique circumstances of isolated Alaska and its far-flung native villages be appropriate elsewhere? In spite of Bill Gordon's prophetic message heard in many places throughout the land, there were doubts. Sometimes ethnic congregations in the inner city and probably some Native American congregations hear propositions for indigenous ministry as yet another attempt to foster second rate or cheaper services off on "second rate" people.

It would be Wes and the people of Nevada who would finally get this cause seriously rolling. Methodically, persistently, drawing on the experience of Alaska and others, they began the developmental work. With a competent and stable commission on ministry at home and Coalition-14 as a larger forum, the strategies were challenged, tested and refined. Then, based in one of the smallest jurisdictions of the American church, the effort was extended outward. Work on the national canons, guest speaker or preacher in many settings (hence, "The Dream," Chapter 1), the Roland Allen conferences, visits to Central American, Africa, Australia and New Zealand, and the influence was felt internationally. We have dipped into his story and present this collection in the interest of keeping his legacy alive and his challenges before the church. We have, it seems to us, assembled an outstanding and well-qualified range of authors to present the subject. One would hope that a generation hence such an assemblage will not be as predominantly white, male and ordained. But it is our call to inspire and move toward that time, and we begin with the realities of our own day. The creation of this book over the past 20 months has been a labor of love, but also one rooted in a sense of urgency and deep positive convictions about the course set, the enterprise taken. Along the way there have been tears and laughter, wonder and joy, and tough work in writing and editing in an attempt to produce something worthy of offering in his name.

And along the way the spirit of Wes Frensdorff has been with us — prodding, joking, challenging — like when faced with a particularly difficult passage one pauses . . . and remembers. . . him. His poking fun at symbols of hierarchy and status, for example. One time when he and I were scheduled to fly to a certain meeting, he offered to purchase my ticket. When we met he informed me that I was flying first class, as coach was sold out. (He had picked up his ticket earlier.) As we boarded the plane, both in clericals, he grinned and said, "I'll come up and join you after we take off." "How are you going to manage that?" I queried. "I'll tell the stewardess that I need to go up to the first class cabin to talk to my bishop." Or his amusement with the foibles of human nature, like the time I met him in Salt Lake City. He was then dean of St. Marks, and in the course of our meeting he got on the subject of a particularly troublesome member of the parish, a holier-than-thou judgmental type who was too critical of someone else. In a tense moment he grasped the table and asked rhetorically and forcefully, "Why can't people accept people the way they are?" We both immediately caught the irony of the question and guffawed — at our own impatience with people "as they are."

We certainly needed that humor in working through all the language problems a writer faces these days and we did, alternately, struggle, wince and laugh. It is, of course, 'local priest' ('community priest' in South Africa and New Zealand), not 'non-stipendiary priest' . . . unless 'non-stipendiary' is the only thing that will work in the context. On the other hand, is it 'priest' or 'presbyter'? We also have to remember that 'priest' doesn't mean professionally educated and employed (nor vice versa), but neither does it mean 'rector'; that's a position, not an order. 'Transitional deacon' seems to work okay. It leaves real deacons without adjectives, which seems to be preferred. It wouldn't be in good taste, however, to speak of a 'transitional priest' unless the intention really is to accuse one of being overly ambitious, or unless a deacon were elected bishop and could only get there (i.e., today's rule) via a transitional priesthood.

It seems acceptable these days — even kind of natural — to alternate She and He in references to God. But 'Lord' and 'Father' are problematical as is *King*dom (*Realm* of God or *Realm* of Heaven should work all right, but hasn't caught on; '*Queen*dom' sounds contrived) These, of course, are sexist issues. 'Father' or 'Mother' in reference to the priest (or presbyter) is also a problem. We have avoided both, believing that both are destined to go out of general usage soon. We have also skipped all those little plusses (+) fore and aft, a relatively new fad that arrived after its time. 'Shepherd' is out too, as is 'pastor', but we had better check with the Lutherans on the latter. Here we are dealing with issues of hierarchy or status. I wonder if 'Father' in reference to God, or 'Father' in reference to priest will be first to go? Probably 'Father' in reference to God, as she is less likely to object.

Deacons and bishops have it a little easier. 'Deacon Borgeson', 'Bishop Frensdorff' — a nice even tone to it, no presumptions. Maybe I could go with 'Presbyter Wilson', or maybe recover the old form of 'Prester Wilson'. Either way it would take some getting used to. Then there are all the redundancies. But you have to watch them; it's easy to be fooled. Sometimes 'local congregation' is appropriate, and 'ordained priest', which used to sound so offensive, is less so today. In the context of discussing the priesthood of all the baptized, we might find it needful to refer specifically to one who is also ordained. But that other one: 'lay ministry', is redundancy of redundancies. It doesn't mean 'amateur ministry' of course, but does it exclude me — an ordained member of the laity? If so, I want back in! After all, if we have broken ministry loose from captivity by the ordained, no need to go to the other extreme and exclude them altogether. Come to think of it, maybe there is some real fear of that in the ranks of the professionals. We could go with "baptismal ministry" or simply "ministry." However, these terms are inclusive. How do we make reference specifically to the ministry of the non-ordained? We certainly can't call people "non-ordained ministers;" that would make them seem illigetimate. It's a continuing problem and maybe "lay ministry" is the only thing that will work sometimes. I can hear Wes chuckle and see the twinkle in his eye as we make our way through the morass of new sensitivities and shifting meanings, trying to write coherently.

Yes, we miss him. But we pray that his spirit will continue in the church he loved so much and served so well, for the enterprise so ably begun is not finished. It is often the case that in remodeling an old house we encounter more twists, problems and opportunities than we expect. Pipes no longer meet the building code; walls are out of square; there is beautiful oak flooring under the tired living room carpet. So, too, in reshaping ministry. It is impossible to predict what issues may arise, how changing one part of the enterprise will affect another. Nevertheless, just as we grapple with new plumbing and employ shims and a square, we change canons, have discussions, start educational programs, have discussions, adopt new policies and, yes, have more discussions. The kitchen is complete; we can sit at the table, sip some coffee and contemplate what has yet to be done in the den. Then it's on to the second floor.

Webster defines 'enterprise' as "an undertaking that is especially difficult, complicated or risky; readiness to engage in daring action . . . ." Asking the hard questions *does* require courage. And in asking them we set ourselves up for a response — through action, or inaction — either way, a response. The partially remodeled house is waiting. Dare we continue the task?

Years ago Ernie Southcott spotted a few of the blocks to church renewal. There have been others and we have been chipping away. Wes stood tall in that enterprise. But, as he always insisted, no block must be allowed to deter us from the *mission* of the church. Not pipe organ, nor pew, nor bricks and mortar, nor prayer book, nor canons, nor education, certification, licenses or orders, nor age, race or gender, nor balloons, banners or slogans, nor anything in God's creation deter us from that mission. As a matter of fact, experience has shown that most of the so-called blocks are resources in disguise; it's our way of seeing them that makes them obstacles. When viewed openly and creatively, we see blessings: solid oak beneath a tired old carpet. The pipe organ is still an asset. Yes, we must look for opportunities where the inclination is to see only problems. Peter Drucker says that when it rains manna from heaven, most people reach for an umbrella, some for a big spoon. Wesley Frensdorff has bequeathed us a *very* big spoon.

Here are some ideas for Part III.
(Numbered items could be used with the corresponding chapter.)

11)   Who are the individuals in your congregation who might be considered signs or icons of the diaconate we all share? Assuming that you have identified lay people, what difference would it make in your church's total ministry if one or two of them were ordained?

Compare Plater's attitude (Chapter 11) toward ordained ministries with those of Sumner (Chapter 5).

12)   Share experiences: An incident in your life (other than in or about the church) where you served as a Christian minister.

Discuss the ways your parish functions as a support base for the ministries (in the world) of members. How about your diocese?

13)   Take each of the four principles considered in Chapter 13 and, one at a time, discuss their application to your parish/diocese.

You are the editorial committee of your diocesan paper. You have just interviewed Borgeson and Kelsey. You are now meeting to decide how much of this you will actually report. Two concerns have been raised: (1) how much the average reader is ready to hear, and (2) whether you might offend someone associated with diocesan headquarters. What are your conclusions?

14)   Matthew claims that all authority is God's. There is no authority in office, title, role, etc., but for people of faith God's authority is in the action. In other words, authority is a function of faithful action, not of office. (See Daniel Patte, *The Gospel According to Matthew.* Fortress, page 291*ff.* on Matthew 21:18-22:14.) Discuss the implications of this for structures of ministry in your church.

Have a brain-storming session (check with someone who knows the rules for this exercise). Describe the qualities and characteristics (local, diocesan and national) of a totally new approach to the theological enterprise.

If you have an EFM group in your parish (or one near by), ask someone from that group to join you for a demonstration session on theological reflection. (They have techniques for doing this. See also, James D. Whitehead and Evelyn Eaton Whitehead, *Method in Ministry*, Seabury.)

One individual who felt a call to a ministry in counseling approached the commission on ministry with a request for ordination to the priesthood. Members of the COM couldn't understand why ordination to the priesthood was desirable for a counseling ministry. The applicant responded, "Because that's where the credibility is." Discuss.

15) Coffee sipping time is over. Take up your big spoon and join the action. Where do you start?

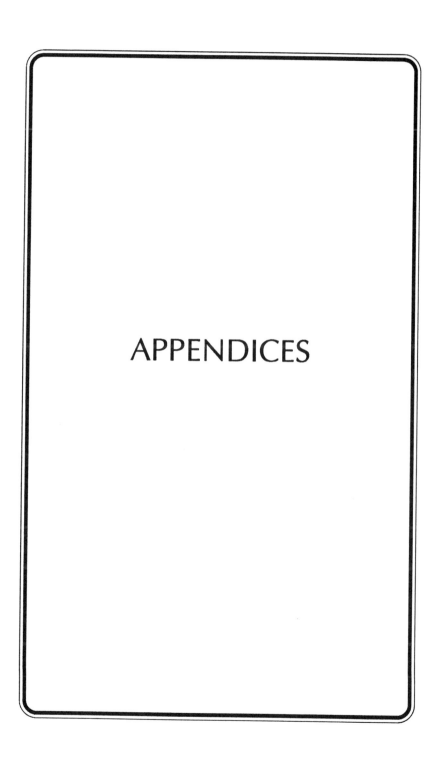

APPENDICES

Frensdorff Bibliography

St. Luke's Journal of Theology
      June, 1983   "An Inaccurate Conception: The Limited Trans-
                        ferability of Clergy"

The Living Church
      Feb. 15, 1981   "The Human Sieve"
      July 12, 1981   "Remodeling the Ministry"
      Oct. 7, 1984   "Moving Church Headquarters" (editorial)
      Aug. 17, 1986   "Pursuing Allen's Vision"

The Witness
      June, 1980   "Theologize, but Indigenize, Too"

Education for Mission and Ministry, The Episcopal Church Center
      1985   "Ministry and Orders: A Tangled Skein"
               (Chapter 3 in this volume)

The Nevada Total Ministry Notebook
      "Holy Orders in Ministry: Some Reflections"
      "Turning Ministry Around"
      "Ministry: Stewardship of Gifts"
      "Total Ministry: An Alternative for Self-support"
      "Extending the Eucharistic Fellowship"
      "Remodeling the Ministry"
      "Renewal of the Church in the City"
              (part of Chapter 4 in this volume)
      "The Church, The Ministry and The Offices"
      "An Inaccurate Conception: Transferability"
      "Servanthood Isn't Color-coded"

Challenge for Change: Clergy and Congregations (with Charles R. Wilson).
Jethro Publications, 1987.

Authors

Part I

William B. Spofford, Jr.

Long known for his contributions to small church and hospital ministries, as well as little theater, Bishop Spofford was the fourth bishop of Eastern Oregon and later, assistant bishop in the Diocese of Washington. He has since retired to Salem, Oregon, where he is a student in theater at Willamette University, and works with the Mid-Willamette Valley Hospice.

Roger White

Bishop of Milwaukee since 1984, Roger White has been involved in ministry development on national, provincial and diocesan levels. He is a member of the Title III Committee, which recently revised the ministry canons of the church, and serves on the Cornerstone Project committee. Bishop White is a native of England.

Enrique Brown

Archdeacon of Region Two, Diocese of New York, and founding director of the Instituto Pastoral Hispano, Enrique Brown is actively involved in Hispanic ministry development in the New York metropolitan area. He was appointed consultant to the 1988 Lambeth Conference, Mission and Ministry Section, by the Archbishop of Canterbury and served as chairman of the 1986 Roland Allen Symposium Steering Committee. The Rev. Mr. Brown, a native of Panama, immigrated to the United States in 1969, and graduated from Yale/Berkeley Divinity School in 1974.

Part II

George R. Sumner, Jr.

The Rev. Mr. Sumner, wife Stephanie Hodgkins and daughter Marta Zoe reside in New Haven, Connecticut, where he is a doctoral candidate in theology at Yale. Since his ordination in 1981, he has served in St. Philip's Theological College, Kongwa, Tanzania, East Africa; at St. Matthew's Church, Worcester, Massachusetts, and the Church of the Good Shepherd, Fort Defiance, Arizona.

Leo Frade

Bishop of Honduras since 1984, Leo Frade is a native of Cuba. He attended college and seminary in the U.S. at the University of the South and served churches in Florida and Louisiana. He is a member of the Executive Council of the Episcopal Church. He is married and has two children.

Clyde M. Wood

Anglican Bishop of the Northern Territory, Australia, since 1983, Bishop Wood was educated in the Diocese of Melbourne and served as dean of Christ Church Cathedral, Darwin, from 1978-1983. He enjoys golf, sailing and cycling. He lives, with his wife, Margaret, and three children, in Nightcliff, Northern Territory.

Richard A. Kraft

Richard Kraft grew up in the Episcopal Church, U.S.A. Upon completing seminary and being ordained deacon in 1961, he went to South Africa where he was ordained priest and has spent the whole of his ministry. After parochial experience which included university chaplaincy, English and Zulu speaking parishes, he was director of Christian education, first in the Diocese of Zululand, and then for the Church of the Province of Southern Africa. In 1979 he became dean of St. Alban's Cathedral, Pretoria, and in December, 1981 was elected bishop of that diocese. He is married to Phyllis; they have four children and three grandchildren.

David W. Brown

The Rev. David W. Brown is a pioneer in cluster ministry development - one variation in the total ministry theme. His formative work took place in the Norwich Area Episcopal Council, of which he was chairman in the early 1960s. In the Northeast Kingdom of Vermont in the '70s, he served as dean and as canon missioner. In 1980 he became senior priest of the Middlesex Area Cluster Ministry, centered in Durham, Connecticut. In mid-1989 he retired and is doing interim work in Connecticut and consultation in regional ministry development.

Charles R. Wilson

In private practice since 1971, the Rev. Mr. Wilson (Chuck) was ordained in Idaho and has served in a variety of parochial, diocesan and national church positions. Specialties include church management and ministry development. He and his wife, Lynne, reside in

Arvada, Colorado, the base of their two enterprises, CRW Management Services and Jethro Publications.

Part III

Ormonde Plater

Deacon Plater, New Orleans, earns his living in the sugar cane country of Louisiana and serves liturgically at St. Anna's. He also coordinates ministry to the sick at local hospitals and edits *Diakoneo*, newsletter of the North American Association for the Diaconate. He has recently taken on a part-time ministry in the men's surgical wards of Charity Hospital, where many of the patients are casualties of urban warfare.

Jean M. Haldane

A consultant, educator, trainer and conference leader in ministry development, Ms. Haldane is a professional church worker. She is past chair of the National Task Force on Ministry, a delegate to the Canterbury Celebration of Women's Ministries, and founding dean of the Lay Academy, Diocese of California. A Fellow of the College of Preachers and the Seminary of the Southwest, she was awarded an honorary doctorate of divinity by the General Theological Seminary in 1987, for her work as an educator. She lives with her husband, Dr. Bernard Haldane, in Seattle.

Josephine Borgeson

Deacon Borgeson (Phina) was ordained by Bishop Frensdorff in 1974, when the diaconate was generally seen as a "transitional ordained role." A patchwork of program responsibilities in Nevada evolved into the position of ministry development coordinator. Through consulting and committee work she influenced total ministry development both within and beyond Nevada. She now serves as Christian Education Missioner in the Diocese of Los Angeles.

James A. Kelsey

The Rev. Mr. Kelsey (Jim) resides in Marquette, Michigan, where he recently assumed a new position as ministry developer in the Diocese of Northern Michigan's total ministry program. His pioneer work in total ministry was in Vermont, a story reported in Chapter 2 of *Against All Odds*. From Vermont he went to Oklahoma, where he launched the Green Country Cluster Ministry.

Also available from Jethro . . .

Against All Odds: Ten Stories of Vitality in Small Churches
Charles R. Wilson and Lynne Davenport
Challenge for Change: Clergy and Congregations
Wesley Frensdorff and Charles R. Wilson
Living Out the Vision: Nevada's Experience in Total Ministry
CRW Management Services
Under Authority: Supervision and Church Leadership
Charles R. Wilson

Jethro Publications
6066 Parfet Street
Arvada, Colorado 80004
(303) 431-6436

Write for a free catalog.